Using Software in Qualitative Research

Using Software in Qualitative Research

A Step-by-Step Guide

Ann Lewins and Christina Silver

SAGE Publications

Los Angeles • London • New Delhi • Singapore

First published 2007

 SAGE Publications Ltd
1 Oliver's Yard
55 City Road
London EC1Y 1SP

SAGE Publications Inc.
2455 Teller Road
Thousand Oaks, California 91320

SAGE Publications India Pvt Ltd
B 1/I 1 Mohan Cooperative Industrial Area
Mathura Road, New Delhi 110 044
India

SAGE Publications Asia-Pacific Pte Ltd
33 Pekin Street #02-01
Far East Square
Singapore 048763

Library of Congress Control Number 2006932844

British Library Cataloguing in Publication data

A catalogue record for this book is available from the British Library

ISBN 978-0-7619-4922-0
ISBN 978-0-7619-4923-7 (pbk)

Typeset by C&M Digitals (P) Ltd, Chennai, India
Printed on paper from sustainable resources
Printed in Great Britain by The Alden Press, Witney

Contents

Acknowledgements

We would like to thank the thousands of researchers and students we have met during our work with CAQDAS who have helped us to understand what works well in software, what they have found easy to use, and what adapts well to their complex range of needs. Freinds such as Graham Gibbs, Duncan Branley and Susanne Friese have contributed so much to our wider understanding of technology.

Special thanks go to the other researchers and organisations who gave us permission and the necessary information to use their work as example projects. Those were Shalni Gulati, Gerda Speller, Karen Whitby and the NFER, the East Surrey Health Authority, the VIA project, of whom in particular Michael Rich, Richard Chalfen, Julie Polvinen, Julia Szymczak and especially to Jennifer Patashnik for talking to us on their behalf and also for reading and correcting many of our first proof chapters.

We would also like to thank our reviewers for very detailed advice and extremely useful broad suggestions about the structure of the book. We were always able to turn, as ever, to Ray Lee and Nigel Fielding to draw on their experience and methodological expertise. Historically we have so much to thank them for in their original inspirational creation of the CAQDAS Networking Project. In the background and always supporting us was the Department of Sociology at the University of Survey and in particular we would like to thank Carol Lee, Agnes McGill, Frank Suffling and Sue Venn for their individual and quiet support while we struggled to finish this book. We thank Jason Teal and Michael Strong for their patience, red wine and common sense.

Last but not least the ever responsive software authors, founders, or developers and their support teams without whom this book would never have been dreamt of. To name but a few they are, Thomas Muhr (ATLAS.ti5), Anne Dupuis and Scott Kinder and Researchware (HyperRESEARCH), Udo Kuckartz and Anne Kuckartz and members of Verbi (MAXqda2), Tom Richards, Lyn Richards and members of QSR (NVivo7), Normand Peladeau (QDA Miner), Ed Brent and Paul Clusaz (QUALRUS), and Chris Fassnacht, Chris Thorne and David Woods (Transana).

And finally we owe a debt of gratitude to our fabulous little laptops and … the comfy chair.

Rationale and Structure

In this book we combine several aspects of Computer Assisted Qualitative Data AnalysiS (CAQDAS) to help make sense of the variety of tools and products. The book will help in choosing the most appropriate package for your needs and in getting the most out of the software once you are using it. We consider tasks and processes, bringing them together to enable a sense of direction without encouraging a linear approach. We do not claim to provide exhaustive information regarding the functionality or potential use of any software package. Rather, our aim is to demystify qualitative software and encourage flexible and critical choices and uses of software in supporting analysis. At various points, we also talk about *doing* qualitative data analysis. In the context of software use, we discuss real projects, illustrating how software can support a range of methodological strategies and practical requirements. We discuss aspects of our own and others' work where projects have used particular software tools to great effect. Sometimes these are innovative or unusual. At other times they are very simple. Where the authors have given their permission we provide brief descriptions and contact details in Appendix A.

BACKGROUND

The CAQDAS Networking Project was proposed and launched by Nigel Fielding and Ray Lee in the mid 1990s to provide information, advice and training in the use of different packages designed to assist qualitative data analysis, and to facilitate debate amongst users and methodologists. The project, funded by the UK Economic and Social Research Council (ESRC), is the only resource of its kind and is independent of any commercial links to software. Our day-to-day practical work for the project involves seeing and using many software packages. We provide different levels of training in several packages and ongoing support to researchers in using software where required. This puts us in contact with a wide range of projects and research settings. We see an enormous variety of expectations, needs, methodological approaches and computer confidence levels amongst researchers. In teaching and using software we inevitably make comparisons and evaluations between packages. We also learn continually from those we support. In this book, we draw on these experiences to provide a practical but analytically grounded guide to thinking about and using software.

HOW TO USE THIS BOOK

The way you use this book will depend on your own starting point with qualitative research and the use of software to support it. You may be an experienced qualitative researcher who has never used software before. You may be exploring software capability or be looking to make an informed choice between products. You may be completely new to qualitative research and be seeking practical advice in conducting analysis and using software. Or, you may have used software before, and just need to explore other options.

The book can be read as a whole, or chapters can be treated on a standalone basis when, for instance, you need ideas on a particular task or software. This said, chapters also build on one another to provide a holistic sense of the iterative and cyclical analytic journey, without advocating a particular sequential process.

Above all, keep in mind your analytic and practical needs, and view the procedures we illustrate with a critical eye. You are always the expert in your own project, and we encourage you to use this book as we would encourage you to use qualitative software and the tools within them: pick your own.

To help you navigate through the chapters we flag up certain features of work using the following icons:

 Software can support collaborative projects in many ways. This icon highlights an aspect of work which may be useful in a team situation.

 This icon indicates a moment when it may be useful to output information about an aspect of your work, either to a file for viewing in another application, or to print off and consider in hard copy away from the computer.

 This icon indicates a point in the process when it may be useful to reflect upon your work by commenting or writing about an observation or idea. This may include noting action points for consideration later.

 At various points, tasks and processes converge. This icon indicates where a particular task can be built upon in the future, or where it relates to previous tasks.

While this book focuses on textual data, we include reference to how software can support the analysis of multimedia data at various points by using this icon.

THE STRUCTURE OF THIS BOOK

In the main body of the book we first outline the general principles and functionality of software, detailing similarities between packages and highlighting core processes and tasks (Chapter 1). We encourage you to read this chapter whatever your needs.

We then focus attention on three leading CAQDAS programs: ATLAS.ti5, MAXqda2 and NVivo7. Chapters 2–12 provide step-by-step support for tasks in these packages, reflecting the cyclical nature of qualitative research while providing practical ways to proceed. We use examples from real projects to ground software tools in analytic and practical contexts.

Some chapters incorporate aspects of qualitative work which have been debated in the literature, and we refer you to seminal works where appropriate (Chapters 4, 5, 6). Other chapters are practically oriented, focusing on the step-by-step tasks you may undertake (Chapters 7, 8, 11, 12). The remaining chapters (9, 10 and 13) encourage a flexible approach to what we call 'the bits in between'.

Usually a fully annotated graphic accompanies each practical task, although as we proceed these become fewer, to reflect increased confidence as you progress with software use. The main body of the book concludes by bringing together the various strands to encourage working in flexible, creative and focused ways (Chapter 13).

In Appendix C we reflect the broadness of available software to facilitate qualitative data analysis by reviewing seven leading CAQDAS packages, highlighting their possibilities and potential uses: ATLAS.ti5, HyperRESEARCH 2.6, MAXqda2, QDA Miner 2.0, NVivo7, Qualrus and Transana 2. The reviews build on the similarities identified in Chapter 1, taking each package in turn to discuss their distinguishing features. We comment at the end of each review on aspects we consider to be particularly useful or somewhat problematic. If you are new to CAQDAS programs, or are looking to this book to help make an informed choice, we recommend you read the software-specific reviews in conjunction with Chapter 1.

THE YOUNG PEOPLE'S PERCEPTIONS PROJECT

As well as providing specific real-life examples from a range of different projects, we also use one project as an example which we follow through the chapters. This is taken from one of the authors' doctoral studies. The project took place between 1998 and 2002 and elements of the analysis were facilitated by the use of QSR NUD*IST version 4. See Appendix A for a project description.

Since the project's completion there have been significant developments in software functionality. In writing this book we took a sample of the data and worked up projects in the three software packages we focus on: ATLAS.ti5, MAXqda2 and NVivo7.

We have learnt a lot by creating these software projects, seeing different ways of working from those originally carried out. Each software project undertaken is the learning ground for the next. This is just as true for experienced qualitative researchers and teachers of software as it is for those new to either area. We hope this book will facilitate you to make informed choices between software packages and to use the tools within them flexibly.

Chapter 1
Processes and Tasks
in Using Qualitative Software

In this chapter, we introduce qualitative software. We first briefly overview types of software for handling qualitative data to provide context for how the packages we discuss fit into the wider field. As much as we can, we define the eclectic Computer Assisted Qualitative Data AnalysiS (CAQDAS) category of programs. We then focus on such software and overview general functionality and the aspects of work that most programs have in common. Finally, we introduce key aspects of working within CAQDAS packages, illustrating different ways in which you can work. The remainder of the book builds on this chapter, describing core tasks you may undertake using a CAQDAS package (illustrated in Table 1.1). This chapter provides commentary concerning what is generally possible in the featured packages. The remaining chapters focus on three leading packages, ATLAS.ti5, MAXqda2 and NVivo7, providing step-by-step, illustrated support and commentary. Appendix B lists keyboard shortcuts for these three packages.

In Appendix C we summarize and review seven leading CAQDAS packages, focusing on the distinctive tools they provide. We do not include the entire functionality of packages and we recommend the reviews are read in conjunction with this chapter. Commentary sections in each chapter and at the end of each software review reflect our own opinions as well as our observations of users' experiences and evaluations. Their most frequently asked questions and issues in working with software ground us in the reality of day-to-day use amongst disparate users. We also recommend visiting software developers' websites as part of your decision-making process.

TYPES OF SOFTWARE SUPPORTING WORK WITH QUALITATIVE DATA

In 1995 Weitzman and Miles developed a typology to differentiate software designed to handle qualitative data. At the time, packages were generally concerned with the analysis of text. Weitzman and Miles distinguished between *text retrievers*, *textbase managers*, *code and retrieve packages*, *code-based theory builders* and *conceptual network builders*. Although the distinctions they made have since become somewhat blurred, we make reference to their typology here, because it provides useful background context.

What types of software do we categorize as CAQDAS?

The acronym CAQDAS is well understood across disciplines as broadly referring to software designed to assist the analysis of qualitative data. It was coined by Ray Lee and Nigel Fielding at the time of the first Surrey Research Methods Conference in 1989 which brought together pioneers in the field. The subsequent CAQDAS Networking Project, funded by the UK Economic and Social Research Council (ESRC) from 1994 and directed by Fielding and Lee, had the effect of 'fixing' the acronym.

However, there has often been rather a fuzzy conception about which packages CAQDAS included, and the way this term relates to the typology proffered by Weitzman and Miles. We make a broad definition here. Software which falls under the CAQDAS 'umbrella' includes a wide range of packages, but their general principles are concerned with taking a *qualitative* approach to qualitative data. Qualitative data include text, visual and multimedia forms of non-numerical information (see Chapter 2). A qualitative approach often includes a need to interpret data through the identification and possibly *coding* of themes, concepts, processes, contexts etc., in order to build explanations or theories or to test or enlarge a theory (see Chapter 5). Qualitative data collection techniques include in-depth interviews, focus groups and participant observation. Qualitative analytic techniques include Grounded Theory, Framework, and conversation and narrative analysis. These approaches are all *qualitative* though each may use different processes to analyse data.

The qualitative approaches to data that we refer to are distinct from 'content analysis' methodology, in which the statistics of word or phrase frequencies and their occurrence relative to other words or phrases are the basis of analytic work (see Holsti, 1969). We refer to tools that support a content analysis approach in varying degrees.[1] These packages are included because their main focus is qualitative.

Code-based theory building software

Both these and the earlier code and retrieve packages assist in managing analysis by enabling thematic coding of chunks of data. Code and retrieve packages allow reduction of data along thematic lines for coded retrieval and limited searching and memo functionality. Code-based theory building packages extend the abilities of search tools, allowing the researcher to test relationships between issues, concepts and themes, to develop broader or higher order categories, or, at the other extreme, to develop more detailed specific codes where certain conditions combine in the data. When the term CAQDAS was coined, it essentially encompassed those packages which fell into the Weitzman and Miles code and retrieve and code-based theory building categories.

Text retrievers, textbase managers

Tools provided in both these categories provide quantitative and 'actual content' based analysis of textual data. For example, sophisticated ways to search for text and language include the use of thesaurus tools to find words with similar meaning, to index all words contained in the text, to provide word frequency tables, to create active word lists, and to provide easy key word/phrase in context (KWIC) retrieval. However, broadly summarizing them in this fashion masks the huge variety of ways they handle the quantitative analysis of content.

Increasingly, with the advances of individual software described in this book, distinctions have become blurred. This has happened, for example, between software formerly labelled code and retrieve and the more extensive functionality in code-based theory builders. Now very few software programs remain solely in the code and retrieve category. Similarly, some of the code-based theory building software has taken on tools more traditionally featured in text retrievers or textbase managers – e.g. content analysis tools which may comprise word frequencies, word indexing with KWIC, and complex text-based searching tools. Conversely, by expanding to provide different add-on software to enable thematic coding, text retrievers and textbase managers are beginning to enable tasks originally only possible in code-based theory building software.

WHICH IS THE 'BEST' CAQDAS PACKAGE?

This is perhaps our most frequently asked question, yet it is impossible to answer! All the packages we use and teach have tools in common, plus their own distinctive features. We bring your attention to our perceptions of their advantages and disadvantages in commentary sections throughout the book.

The purpose of software is not to provide you with a methodological or analytic framework. The tools available support certain tasks differently and there is some debate about whether a particular package may 'steer' the way you perform the analysis. Users should take into account practicalities such as the way software programs are taught, and how much emphasis is placed on an 'ideal' way of using software. To promote only one ideal way of using any package undervalues both the software and the methodological independence of the researcher. Creeping homogeneity helps no-one in the long run except the person who is trying to sell a method to you. As the researcher, you are the expert. You remain in control of the interpretive process and you decide which tools within a software package best facilitate *your* approach to analysis. You also have the responsibility for documenting your processes.

Whichever package you choose, you will be able to utilize a selection of tools which will facilitate data management and analysis. Software developments and blurring boundaries mean that tools within a given package may not be appropriate for all qualitative approaches. Just because a function is available does not mean you have to use it. We also caution against choosing a package simply because it seems the most sophisticated.

BASIC FUNCTIONALITY AND ASPECTS OF WORK IN CAQDAS: KEY SIMILARITIES

Table 1.1 lists basic functionality provided by CAQDAS packages as they relate to analytic tasks. We reference which of the following chapters discuss and illustrate these tasks in further detail so that you can easily jump to those which support your particular needs, as required. Your methodology and style of working will affect which software tools are utilized, and the order in which tasks are carried out.

Structure of work in CAQDAS packages

The software 'project' acts as a container for, or a connector to, all the data files and other information relevant to your research study. Some programs contain the individual data files, by copying them into a project file. We call these 'internal databases'. Other programs connect to data files which remain outside the software. We call these 'external databases'. In either case, once relevant files have been 'imported' or 'assigned', opening the project enables immediate access to all of them. There are varying benefits and disadvantages to either system (see Chapter 3).

Table 1.1 *Main tasks of analysis*

Task	Analytic rationale	Chapters
Planning and managing your project	Keep together the different aspects of your work. Aid continuity, and build an audit trail. Later, illustrate your process and your rigour	3 and 10
Writing analytic memos	Manage your developing interpretations by keeping track of ideas as they occur, and building on them as you progress	9 and in most chapters
Reading, marking and commenting on data	Discover and mark interesting aspects in the data as you see them	4
Searching (for strings, words, phrases etc.)	Explore data according to their content, discovering how content differs, how it helps you understand	4
Developing a coding schema	Manage your ideas about your data, in themes, concepts etc. Structure and function may depend on methodology and style of working	6
Coding	Capture what is going on in your data. Bring together similar data according to themes, concepts etc. Generate codes from the text level or according to existing ideas as necessary, define the meaning and application of codes	5 and 7
Retrieval of coded segments	Revisit coded data to assess similarity and difference, to consider how coding is helping your analysis, and 'where to go next'	8
Recoding	Recode into broader or narrower themes or categories if appropriate and necessary. Perhaps bring data back together and think about them differently…	8
Organization of data	Organize data according to known facts and descriptive features to allow consideration of how these aspects play a role in your understanding	11
Hyperlinking	Link data to other data segments and/or to other files to track process, contradiction etc.	4
Searching the database and the coding schema	Test ideas, interrogate subsets for similarity and difference, or generate another level of coding	12
Mapping	Manage analytic processes by visualizing connections, relationships, patterns, processes, ideas	10
Generating output	Report on different aspects of your progress and the project at any stage. Save as files to capture status at an analytic stage, or to work in other applications. Print off to get away from the computer and think and work in more 'traditional' ways …	Most chapters

Data types and format

Most of the packages we discuss were originally created to support the analysis of text.[2] Any digital textual information can be regarded as 'data' by software, including field notes, transcripts, literature lists, downloaded documentation, emails and diary data. There are few limitations in the types of textual data that can be 'managed' by CAQDAS software. The formatting of the text, however, matters in each package and should be taken into consideration in planning for the use of software (see Chapter 2).

 Some packages also directly handle multimedia data, for example allowing audio/video data to be segmented and coded using similar processes as for text. These packages function using the 'external database' structure, for example ATLAS.ti5, HyperRESEARCH, Qualrus and Transana. (see Chapter 2 and relevant reviews in Appendix C).

'Closeness to data' and interactivity

Software increases the access you have to whole data files and parts of them, and at the basic level this is the key benefit of using software. Whatever tools are used, 'live' contact to source data is always easy, increasing the researcher's 'closeness' to data. Interactivity between different tools and functions within software is also a key aspect of its flexibility. The level of interactivity varies across packages in some views and functions, for instance in the coded information in the margin or between different panes (see Chapters 7 and 8).

Exploring data

Once incorporated into the 'project', data can be easily explored. Text search tools offer automated ways to search for words and phrases. Such searches usually provide good access to the source context. Text-level annotation and marking goes hand in hand with exploration (see Chapters 4 and 9).

Code and retrieve functionality

All CAQDAS packages offer code and retrieve functionalities. User-defined key words (codes) can be applied to selections of text, and as many codes as required can be applied to the same or overlapping text selections. Code generation is both easy and flexible, and the researcher is free to use a combination of strategies if desired and to refine coding when necessary. In all but one of the software packages discussed in this book, the responsibility for identifying suitable codes and applying them rests entirely on the user.[3] In all packages, coded data can be retrieved, recoded and outputted with ease. Software differs in the way coded information is provided in the data file itself, for instance in the margin area (see Chapters 5, 7 and 8).

Coding schema

The user has complete freedom concerning the structure of the coding schema. If using an inductive approach, for example, the user can identify codes in a grounded way while reading the data. If using a deductive approach, or a combination of both, codes can be built into an *a priori* structure before coding of the data begins (see Chapter 5). The coding schema can always be restructured and refined (see Chapters 6, 7 and 8).

Data organization

All the packages offer ways to manage the research project as a whole. Known characteristics about the data, including for example their origin and type and the socio-demographic facts and figures about respondents (age, gender etc.), can be included. This allows for the comparison of data across subsets. In most software, such information can be imported in a table from other applications (see Chapters 2 and 11).

Searching and interrogating the database

Software packages offer means by which to interrogate the dataset at any time. This includes searching the content of data based on the language used and *auto coding* the results (see Chapter 12). The units of text that can be returned or auto coded around the actual finds or hits vary between packages. Not all contextual options are provided in each software package and this may matter if much dependence is placed on this tool (see Chapter 2 and Appendix C).

Searches to discover relationships between codes as they have been applied to data are also possible. These include co-occurrences, proximity etc. (see Chapter 12). This can produce a secondary level of analytic coding. Search tools also allow you to combine the interpretive or conceptual coding and organizational or descriptive dimensions of your work. Searches can be used to play with ideas in an exploratory fashion, to confirm or reject theories or hypotheses. The central and most important principle of any search, however, is that the findings it produces are based on the earlier coding and organization of data.

Writing tools

The process of qualitative data analysis is rarely linear, and the various writing tools (memoing, commenting, annotating etc.) offered by CAQDAS packages provide ways to increase contact with thoughts and processes. Each package provides different writing tools and ways to sort and retrieve memo content (see Chapters 4 and 9).

Output

All reviewed software packages allow the generation of output reports for viewing in hard copy or in other applications, e.g. Word, Excel or SPSS. Standard reports can include documents or coded segments. Usually, simple tabular output is available, providing a breakdown of code frequencies, which can be exported to Word, Excel or SPSS. Often, results of searches can be viewed in both output format or inside the software. When the software supports the use of mapping or more graphic representations of coding schemata, these can usually be copied or exported in file format, or pasted or inserted into Word files.

MAKING SOFTWARE WORK FOR YOUR PROJECT

Starting points

There is no single process for handling qualitative data in a CAQDAS package. It is desirable to know your methodological standpoint first rather than seeing the software as being the architect of your method. This is the ideal, of course, but in practice the software will tend to modify the way you imagined you were going to work, or when you know a software program well, you may be tempted to draw on what the software can do, in designing your next project. Using a customized CAQDAS package can open up additional possibilities of handling and analyzing data.

Familiarization

It is noticeable when teaching software packages that no two sessions are the same. Sometimes a methodologically motivated participant, with a clear idea of his/her requirements, will vary the direction of the workshop. That participant will know what is wanted at an interim stage of analysis. The way to achieve the task may not be immediately obvious. Eventually, between us, we will work out a strategy, maybe a two- or three-stage process, that will produce the required outcome. Your methodological preparation will enrich the way you look at your data. As you become more familiar, you will be more prepared to mould the software tools to serve your objectives, and you will become more creative in combining different tools together to achieve a complicated objective. Your objectives and the conceptual progress you make, however, will come from *your* methodological underpinnings, *your* observations, *your* thinking.

What the software project represents

One software 'project' should usually be created to represent one research project, i.e. not a separate project for each type of data, case or respondent. Having organized data into subsets within the project (see Chapter 11), it will be possible to filter work to isolate these elements. If different aspects of a research project are in discrete software projects, it will be more difficult to compare across them. There may be situations in very

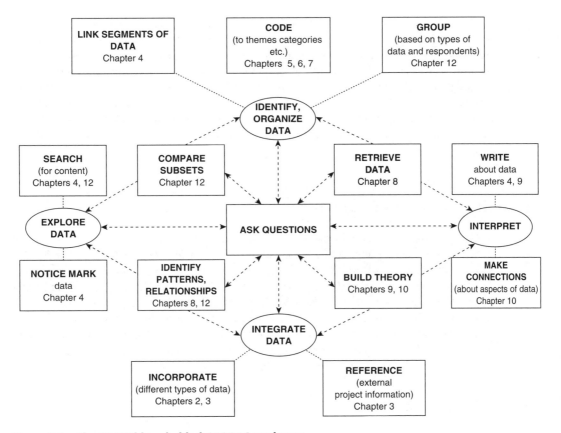

Figure 1.1   The BASIC ideas behind CAQDAS packages

large projects where separating cases into individual projects is useful, but this needs careful thought.

CAQDAS packages as project management tools

The CAQDAS project is the container for your work, providing continuity and linking different aspects of work into a coherent unit. This is illustrated in Figure 1.1. Since none of these things happen automatically, your role as the user of the software and the manager of your work is crucial.

The right tools for the job

The tasks of qualitative analysis discussed above and listed in Table 1.1 can be used selectively. As already mentioned, you can pick and choose which tools will be useful and, to an extent, in what order they are used most effectively. Several factors vary the way software is used. Practical issues concerning resources, expertise or time available will often determine the number of different functions used, and the extent of reliance on the software. Silverman (2000: 42–3) reminds us that once you have chosen a methodological approach you can 'treat it as a "toolbox" providing a set of methods and concepts to select your data and illuminate your analysis'. That methodological toolbox starts at a rather conceptual level. The CAQDAS package acts as another toolbox at a more practical level. Be selective and sceptical about the tools and do not be 'seduced by the convenience and credibility of the program's rendering of sense' (Fielding and Lee, 1993).

Flexibility in the sequencing of tasks

CAQDAS programs do not dictate the order in which you might perform various tasks, but they might influence you in terms of the number and complexity of the tasks you undertake, or your readiness to perform them. It is a paradox of software that, while systematizing the management and storage of data and your ideas about them, it in fact frees you from having to be quite so systematic in the order in which you do things. Using the software liberates you from the clerical constraints which may have prejudiced flexibility using more traditional 'craft' methods. Although the chapters that follow happen in a certain order, they do not aim to recommend one sequence or one process. One of the principal benefits of using software is that you can flexibly revisit tasks and rethink areas of interest as you go.

The bits in between

Reducing work that is done with data to a set of tasks inevitably misses those parts of the process which change your account from a straightforward description to something at an analytically higher level of abstraction. However you proceed, different aspects of your work will need to come together to form a coherent whole. We emphasize two main aspects of work that will facilitate this:

- *Become thoroughly familiar with writing/memo tools.* This is a useful exercise, particularly early in your use of software, and will be something you should return to constantly. Use the relevant tools to help you to retain insights and remind you of small impromptu action plans that might bear fruit later. This will help you feel less isolated within coding devices.
- *Come out of the software when you need to.* To do that, we encourage the printing of output on a regular basis. Print all your important memos. Print reports of coded data. Go back to basics: use coloured highlighters and pens to deconstruct coded data reports. Print tabular summaries of code frequencies; look especially for gaps, investigate them, and print whole files where these gaps exist. Print code lists; draw connections or mark codes you think belong together in some way. While we believe that software can help with most projects, this may not always be the case, and even when it is, using software does not mean you need to become a slave to your computer.

Teamwork

There are certain types of project where the focus on efficient management of work is more prominent. Large or complex datasets and projects where multiple research partners or sites are involved will be facilitated by the orderliness of project work in the software. In the case of teamwork, competent organization means thinking ahead, and being aware of potential logistical problems in the handling and sharing of data. Only one of the software packages featured in this book allows concurrent use on more than one workstation, feeding into one central project on a shared network drive.[4] Most software, however, allows individual projects to be merged into one master project, though the detailed procedures and preparation for doing so can be quite different. The logistics and protocols of teamwork need to be carefully planned. However, they are software specific and outside the remit of this book.

The following chapters illustrate and discuss ways software can support various processes involved in conducting qualitative analysis. While we present these in a particular order, we cross-refer between tasks and chapters to promote flexible combining of tools and we encourage you to consider software tools in the context of your own needs.

NOTES

1   Content analysis support to varying degrees: QDA Miner (high statistical support), MAXqda2 (interactive word frequency support with key word in context (KWIC), ATLAS.ti5 (basic word frequency support).
2   Transana was developed to support video data, but allows the development of parallel transcription or notes.
3   Qualrus has an optional code suggestion device, based on patterns in the data and how the document has previously been coded (see Appendix C).
4   Transana allows concurrent work on the same project from different workstations.

Chapter 2
Data and Their Preparation for CAQDAS Packages

As mentioned in Chapter 1, one of the main advantages of CAQDAS programs is their project and data management capabilities. This chapter focuses on the various forms of textual information and data that may be used within a project, although we make reference to non-textual forms of data. There may be several types of information relevant to the project which need to be managed and integrated. This can be achieved either by directly importing or assigning data to the software project, or by referring to information held outside the software project. CAQDAS packages provide flexibility in the ways various stages of research are managed and data are handled.

As with all tasks and processes, the user is responsible for the ways in which tools are used. An understanding of potential software tasks at the outset of the project may, however, significantly affect the ways certain data are formatted before being imported or assigned. Once documents relevant to the project are incorporated within the software project, you can move between them without having to open separate files, as you would if using a word processing application.

TYPES OF QUALITATIVE DATA

In Table 2.1 we list some types and origins of qualitative data, although in this chapter we focus mainly on textual documents. Not all research projects will use all the forms of data listed, or necessarily require their direct incorporation into the software project. However, primary data, supporting or secondary data, or just useful 'information' may all be integrated at some level and cross-referenced within the software project as a whole. Consider how different stages of the research project may be represented and facilitated in this way, including:

- *background information* – project brief, notes of meetings with team members/ supervisors, email exchanges etc.
- *primary data* – interview and focus-group transcripts, responses to open-ended questions in questionnaires, field notes etc.
- *secondary data* – official documentation, newspaper articles etc.
- *relevant supporting information* – existing literature, supporting quantitative evidence, relevant websites, media coverage etc.

INCORPORATING DIFFERENT TYPES OF DATA INTO THE SOFTWARE PROJECT

Any information that can be converted into an appropriate format and assigned or imported is data as far as the software is concerned. You may incorporate some forms of data into the project and not perform any other tasks on them, but they will be listed alongside all the other relevant information and data. This will help keep various strands of the project together, aiding continuity and cross-referencing. Most forms of textual data can be treated similarly by the software, but you may wish to treat different data types

Table 2.1 *Types of qualitative data*

Computer readable (Transcribed text or digital formats)	Not computer readable[c]
Interview data: structured, semi-structured, unstructured	Archival material, official documentation etc.
Survey data: open-ended questions and answers	Video, film
Narrative accounts: life history etc.	Audiotapes
Discourse: political, journalistic, conversation	Paintings
Bibliographic material:[a] Lists, online abstracts	Photography
Field notes, observations	Diaries, letters: any handwritten material
Online data: email exchanges, chatroom discussions, websites etc.	
Multimedia data:[b] graphics (e.g. .bmp), digitized photos (e.g. .jpg), video (e.g. .avi, .mov), audio (.wav, .mp3) etc.	

Notes:

[a] *Lists can incorporate references to any data that are not online or machine-readable, e.g. see right-hand column. The list can be imported as data, and integrated into the analysis and cross-referencing processes.*

[b] *Only certain software packages can 'directly' analyse (incorporate) multimedia data. At the time of publication ATLAS.ti5, Qualrus, HyperRESEARCH and Transana 2 directly handle whole multimedia files. MAXqda2 and NVivo7 only allow objects, including multimedia files, to be embedded into rich text format documents (see Appendix C).*

[c] *All of the data in this column can be digitized (e.g. audio) or scanned (e.g. handwritten diaries). Alternatively they can be incorporated as references in lists or summarized in computer readable textual form: see left-hand column.*

differently, in which case the data management tools will facilitate handling them separately and/or together when necessary (see Chapter 11).

Consider using the management potential of CAQDAS packages to improve cross-referencing to information not 'directly' readable by the software (see Table 2.1). Data can be formatted as lists, summaries or abstracts, incorporated into the software and then treated in the same way as any other data.

Once incorporated into the software, data files are usually referred to as 'documents' (although MAXqda2 refers to them as 'texts' and NVivo7 as 'sources'). The distinction between *documents* and *memos* is complicated in some packages, but it is usually possible to treat your own writing as data, identical to any other form of text. Various writing tools provided by CAQDAS packages are discussed in Chapter 9.

Incorporating different types of data into the Young People's Perceptions Project

The Young People's Perceptions Project used many different forms of data and incorporated them into the software (see Appendix A). The project comprised a comparative exploration of the historical development, provision and experience of school-based sex education in England and Wales and the Netherlands. The project involved large amounts of primary and secondary data, including the following:

- *questionnaires* concerning aspects of life as a young person living in England
- *focus groups* with young Dutch people living in England and young English people living in the Netherlands
- *in-depth one-to-one interviews* with young people and school sex education teachers in both countries
- *materials used in school sex education lessons* including textbooks and other materials
- *documentary evidence* including official documents, Parliamentary debates, voluntary organization activities, historical texts concerning Dutch and English society etc.
- *newspaper articles* relating to young people's sex(uality), 'teenage' pregnancy and school-based sex education
- *young women's magazines,* in particular 'problem pages', articles relating to relationships and sex(uality) and contraception advertisements.

The variety and nature of the data necessitated a flexible and open approach to the research process and the analytical tasks performed. As described more fully in Chapters 5 and 6, the various forms of data were handled and analysed differently according to both their inherent nature and their function within the project.

TEXTUAL DATA PREPARATION CONSIDERATIONS

While a CAQDAS project can contain and reference all aspects of the project, transcribing and preparing primary data files is usually done outside the software. There are particular necessities and protocols for transcribing data for different methodological approaches, but it is useful to be aware of how software packages can handle textual data as early as possible. Pay attention to the format in which the software expects these files to be saved. Most packages provide text searching tools, which allow for the quicker organization (auto coding) of structures in data (see Chapter 11). This is useful for structured interview data, focus-group transcripts, open-ended questions to survey data and many other forms of structured data. It may well be cost effective to follow a simple set of rules when transcribing, which will save a lot of tidying up later. On the other hand, do not become too obsessed with what makes for efficient data formatting, as it would be a great mistake if this influenced the way data are collected, the design of the interviews and the rigidity of the interview framework, or generally led to a loss of the 'qualitative' dimension of the dataset.

GENERAL GUIDELINES FOR TRANSCRIBING DATA

The three software packages we focus on in this book all handle rich text format (RTF, file extension .rtf) data. We concentrate on RTF for ease of comparison, although many issues discussed are relevant to other textual formats. Documents saved in RTF allow editing within the CAQDAS package. Each software program handles text structures slightly differently but there are some general guidelines which are useful to consider before transcribing data.

Transcription formats

Primary data are often transcribed into tables, allowing for codes and comments to be handwritten in the margin. Some software packages accept embedded objects such as tables in RTF files, but others will not. In any case, this way of transcribing is not necessary when using a CAQDAS package, as the software incorporates its own, much more powerful and flexible, facilities for annotating and coding the text (see Chapters 4 and 9, and Chapters 5 and 7 respectively). Converting tables to text may be a fiddly process, but should be achievable using word processor applications. Software will automatically number different units of context (see below). In many cases line numbering inserted by hand into documents will not transfer neatly into the software project.

If your methodology necessitates particular transcription protocols (for example, when conducting conversation analysis), it is useful to pilot your use of the software to ascertain how your chosen software displays the data. Software user forums and discussion lists are good sources of information on other researchers' experiences of software and particular transcription conventions. For discourse and conversation analysis see Silverman (2000), ten Have (1990), Atkinson et al. (1984) and Appendix D.

Using rich text features to indicate important aspects of the data

When saving files in RTF, most style and formatting features will be maintained. There may be distinct advantages to using such features to indicate various important aspects of the data.

Coloured fonts (but not coloured highlighting) are preserved in the conversion from the standard Microsoft Word .doc file to RTF. At the time of writing, no CAQDAS package allows searches for text based on its colour.[1] However, in projects we have undertaken, it has often been useful to indicate different speakers in interview data with contrasting colours as a way of enabling quick visual identification of who is speaking when retrieving data later on. Remember, though, that it takes time to colour data during transcription, and it will help only in a visual sense once inside the CAQDAS package.

RTF also maintains **bold**, underlining and *italics*. Again, CAQDAS packages cannot search text based on these features, but in research projects where the language or terminology of the data is of interest, it may be useful to identify relevant characteristics using such features.

Formatting structured data

Some types of data are inherently structured. These include the following:

- structured and semi-structured interview data
- focus-group data
- open-ended questions to survey data
- some forms of field notes and observational data
- secondary qualitative data such as some forms of official documentation, newspaper articles or online data.

It can be useful to identify repeated structure so that the software can find and automatically code it (see Chapters 5 and 11). Only use these data formatting structures where they are necessary. Unstructured forms of data do not need these automatically recognized units; so, as with any tool, do not feel compelled to make use of auto coding just because it is available.

Recognizable units of context: sentences, paragraphs and sections

Punctuation and text breaks which are useful might include the following:

- *Sentences* are only recognized in some software (indicated by full stops, exclamation marks, question marks). If the software you are about to use recognizes sentences *and* you are intending to make use of auto coding tools, consider adding extra full stops and/or hard returns into unstructured data.
- *Paragraphs* are always recognized (identified differently in different software, but frequently by one hard return). Find out what indicates a paragraph in your software and consider how they may be useful to you.
- *Sections* are only recognized in some software (where a section may contain several paragraphs). Software which recognizes sections as well as paragraphs or different levels of paragraph will provide more sophisticated ways of structuring data (see software-specific areas below).

In semi-structured or unstructured data, it may not be desirable or possible to use shortcut methods of coding (as with the auto code tool mentioned above). There is therefore no need to adopt any special paragraph structure: simply break data up into paragraphs as you would normally.

Speaker and topic identifiers

For group and survey data, identifying speakers or respondents may be of interest, and in such cases it is imperative that repeated identifiers are absolutely uniform throughout. You will depend on consistency when performing text searches and saving or auto coding the results (see Chapters 4 and 11).

Use a clear question, speaker or topic identifier, preferably in UPPER CASE. This will allow case sensitive searches for the identifiers, e.g.

QU1: What did you think of the sex education you had at school?

If you are anonymising speakers or respondents at transcription stage, consider codifying important aspects of information about the respondent in the speaker identifier. For example:

IV: So tell me how you feel …

R33-F-CR: Well, it's hard to describe but I think that when I'm anxious my brain seizes up and I don't say half the things I should have said.

In this case, 'R33-F-CR' might represent respondent 33 who is a female carer. Use find/replace tools in a word processing application to quickly fix speaker IDs and use hyphens to isolate the different codified information in the identifier. This will enable easier auto coding of the discrete elements codified in the identifier. If anonymising data at the transcription stage is not necessary, using CAPITAL LETTERS and a colon at the end of the identifier will facilitate searching for where 'CAROL:' is speaking herself, rather than where Carol is spoken about by somebody else in a focus group, for example.

These are not necessarily vital aspects of transcription or *cleaning up*. If data are already fully transcribed, the time it takes to clean up data may not justify the benefits of doing so. However, consistent formatting will enable fast and reliable organizational coding functions, and if nothing else, will remind you of additional factual information each time you see the speaker's ID.

Speaker identifiers are particularly useful where you are conducting a mixed-methods project. For example, you may have open-ended questions to survey data for the same respondents who were interviewed, and you wish to integrate the quantitative data with the qualitative analysis. It is possible to import into the CAQDAS package the quantitative information from a statistical package (e.g. Microsoft Excel or SPSS) (see Chapter 11).

When transcribing structured primary data, consider developing a transcription template in order to ensure consistent speaker/respondent/topic identifiers across files. This may be particularly useful if contracting out transcriptions and where large datasets are involved. Software packages differ in the way they recognize structures in data, so be clear about this as early as possible as it may have implications for the ease with which data can be accordingly auto coded (see below).

What to avoid when transcribing identifiers

When *initially* transcribing, never use a single letter for speaker IDs without something exclusive (like a colon) next to it which turns it into something that the find/replace tools can identify as a speaker identifier rather than normal text. For instance, the following is not recommended:

I   So tell me how you feel about …
R   It's hard to explain really.

You will not be able to replace these quickly because you will find many Is and Rs in other places in the text.

Naming and saving data files

Systematic file names that codify important information are also useful: for example, R33-F-CR-PH2 (second-phase interview with female carer). If you have an interview respondent who also took part in a focus group or completed a questionnaire, make sure the speaker ID in the focus-group transcript is the same as the file name for the interview transcript.

In most packages, files can be renamed after import. However, earlier, efficient file naming is especially useful when working in CAQDAS packages which use an external database system (see software-specific reviews in Appendix C). It will also be useful if retaining copies of original data files outside the software for reference purposes. Grouping files by the order they are listed in the software, however, is usually just a way of more easily locating them. Each package discussed in detail in this book provides more sophisticated ways to group files according to (combinations of) known characteristics such as the socio-demographic characteristics of respondents (see Chapter 11).

Save a copy of your cleaned-up file in your word processing application first, then save as RTF (see Figure 2.1).

 With the above considerations in mind, before transcribing too many data, it is advisable where possible to prepare a small pilot project with one or two files inside the chosen CAQDAS package. Do some coding and retrieval (see Chapters 7 and 8); carry out some auto coded text searches (see Chapter 11); and generate some output reports (see various chapters) to test that the formatting of the data seems to work for your needs. If you see where improvements can be made, they are more easily applied at an early stage of transcription.

SOFTWARE-SPECIFIC TEXTUAL DATA PREPARATIONS

The following sections should be read in combination with the general discussion above. Here we provide software-specific information for formatting data files for use in

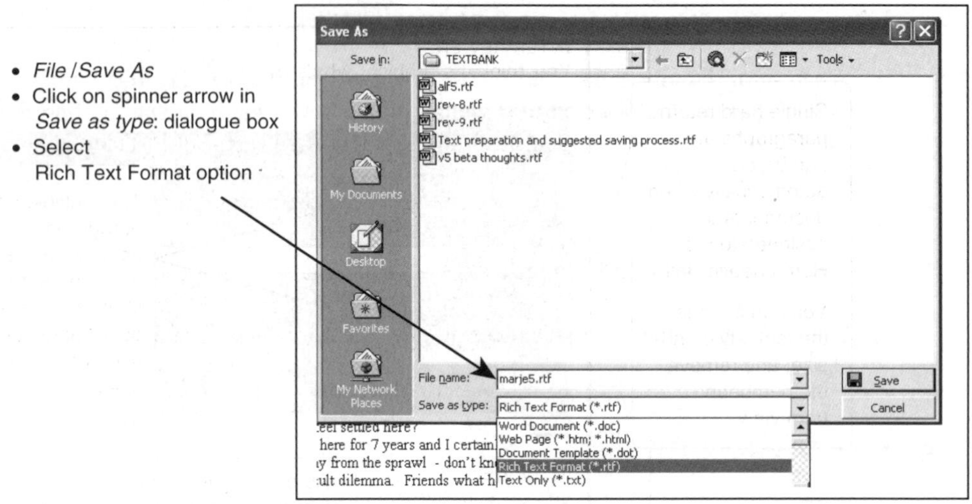

- *File / Save As*
- Click on spinner arrow in *Save as type*: dialogue box
- Select Rich Text Format option

Figure 2.1   Save the word processed file as rich text format

ATLAS.ti5, MAXqda2 and NVivo7. We assume that files will be initially prepared in a word processing application. However, editing ability in RTF documents means they do not need to be complete before they are assigned or imported into the software project.

Preparing textual data for ATLAS.ti5

ATLAS.ti5 handles data in textual, graphic and multimedia formats. Textual data formats include plain text (.txt), RTF (.rtf) and Microsoft Word documents (.doc). Files saved as RTF can be edited within the software, whereas those saved in .doc format cannot. Blank RTF documents can be assigned and used as memos, although there is a separate and very flexible memo system (see Chapter 9).

Of the three software packages we focus on, ATLAS.ti5 is the only one which allows non-textual data files to be directly incorporated into the software project. A large variety of graphic, audio and video formats can be assigned and marked, coded, annotated and retrieved using similar processes as those for text (see developer website for list of accepted formats). This is enabled by the 'external database' structure and allows flexible integration of a large range of data and information which may contribute to a research project. If working directly with audio/video files, it may be useful to split long files into shorter segments before assigning them to the software, as long sequences may be cumbersome to handle when coding (see Chapter 7). Graphics can be assigned to ATLAS.ti5 as individual files or embedded into RTF files. The way you work with multimedia data will depend on the status and function of such data within the research, for example photos may be data in themselves, or simply serve to remind you of a research setting or context etc.

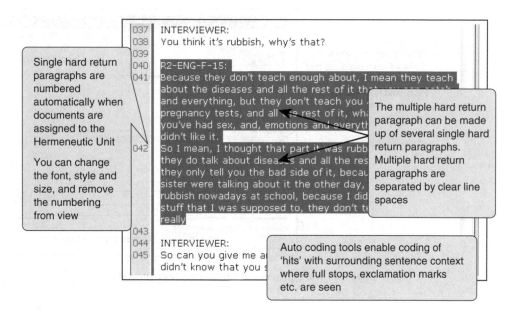

Figure 2.2   Recognizable units of context in ATLAS.ti5

Units of context in ATLAS.ti5

ATLAS.ti5 allows the semi-automatic and automatic selection of text to certain units of context, either by double clicking or when using the auto code tool (see Chapter 11):

• the *word*	1 double click
• the *sentence* – identified by a colon or a full stop	2 double clicks
• the *paragraph*	3 double clicks
• the *whole document*	4 double clicks

There are two levels of paragraph: those separated by one hard return, and larger units of context separated by more than one hard return. In the auto coding tool these are referred to as 'single hard returns' and 'multiple hard returns' (see Figure 2.2 and Chapter 11).

In structured data, if you intend to auto code, keep speaker or question identifiers attached to the paragraph to which they refer. For example, text or speech begins on the same line or the very next line as the identifier (see Figure 2.2 and Chapter 11). Ensure there are multiple hard returns between contextual sections in the data, for example between the speech of focus-group respondents.

Embedded objects in ATLAS.ti5

Objects including Excel tables, images, PowerPoint slides etc. can be embedded in RTF primary documents.[2] As long as the host application is installed on the computer, most

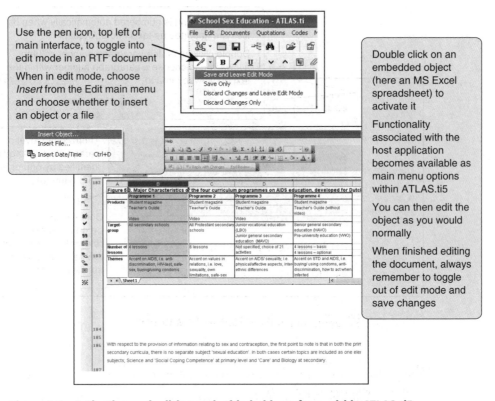

Use the pen icon, top left of main interface, to toggle into edit mode in an RTF document

When in edit mode, choose *Insert* from the Edit main menu and choose whether to insert an object or a file

Double click on an embedded object (here an MS Excel spreadsheet) to activate it

Functionality associated with the host application becomes available as main menu options within ATLAS.ti5

You can then edit the object as you would normally

When finished editing the document, always remember to toggle out of edit mode and save changes

Figure 2.3 **Activating and editing embedded objects from within ATLAS.ti5**

objects can be activated and edited from within ATLAS.ti5 without opening the host application (see Figure 2.3). If documents contain graphics when assigned to the Hermeneutic Unit, they cannot be activated in this way, so it may be more flexible to assign graphics as files (primary documents) in their own right.

Upon activating the object, the host application's toolbars and menus can be directly accessed within the ATLAS.ti5 windows (see Figure 2.3). For example, if you insert an Excel table as an embedded object and double click on it, the ATLAS.ti5 main menu and toolbar are replaced by the Excel menu and toolbar. All Excel functions can be used to modify and work on the embedded table. This is called *in-place activation* or *editing*. If you don't have Excel on your computer, you will see the image of the table, but it will not be possible to activate or edit it.

Preparing textual data for MAXqda2

MAXqda2 handles data in RTF only. Once imported into the project, files are referred to as 'texts'. Texts are fully editable within the software when in edit mode. New blank texts can be created within the software and can be treated in the same way as imported files.

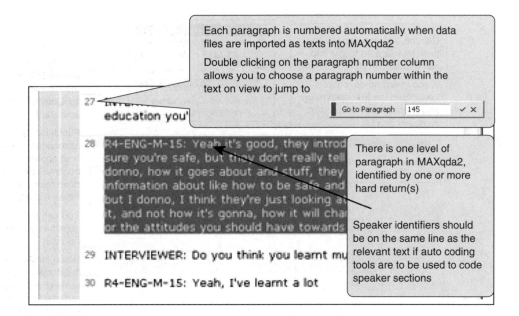

Each paragraph is numbered automatically when data files are imported as texts into MAXqda2

Double clicking on the paragraph number column allows you to choose a paragraph number within the text on view to jump to

Go to Paragraph   145

There is one level of paragraph in MAXqda2, identified by one or more hard return(s)

Speaker identifiers should be on the same line as the relevant text if auto coding tools are to be used to code speaker sections

Figure 2.4   Recognizable units of context in MAXqda2

These blank texts can be used as memos, although there is a separate and very flexible memo system (see Chapter 9).

Units of context in MAXqda2

MAXqda2 allows the semi-automatic and automatic selection of text to the word or paragraph. MAXqda2 does not automatically recognize the sentence.

• the *word*	1 double click
• the *paragraph*	2 double clicks

In structured data, you will need to keep speaker or question identifiers within the same paragraph as the associated speech or text if you intend to auto code. Paragraphs are automatically numbered within the software, and are identified by one hard return (see Figure 2.4). Line breaks can also be forced using Shift + Enter on the keyboard. Small paragraphs, where the respondent identifier appears at the beginning of the first line of each paragraph, may be useful if you need to auto code for structure (see Chapter 11).

Embedded objects in MAXqda2

Objects including graphics, Excel tables, PowerPoint slides etc. can be embedded into RTF files. Embedding creates a link to the original file. Double clicking on the link within MAXqda2 opens the file in its host application. Embedded objects can be coded in their

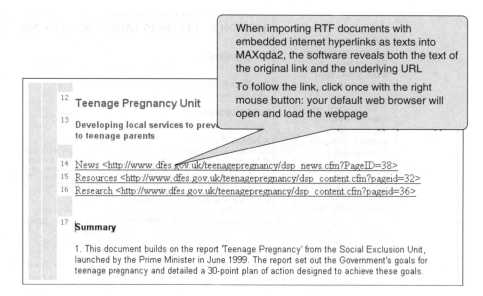

When importing RTF documents with embedded internet hyperlinks as texts into MAXqda2, the software reveals both the text of the original link and the underlying URL

To follow the link, click once with the right mouse button: your default web browser will open and load the webpage

12 **Teenage Pregnancy Unit**

13 **Developing local services to prev** **to teenage parents**

14 News <http://www.dfes.gov.uk/teenagepregnancy/dsp_news.cfm?PageID=38>
15 Resources <http://www.dfes.gov.uk/teenagepregnancy/dsp_content.cfm?pageid=32>
16 Research <http://www.dfes.gov.uk/teenagepregnancy/dsp_content.cfm?pageid=36>

17 **Summary**

1. This document builds on the report 'Teenage Pregnancy' from the Social Exclusion Unit, launched by the Prime Minister in June 1999. The report set out the Government's goals for teenage pregnancy and detailed a 30-point plan of action designed to achieve these goals.

Figure 2.5   Active internet hyperlinks in RTF documents in MAXqda2

entirety, but not parts of them. Internet hyperlinks embedded into RTF files are active in that just one click will open your internet browser and load the website (see Figure 2.5).

Preparing textual data for NVivo7

NVivo7 will directly import plain text (.txt), RTF (.rtf) and Microsoft Word (.doc). All formats are fully editable within NVivo7. It is possible to set document properties to read-only to prevent accidental editing. If source documents contain hyperlinks, they are visible but not active. Objects can be embedded into documents, but those containing images may significantly increase the size of your project file. Whole embedded objects can be coded, but not parts of them. Tables can therefore be included for reference in documents but data should not be wholly transcribed into tables.

Units of context in NVivo7

NVivo7 allows the semi-automatic and automatic selection of text when browsing a document. Note that NVivo7 does not recognize the sentence.

- the *word*   1   double click
- the *paragraph*   2   double clicks

In structured data, you can make use of Microsoft Word styles to insert up to nine levels of heading. These are recognized as sections within NVivo7 and data can be auto coded according to their presence (Figure 2.6). Sections can comprise multiple paragraphs. They may be useful in some forms of structured data.

NVivo7 recognizes sections identified by different heading levels (styles in Microsoft Word)

In this example, each interview topic is identified by a section heading at heading level 1

Each speaker section is identified as a subsection (heading level 2)

Sections can comprise multiple paragraphs

SECTION A : LEARNING ABOUT SEX - SCHOOL
...

INTERVIEWER:
So have you ever had any sex of relationships education at school?

R2-ENG-F-15:
Yes, and I think it's rubbish

INTERVIEWER:
You think it's rubbish, why's that?

R2-ENG-F-15:
Because they don't teach enough about, I mean they teach about the disea all the rest of it that you can catch, and everything, but they don't teach y taking pregnancy tests, and all the rest of it, what happens after you've ha and, emotions and everything like that, I didn't like it, so I mean, I though part it was rubbish.

But I mean they do talk about diseases and all the rest of it, I mean they c you the bad side of it, because me and my sister were talking about it the ...

Sections and paragraphs are numbered automatically when data files are imported as documents into NVivo7. They do not appear when browsing a document within the software but can be included in text reports

When reducing the width of the document window, the data do not line wrap

Figure 2.6 **Recognizable units of context in NVivo7**

Embedded objects in NVivo7

Pictures, tables and text boxes can be embedded in documents to be imported into NVivo7. Internet hyperlinks embedded into RTF files are active in NVivo7 in that clicking on the URL will open the internet browser and load the website (Figure 2.7).

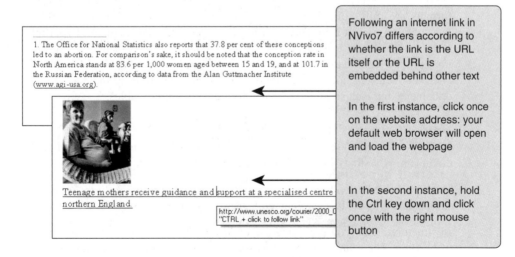

1. The Office for National Statistics also reports that 37.8 per cent of these conceptions led to an abortion. For comparison's sake, it should be noted that the conception rate in North America stands at 83.6 per 1,000 women aged between 15 and 19, and at 101.7 in the Russian Federation, according to data from the Alan Guttmacher Institute (www.agi-usa.org).

Teenage mothers receive guidance and support at a specialised centre northern England

http://www.unesco.org/courier/2000_0
"CTRL + click to follow link"

Following an internet link in NVivo7 differs according to whether the link is the URL itself or the URL is embedded behind other text

In the first instance, click once on the website address: your default web browser will open and load the webpage

In the second instance, hold the Ctrl key down and click once with the right mouse button

Figure 2.7 **Active internet hyperlinks in RTF documents in NVivo7**

SUMMARY: DATA PREPARATION ISSUES

CAQDAS packages allow for the direct incorporation of many different data types and formats, and as packages continue to develop, acceptable formats increase in variety. It is useful to be aware at the outset what data formats your chosen software can handle and to consider carefully how structures may be useful for later tasks and processes. In particular, the automatically recognizable units of context can have important implications for your use of content searching and auto coding tools (see Chapters 4 and 11). It would be wrong, however, to build an interview schedule around the capabilities of any package, or to overly structure data which are inherently unstructured. Try to reach a workable balance between the needs of your project and methodology, and the capabilities of your chosen software.

COMPARATIVE COMMENTS ON DATA AND THEIR PREPARATION FOR CAQDAS PACKAGES

These comparisons draw together some of the considerations discussed in this chapter to highlight the main differences between ATLAS.ti5, MAXqda2 and NVivo7 with regard to data and their preparation for software. We also make reference to aspects of later work which may be affected by the way data are prepared, indicating where following chapters discuss these tasks.

Directly handled data formats

ATLAS.ti5 can directly handle a far greater range of data types than either MAXqda2 or NVivo7. This ability relates to its 'external database' structure (see Chapter 3). External systems usually allow for many more forms of data to be directly incorporated, as they are not contained within one project file as is the case with MAXqda2 and NVivo7. This aspect of ATLAS.ti5 potentially provides immediate access to all relevant online materials. Since the user can code and hyperlink parts of any file in acceptable multimedia formats including video, and play back those coded segments or clips alongside the retrieval of coded text, the software places fewer limitations on what can comprise 'data'.

Embedded objects

ATLAS.ti5 provides sophisticated activation and editing of embedded objects from within the software. This is not available in MAXqda2 or NVivo7.

Internet hyperlinks

MAXqda2 and NVivo7 both support active internet hyperlinking. Any hyperlink to a URL embedded in an RTF document will open that webpage in the default internet browser application by clicking. ATLAS.ti5 shows the hyperlinks and the URL, but you cannot directly link to the webpage.

Units of context

The units of context that each software package automatically recognizes differ. When selecting text in a document by double clicking the left mouse key, ATLAS.ti5 recognizes the widest variety. Precise text segments at the lower levels (word, sentence, paragraph) can be useful in ATLAS.ti5 when coding because of the way it handles quotations (discrete selections of text). MAXqda2 and NVivo7 do not recognize the sentence, which is restrictive when searching text for content and auto coding the results. Also see below concerning structured data. (See Chapters 3, 4, 11 and 12.)

Line wrap

When viewing data within the software, ATLAS.ti5 and MAXqda2 both provide line wrapping of text when the window size is reduced. NVivo7 does not line wrap: this increases the sensation of being in a cramped user interface.

Formatting/organizing structured data

NVivo7 provides the most sophisticated possibilities for auto coding repeated structures across data files. This is useful where you have focus-group data or open-ended questions from survey data since it subsequently provides devices for assigning quantitative/descriptive values to the different structured elements of such files (see Chapter 11). ATLAS.ti5 and MAXqda2 also provide such auto coding of structured data, though the options for later organization of the structure are less developed.[3]

NOTES

1 Although MAXqda2 allows the annotation/colour coding of text in up to four colours, which can be searched for (see Chapter 4), this is not the same as manually colouring text as is discussed here.
2 They can also be embedded into comments (see Chapters 5–8) and memos (see Chapter 9).
3 At the time of writing

Chapter 3
Getting Started in Qualitative Software: Practical Tasks

This chapter is about using software early, possibly before you even have data. Familiarize yourself with your chosen software as soon as possible. We encourage you to try out things that do not matter if they go wrong, but at the same time to use this process productively for your project. When you are ready, you can import textual data into the software. Since your research project probably exists long before you have data, minimize the obstacles that will come between you and your data, and start to do anything with the software to get comfortable with it, to realize you are its boss, and to knock it into shape! Locate your ideas and experimentation in tasks that might be useful for your particular methodological approach. Above all, think creatively and laterally about the software and what it might do for you.

GENERIC TASKS: WHAT CAN BE DONE BEFORE PRIMARY DATA ARE READY?

We do not cover all possible tasks in this chapter, but aim to get you started in an organized way and to refer you elsewhere in the book for step-by-step help.

TASK 3.1   CREATING AND NAMING THE PROJECT, DATA FILES AND REPORTS

Naming your project

Bear in mind that once you start serious work with your project, you may make duplicate versions of the software project as backups or so that you can move around and work on other computers. Plan for the need to bring that project back to your original computer, adequately named, so that it does not get confused with the earlier version of your project. Start thinking now about a project naming convention. Keep it simple. The first time a project called 'Community' is backed up, saved as or duplicated, call it e.g. 06-08-23Comm or Comm06-08-23 (23 August 2006). When you use a date suffix, or prefix, use a convention that will sort the file listing by the whole date rather than by the day of the month, that is in YY-MM-DD order. Then, you can track the chronology of change or movement from the project title itself. Each time you move it to another location, ensure the name is such that it does not overwrite the earlier version. Also, plan now to duplicate or back up your project before you change analytic direction, for example when about to modify a coding schema (see Chapter 6). If things go wrong at this stage you might accidentally undo weeks of work, so you do not want to lose the original version of the project.

Note that the movement of projects between computers is different in each software and requires different safeguards. Note also that there is rarely an effective *Undo* button in complicated database type software, although NVivo7 does include this functionality. See also saving and backing-up instructions in the subsequent exercises for each software.

Naming your data files

Even if you have not yet collected data, establish a convention for naming files. This is more relevant to large datasets but will be useful however many data files you have. Each data file name can contain information. Make the file name as economic as possible and, if you think it will help, add codified information relevant to the project (see Chapter 2).

 ### Naming reports/output and placing them

Although it might seem early to be thinking about this, structures established now will pay off later. Create at least one new folder on your computer, within My Documents or elsewhere, to house subsequent reports and outputs from the software project. Think systematically about a naming convention for reports, so that all like reports sit together in a list. You will be asking the software for document printouts/files (e.g. for paragraph numbers) coded data printouts, memos and code lists. Use a prefix which tells you the type of each report, e.g.

Code-coping-strategies-06-01-15
Code-communication-issues-06-01-16

As in the naming of data files themselves, it is always useful to date stamp an output or report in the name of the file, as you may have several versions of the same output over the life history of a project and this allows you to see clearly which one you want without having to carefully compare the computer's system date 'details'. Date stamping using a consistent protocol is important (see Chapter 2).

 When working in teams, it is especially important to think ahead about report (and project) naming. One element of each report name you may pass to other colleagues will be your own identifier. For example, DS-C-coping-strats-06-01-15 might be Deb Smith's report file about the code 'coping strategies', 15 January 2006. Clarity regarding date-stamping protocols is particularly important in international collaborative projects.

TASK 3.2   FAMILIARIZE YOURSELF WITH THE SOFTWARE

You cannot do any damage by just having a go with menus, buttons and windows. Explore the main interface, look at main menu options and right mouse button menus, which are often different depending on where you right click. Get used to flicking between different views and windows. Fluid movement will be important when you are in serious coding or thinking mode, so familiarize yourself with the available options and different ways of accessing them.

Many CAQDAS packages encourage heavy use of the mouse, with different menu options being available by right clicking. There is increasing concern amongst software users about the risk of repetitive strain injury (RSI), and the role CAQDAS may have in exacerbating it. You may therefore wish to explore the keyboard shortcut keys provided by your chosen software. For ease of comparison, we provide a list of keyboard shortcuts in ATLAS.ti5, MAXqda2 and NVivo7 in Appendix B.

TASK 3.3   MEMOING

Create a project journal
Reflections about your project can be recorded in memos which represent different aspects of the research. It is useful to create a project log or journal straight away, to note the day-to-day tasks you perform and the questions occurring in your mind. Importantly, at the end of a work session note any follow-up actions to improve your continuity next time you work in the project. Investigate memoing procedures, and think early on about how you intend to organize your writing. It will help to be systematic about the management of this aspect of your work (see Chapters 4 and 9).

Standalone memos as full documents
You may be writing memos as standalone documents in your project, in which case assign codes to parts of memos and start the process of efficient cross-referencing early (see Chapters 7 and 9).

TASK 3.4   CODE CREATION

Play with ideas about your coding schema
This will give you practice at code creation, since codes need not yet be associated with data (see Chapter 6).

Theoretical codes
If you are using a theoretical approach to coding, practise creating main codes in a logical way, based on theoretical concepts or sensitizing ideas, so that they are ready to apply to *any* data when they become available. If using a constructivist approach, codes may be used as linking devices to particular patterns of speech or discourse. If you are using a 'grounded' approach, code creation at this stage may just give you a chance to practise. You can always rename and delete codes. (See Chapters 5, 6 and 7 on coding processes.)

Codes relating to literature

Whatever your approach, practise code creation which relates to the literature in your substantive field and your review of it. Consider prefixing codes to note their function. (See Chapter 6 on coding schemata and Chapter 7 on coding tasks.)

Define and describe all codes, adjust meaning and labels

It will help to begin in a disciplined way in this respect. The meaning of a code and its parameters will be important to you as a reminder of what you mean when dealing with subtle and slippery concepts, complex or ambiguous terms. You can *always* abandon any codes or adjust them, rename and redefine them, split them and merge them with others. (See Chapters 5, 6 and 7 on coding processes.)

TASK 3.5   EXPERIMENTING WITH IMPORTING/ASSIGNING DATA

Import pilot data

If you do have pilot project data, or any information about your project at all, go through the data preparation stage and the data import/assignment stage. Practise this to be sure you like the way data appear within the software, and to see if anything unexpected happens! (see Chapter 2 and later in this chapter.)

Import literature lists, abstracts

In any package, you can import abstracts or bibliographic lists as standalone documents. These may be coded and/or act as memos (see Chapter 9). It will help to have such background information available or referenced in the software project to enable continuous cross-referencing throughout your work.

TASK 3.6   EXPERIMENT WITH DATA

Once you have assigned a couple of files of any sort, experiment with moving between them and practise different tasks with them (e.g. annotating, coding, searching).

 Practise getting simple output of these files from the software. It is very useful to have a printout generated from within the software because it will include paragraph numbers. This is useful for any subsequent *armchair annotations* that you make in hard copy. You will be able to input them much more easily if you can navigate easily to the relevant paragraph number. (See Chapter 2 and later in this chapter.)

TASK 3.7   EXPERIMENT WITH MAPPING TOOLS

If you have software which has a mapping capability, you can use it to map processes and project timetables, or if your project is theory driven, theories and relationships between abstract categories that you wish to test later in your project. Practise by creating a map of how you see the project at its outset. You can then compare later as your analysis progresses, helping you to visualize your analytic journey (see Chapter 10).

TASK 3.8   USE OR THROW AWAY

 If you are working in a team, think carefully about how you intend to share work. Communication about the technical aspects of using software in a team situation is as important as communicating about the theoretical and analytic aspects of the project. Experiment with backing up and moving projects between team members and computers early on if you will be doing this frequently. Copy one project (with a coding schema prepared) between members as a way to get everyone started with the same coding schema structure. There need be no data to copy (unless you choose to include a couple of files for a coding reliability check between you).[1] Continue to communicate and modify this during subsequent work. Copying the whole project between team members can be an effective way to start work on a project in a software program, particularly if, in the long term, you intend to merge team members' individual work into one large software project.[2]

 These eight tasks are useful for familiarizing with software and planning for its use. Often, playing with software early on produces material and items which are quickly superseded when you get down to real work, so be prepared to throw the early work away!

SOFTWARE-SPECIFIC VARIATIONS: GETTING STARTED WITH SOFTWARE

Exercises in ATLAS.ti5

Reminders about the structure of the project in ATLAS.ti5

ATLAS.ti5 has what we call an 'external database' (see Chapter 2). There are two main parts to your work in ATLAS.ti5: the Hermeneutic Unit (HU) or project file and, separately, your documents or data files. This has very important implications for saving, backing up and moving your project. A clear understanding of the basic architecture and movement of files and folders on your computer is an absolute prerequisite for using ATLAS.ti5.

Different types of work/methods/methodology

ATLAS.ti5 offers the most extensive range of ways to handle different types of data. In addition to the usual code and retrieve functionality appealing to many interpretive researchers, it has in particular many 'text-level' tools which are rather different from other software. The architecture of the software makes quotations (see below) into independent objects which can be commented on, included in networks, and hyperlinked together (see Chapter 4). Thus it may be that users who are interested in more micro-level interactions in the text can consider the use of this software to manage them. If working in teams, merging work is possible in ATLAS.ti5, since various different micro or macro models of merge can be utilized.

The Hermeneutic Unit

Once your software project or HU is created and you assign data files to it, it will gradually contain links *from* all of these documents *to* and *between* other project objects, for example analytic memos, codes, 'quotations' (selections of significant text that you have made) and networks (visual maps of connections that you have made).

Data files

It is important to understand that the HU only 'reads' the data you have assigned. The data files (documents) remain physically outside the HU. This type of 'external system' allows you to assign any file recognized by ATLAS.ti5 to the Hermeneutic Unit, including non-textual data such as graphics and audio/visual files. Textual data can be in Word, rich text format or text only. The latter two options will allow editing inside ATLAS.ti5, but if Word files are assigned you will not be allowed to edit inside ATLAS.ti5. Once files are assigned to the HU, you must not edit them in any other application. For safety reasons due to the external database architecture, we strongly recommend that you use MS Word files for transcript style data, and only consider using rich text format where it is absolutely essential that you have editing rights over your data. (See Chapter 2 for further information about file format and units of context.)

It makes practical sense to store all the data files you intend to assign to the ATLAS.ti5 HU in the same folder on your computer. The software creates a default folder for this purpose when you install the software. This can usually be found at My Documents/Scientific Software/ATLASti/Textbank.

Whether you use this default location or not, we strongly recommend you save your textual data files and HU into the same folder where possible. Whichever folder you use, the HU will expect to find those files – exactly the same versions of them – in the same path relative to the HU each time it is opened. For instance, if you move the HU to another computer, it will look for the data files in the same place relative to the HU on the new computer. (See Copy Bundle in Exercise 3.4 for more information on this.)

Note: once data files have been assigned to the HU, never move them or open them again from within that folder in any other application. If you move or edit them, ATLAS.ti5 will no longer recognize them, and you will not be able to connect to them from within ATLAS.ti5.

Quotation structure

ATLAS.ti5 is the only software which creates 'quotations' or segments of data as independent objects. This allows you to work with quotations entirely independently of coding processes, for example by annotating them, linking them to one another (see Chapter 4) and visualizing them in a network (see Chapter 10).

 Quotations can be created in different ways and from different types of data (e.g. text, graphic, audio/video). However they are created, all quotations are listed in the Quotation Manager. Each independent quotation can be renamed and annotated in an individual comment bar. When working with multimedia data, renaming quotations more descriptively can facilitate a much more explicit list of pointers to the different happenings in the data. Secondary commentary can be noted in comment bars either as a precursor to coding multimedia quotations, or as a supplement to this process. Developing consistent protocols for using these descriptive functions will make it easier to retrieve certain related quotations later, and the content of labels and comments can later be searched for by using the Object Crawler (see Chapters 4 and 9).

Exercise 3.1   ATLAS.ti5: create a new HU and assign data

The numbering of steps corresponds to Figure 3.1.
Prepare two data files, e.g. a transcript, a literature list, a literature abstract or field notes. For full instructions on how to prepare data files for ATLAS.ti5, see Chapter 2. See also the commentary about this process in Task 3.1 earlier in this chapter.

1   Open ATLAS.ti5. Software will be listed in your Start menu, or a submenu of Program Files/Scientific Software/.
2   Save and name the Hermeneutic Unit (project). Save the HU into the same folder from which you assigned your data files using *File/Save*.

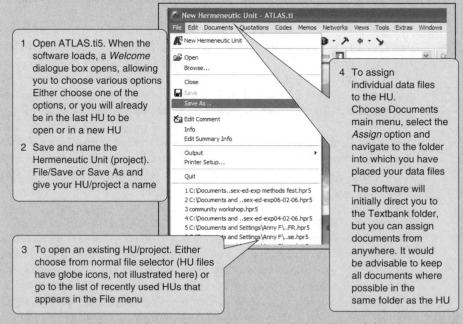

1   Open ATLAS.ti5. When the software loads, a *Welcome* dialogue box opens, allowing you to choose various options Either choose one of the options, or you will already be in the last HU to be open or in a new HU

2   Save and name the Hermeneutic Unit (project). File/Save or Save As and give your HU/project a name

3   To open an existing HU/project. Either choose from normal file selector (HU files have globe icons, not illustrated here) or go to the list of recently used HUs that appears in the File menu

4   To assign individual data files to the HU. Choose Documents main menu, select the *Assign* option and navigate to the folder into which you have placed your data files

The software will initially direct you to the Textbank folder, but you can assign documents from anywhere. It would be advisable to keep all documents where possible in the same folder as the HU

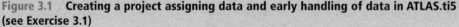

Figure 3.1   Creating a project assigning data and early handling of data in ATLAS.ti5 (see Exercise 3.1)

(Continued)

3 To open an existing HU/project: use *File/Open* or go to the list of recently used HUs that appears in the File menu.

4 Assign individual data files to the new HU. It is simpler if you first collect all your data files into the same folder. You can assign documents at any stage of analysis. Remember that textual files can be in either RTF or Word (.doc). If they are .doc, you will not be able to edit them inside ATLAS.ti5 and this can be a much safer option. Use the Documents menu to find the folder where you have placed data files and select them one at a time or choose several all at once. (To multiply select, hold down the Ctrl key and click carefully on each file in turn.)

5 Get printed output of each data file. Choose numbered paragraphs if you feel it might be useful (not illustrated). Use *Documents/Output/Print with Margin* to print documents with codes, hyperlinks and memos in the margin.

Note: the most frequent problem encountered by users is that the HU file, when it is moved to another computer, will not connect to the data files themselves, although it will list documents, codes and the quotations. This may happen for a number of reasons. The documents also need to be moved into the same relative path compared to the HU. One way to reduce potential path errors is to start off by assigning from, and keeping textual data documents in, the same folder as the HU. (see also Copy Bundle in Exercise 3.4.)

Exercise 3.2 ATLAS.ti5: exploring the user interface

See Figure 3.2. Experiment generally with these options before going on to the structured step-by-step exercises in Exercise 3.3.

• *The user interface* and its functionality are operable via a set of main menus. Look at all main menu options.

• *Combo boxes* with dropdown lists are important. They contain the main analytic objects in ATLAS.ti5. They are Documents, Quotes, Codes and Memos (see Figure 3.2).

• *Manager windows* are associated with each combo box. They list the contents and can be organized and sorted.

• *Shortcut icons* tell you their functionality as you pass your cursor slowly over them.

• *Context-specific right button menus* vary depending on the exact position of your cursor arrow. Some but not all of the right button menu options in the manager windows replicate options found in the main menus for that respective object.

(Continued)

(Continued)

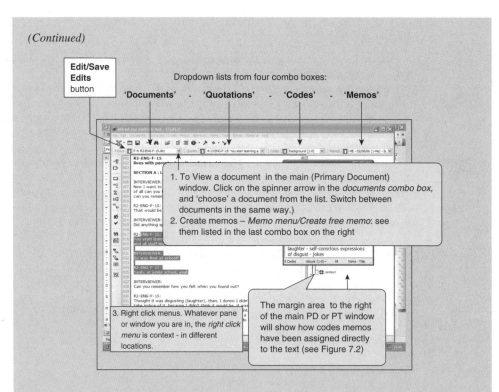

Figure 3.2   The ATLAS.ti5 user interface
See additional step by step information in chapter sections – 'EXERSISE 3.2 ATLAS.ti5' in which numbering of steps corresponds to numbersbelow

Exercise 3.3   ATLAS.ti5: early handling of data

The numbering of steps corresponds to Figure 3.2. See also Tasks 3.5 and 3.6 earlier in this Chapter. After assigning several files, literature lists, pilot data or any textual data, try these exercises.

1 View a document. Click on the spinner arrow in the Documents combo box, and 'choose' a document from the list. (This has to be done even if you only have one document, and always has to be done on first opening the HU in each work session.) Switch between documents in the same way.
2 Create memos. Use *Memo/Create Free Memo*: see them listed in the last combo box on the right. (Leave the date in the title bar when the Memo window pops up, but add a meaningful title just before the date.) Hit the checkbox to save any writing you do in the memo. (See Chapter 9 for more ideas.)
3 Right click menus. Whatever pane or window you are in, the right click menu is context specific, i.e. the exact location of your cursor arrow over a selection, or in space not selected, will determine which right button menu appears. Practise this in different locations.

(Continued)

4   Practise these operations on the right click menu over selected text, e.g. right click and Create Free Quotation. See it listed in the Quotes combo box.

5   Print out a numbered version of your document. To do this, go to *Documents menu/ Output/print with margin*. This will be useful when coding or making armchair annotations to hard copy. (In the vertical tool bar on the left side, the **99** icon toggles paragraph numbering so that you can relate the hard copy to what appears in the software.)

Free quotations: what can you do with free quotations? Navigate between them in the quotations list. Assign codes to them (though the free quotation stage is not a necessary part of assigning codes). You can drag text selections into a network view as a way of creating quotations or to arrange them in a graphic for a report or presentation (see Chapter 10). You can make links between them (see Chapter 4) and put quotations in networks (Chapter 10).

Exercise 3.4   ATLAS.ti5: routine saving and backing up

The numbering of steps corresponds to Figures 3.3 and 3.4. See also Task 3.1 earlier in this chapter.

1. *Prepare for the backing-up operation*
First save your HU. *File menu/Save*

2. *Rename HU*
File menu/Save As and rename your HU by giving a date stamp. e.g.Sex-ED-06-06-31 (yy,mm,dd)

3. *Copy bundle* to condense HU and documents into one file.
*Tools main menu /
Copy Bundle/Create Bundle*

You can choose files to exclude from the bundle in the right hand pane (e.g. exclude large multimedia files) in order to create a more manageable file size.

4. *Condense and back up -Create bundle –* adding the new date stamped file name to the bundle file. You can save it to any desired location. It is a good idea to have created a folder for these bundles.

Copy Bundle Document Selection

Documents not in bundle:

Name	Path	Size	Type

Total size of 0 selected documents: 0 Byte

Bundled documents:

Name	Path	Size	Type
R4-ENG-...	C:\Docume...	130 KB	ric...
R1-ENG-...	C:\Docume...	106....	ric...
FG1-ENL...	C:\Docume...	133....	ric...
FG2-NLIE...	C:\Docume...	115 KB	ric...
R3-ENG-...	C:\Docume...	93 KB	ric...
R2-ENG-	C:\Docume...	109....	ric...

Total size of 6 bundled documents: 687.50 KB plus size of HU 6 KB totals 693.50 KB

Documents which cannot be bundled:

Name	Path	Conflict

Report:

all documents will be bundled

Sometimes you just wish to preserve a version of an HU with all the documents exactly as they were at that point in time. Simply Copy bundle with HU and all documents.

Cancel

Figure 3.3   Backing up in ATLAS.ti5 – Copy Bundle (see Exercise 3.4)

(Continued)

The way you save, save as, condense and move your project from computer to computer in ATLAS.ti5 is very important. Establish an efficient routine early, before you have done too much work. We suggest three basic example scenarios. Decide which one fits your current circumstances.

- *Scenario 1.* Working on the same computer throughout: backing-up process.
- *Scenario 2.* Moving HU and all data files from one computer to another for the first time.
- *Scenario 3.* Moving HU and documents which you have edited to another computer where there is an older (or newer) version of your HU with its associated documents.
- *Scenario 4.* Moving HU ONLY, because all data files are already in both places

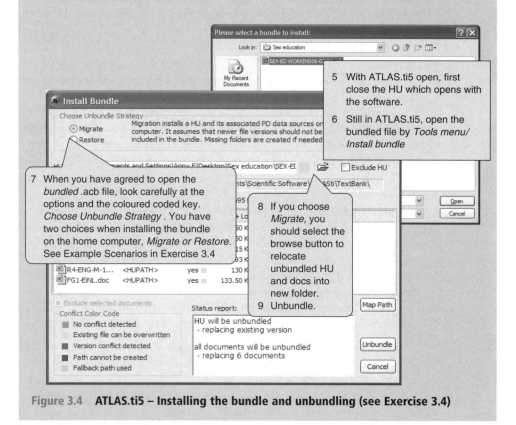

Figure 3.4   **ATLAS.ti5 – Installing the bundle and unbundling (see Exercise 3.4)**

Scenario 1

You are working on the same computer throughout the work process. You simply want to create deliberate, dated backups to preserve your work – just in case. Use steps 1, 3 and 4 *only* from the following (see also Figure 3.3):

1 Prepare for the Copy Bundle operation. Always save your HU as the first step: *File/Save*.

2 Rename the HU using *File/Save As*, but *only* if you are about to move from one workstation to another or to make a deliberate renamed version of the working HU. (The software creates a backup each time you close the HU, but the backups always get overwritten by the next one.) Suggestion: save as e.g. Sex-ED-06-06-31 (see Chapter 2 for advice on consistent naming protocols).

3 Copy Bundle to condense HU and the separate PD entities into one file – *Tools/copy bundle*. Refer to Figure 3.3. You can exclude some files from the right-hand pane (e.g. large multimedia files) in order to create a more manageable file size.

4 Condense and back up *both* the HU and the separate PD entities into one file – *Create Bundle*. Suggestion: give the bundle file the same date stamped name that you may have used already, (see 2. above). It would be a good idea to save this file to a network drive or separate folder.

Scenario 2

You are moving the HU and the documents from work to home for the first time. Follow steps 1–4 in Scenario 1 (see also Figure 3.3). Then:

• Take the bundled .acb file home on a memory stick or email it to yourself. (From the email, *Save As* onto your desktop or into My Documents.)

• Now see Figure 3.4. Use the *Restore* or *Migrate* options.

Scenario 3

You are moving the HU and documents which you have edited to another computer where there is an older (or newer) version of your HU with its associated documents. Follow steps 1–4 in Scenario 1 (see also Figure 3.3). Then do the following (see Figure 3.4):

5 Open ATLAS.ti5 at home, and close the HU which automatically opens. (This will be the one that was previously worked on here.)

6 Use *Tools/Copy Bundle/Install Bundle* to open the bundled file.

7 Consider the *Migrate/Create New Folder* option if:

   (a) You want to preserve the older version of your HU with all its older matching document files (PDs) that you have on your home computer.

   (b) You are not sure what to do.

   (c) You see some conflicts colour-coded pink. Although the software will try to resolve these conflicts if you go ahead, you may feel it is easier just to select the *Browse* button to create a new folder to unbundle the HU and document files.

8 If you choose *Migrate*, select the *Browse* icon at HU path bar to relocate the unbundled HU and documents into a new folder. If you choose *Restore*, all documents and HUs with the same names will be overwritten. If you have Word files as your

documents, you can usually choose *Restore* unless you do not wish to overwrite similarly named work.

9   Select *Unbundle*: the HU will open, giving you contact with each of your documents and all work done so far.

 If you have progressively saved bundles as part of the backing-up process, go to Windows Explorer and delete the older versions (easily identifiable because you have a date stamp in the name of the bundles).

Note: the above options can be confusing. Talking through your own requirements with an experienced user or an advisor can be very productive (see Appendix D).

Scenario 4

Moving HU only because you already have all the documents on both computers.

Just use *File/Save as* process to save HU only. Make certain of efficient renaming so that the correct HU can be identified and opened. Also ensure that each time the new HU file is re-introduced to each computer it is transferred into the correct folder.

Exercises in MAXqda2 M

Reminders about the structure of the project in MAXqda2

MAXqda2 operates using what we call an 'internal database' structure (see Chapter 2). This means that data files (texts) are imported into a MAXqda2 project and, therefore, the project file contains all your work. With the addition of MAXDictio, the program provides content analysis with word frequency tools, key word in context retrieval, and word indexing (see Chapter 4). MAXqda2 will only directly handle RTF files, although objects can be embedded in texts and accessed from within the software (see Chapter 2).

Different types of work/methods/methodology

The simple interface of MAXqda2 provides lists of documents, an easy (and safe) editable text browser, a codes list and the retrieved segments, in windows arranged as quadrants of the screen. The margin display gives you interactive connection with codes or memos assigned to segments of text. Whether your methodological interest is based interpretively or in a more constructivist interest in discourse and patterns of speech, you can choose effective tools to enhance your management of data. The Word Frequency tool added in MAXDictio provides a closer examination of actual verbatim content. Full editing rights over the data means that you can embed in-depth comments either in the data themselves or in memos which are flagged to one side of the text. Teamwork is ideally enabled in MAXqda2, with colour-coded differentiation, memos and the ability to merge different elements of work.

Activation as the central filtering principle

After you have coded the data, if this is how you work, the process of *activating* files or codes is central to how the software will allow you to filter to your current interest within the project, e.g. in retrieving all coded segments but just for particular documents. At the simplest level, you will be switching on (activating) and switching off (deactivating) codes or documents or a combination of both (see Chapter 8).

Data files

Textual data files can have graphics embedded in them, but must be in rich text format for the software to recognize them (see also Chapter 2).

Exercise 3.5   MAXqda2: create new project, create text groups, import data

The numbering of steps corresponds to Figure 3.5. See also Task 3.1 earlier in this chapter.

Prepare two data files, e.g. a transcript, a literature list, a literature abstract or field notes. Data files must be in rich text format (RTF). To remind yourself of full instructions on how to prepare data files for MAXqda2, see Chapter 2.

1   On opening the software, either *Create and Open New Project* or *Open Existing Project*.
2   If creating a new project, in the next file saving pane, enter a short name for your project (see Task 3.1).
3   Create text groups prior to data import. Click with right button on *Text Groups*, then click *New Text Group* and rename it while in edit mode. Create enough text groups to manage the different types of data you have including focus groups, observation notes, literature etc. Click with right button on the relevant group to import or create file to go into that group. (It's up to you what text groups represent.) You can drag files to move them out of one group into another.
4   *Either* create new files: right click a text group and click on *Create Text,* giving an empty file to write analytic, abstract or process-related notes. (See Exercise 3.7 on how to edit this new document.)
5   *Or* import ready prepared texts (existing files saved as rich text format): right click on a text group, click on *Import Text(s)* and navigate to where you have saved data files to select and import.
6   Get printed output of each data file with numbered paragraphs if you feel it might be useful (not illustrated). Go to *Project/Print/Text Browser* to print memos and documents with or without codes in the margins.

Experiment with creating sets of documents underneath the text groups, e.g. a set of phase 1 interviews, a set of phase 2 interviews and so on. Sets consist of shortcuts to existing files. As with text groups, sets can be activated to show retrieval from the files within the set.

(Continued)

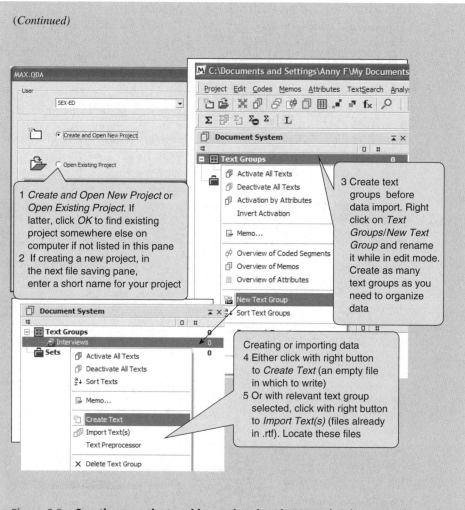

(Continued)

1 *Create and Open New Project* or *Open Existing Project*. If latter, click *OK* to find existing project somewhere else on computer if not listed in this pane

2 If creating a new project, in the next file saving pane, enter a short name for your project

3 Create text groups before data import. Right click on *Text Groups/New Text Group* and rename it while in edit mode. Create as many text groups as you need to organize data

Creating or importing data
4 Either click with right button to *Create Text* (an empty file in which to write)
5 Or with relevant text group selected, click with right button to *Import Text(s)* (files already in .rtf). Locate these files

Figure 3.5 **Creating a project and importing data in MAXqda2 (see Exercise 3.5)**

Exercise 3.6   MAXqda2: exploring the user interface

Experiment generally with navigating around the interface and familiarizing with menu options. Refer to Figure 3.6.

The *user interface* consists of four main windows. Experiment with switching them on and off (look for the four shortcut icons grouped together near the centre of the top button bar). Functions are either in main menus or in right button menus on each object in each pane.

(Continued)

- *Document System* lists text groups and texts (data files). Sets of shortcuts can be created here too, to provide instant devices to activate (filter to) particular text groups.
- *Text Browser* allows viewing and work on data files. Open a file or navigate between them by double clicking in the Document System.
- *Code System* houses the codes you create. Codes can be created in hierarchies but they do not have to be.
- *Retrieved Segments* shows text segments based on the codes which have been activated in the Code System.

These windows can be opened together and will auto arrange (or can be manually resized). You can close any selection of the windows – and the remaining windows will auto arrange to an optimal but resizable setting.

You can also:

- *Experiment with resizing* windows at each of the splitter bars, up–down and, left–right. Open and close each of the panes to focus on an area of work.
- *Edit a text*: edit a blank document by choosing the *Edit* icon.

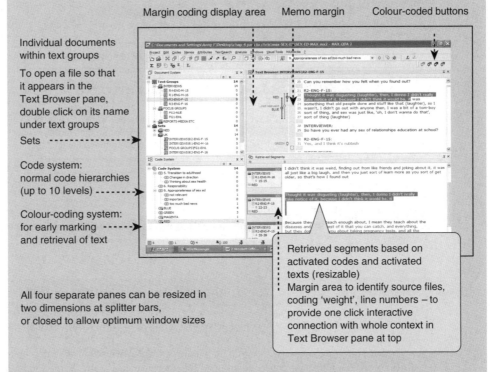

Figure 3.6   **The MAXqda2 user interface (see Exercise 3.6)**

Exercise 3.7   MAXqda2: early handling of data

The numbering of steps corresponds to Figure 3.7 (see also Figure 3.6).
Having created a new (empty) text and imported several files (see Exercise 3.5), literature lists, pilot data or any RTF data, try these exercises.

1   Open a text in the Text Browser and switch between files viewed in the Text Browser by double clicking on a document in the Document System window.
2   Editing data: click on the *Edit* icon to get the open text into edit mode. The text style formatting buttons and text colour buttons only change the colour or style of text in a *visual* sense.
3   If you wish to use functional colour coding, select text and use one of the four colour-coding devices. (Can't see them? Go to *Windows/Show colour coding bar*.) What could you use colour coding for?

   (a)   They can represent a very early non-committal coding process.
   (b)   You can mark interesting segments, knowing that you will be able to retrieve e.g. all the red segments by activating the red code and activating documents of interest.
   (c)   Colour coding can stand for whatever you want it to!

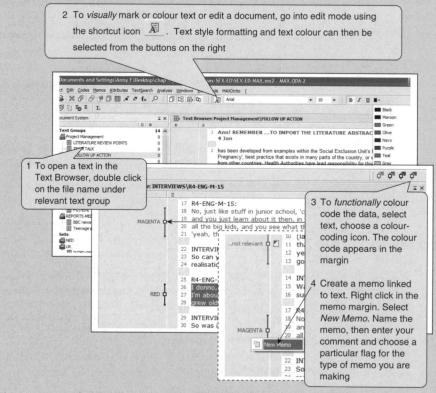

Figure 3.7   Early handling of text in MAXqda2 (see Exercise 3.7)

(Continued)

4   Create a memo at some text by clicking with the right button in the memo margin and
    selecting the *New memo* option. Name the memo, enter the comment, and choose a
    particular flag for the type of memo you are making.

If you are working as part of a team, always fill in the *Author* part of the memo box. There are
always several areas in planning for teamwork which can be considered early on. One of them,
in MAXqda2 particularly, is giving colour attributes to codes for each different team member
(this is different from colour coding). Thus at a later merging of work, coloured codes in
the margin can identify each team member's work. Investigate this now if you are part of a
team.

Variables: you may also use variables to enable more complex organization and complex
activation of data, based e.g. on known aspects of the respondents and data. See Chapter 11.
Variables can be imported in a table created e.g. in SPSS or Excel.

Exercise 3.8   MAXqda2: routine saving and backing up

There is no save option in MAXqda2. Instead, the software saves automatically. The only
option you are given when closing the project is to back up. Consequently, backing up is very
easy. Just be consistent in your naming process.

In *Project/Backup Project*, click on the spinner arrow at the top of the *Save Project as* box
to save into an area other than the one you are working in, such as a memory stick or network
drive, so that you have something to go back to. It is very important to make regular backups
which are thoughtfully named so that you can tell by the name when you saved it, and safely
delete older versions (see advice notes in Task 3.1 earlier about project and backup naming).

Note: the file you create by backing up is fully condensed, but nevertheless, in order to protect
it further, create a compressed or zipped file (in Windows Explorer) if you need to send it by
email.

Exercises in NVivo7

NVivo7 functions using an 'internal' database, so importing data copies each data file
(document) into the database. There is only one file, the *project*, which can be copied if the
project needs to be moved to another computer.

Different types of work/methods/methodology
NVivo7 has adopted a user interface similar to that used by Microsoft Outlook. Navigating
between functions may therefore be familiar to many users. The folder structure that you

can create for documents (and import into) reflects normal file management outside the software. Full editing rights over the data files means that those needing to write copious notes – whether interpretive or more discourse based – can embed comments in any place or use *annotation* tools to enable footnoted reports (see Chapter 4). NVivo7 does not, for those needing such information, provide word frequency tools. At another level, the software is an ideal environment for the integration of quantitative or subset information. This is particularly the case when organizing different types of qualitative data within one project, e.g. focus group, open-ended questions and one-on-one interviews (see Chapters 11 and 12).

Data files
Only textual data files (sources) are directly importable, e.g. in MS Word, rich text format and text only, although graphics can be embedded (see Chapter 2).

Nodes
Coding is central to work in NVivo7. The coding schema and other types of coding are contained within the Nodes area. Different types of coding, free nodes, tree nodes, cases, relationships and matrices are located in different folders within the Node area. (see Chapter 7). Other software functions are listed as navigation buttons down the left side of the interface.

Exercise 3.9   NVivo7: create new project, import data

The numbering of steps corresponds to Figure 3.8.
   Prepare two data files, e.g. a transcript, a literature list, a literature abstract or field notes. Data files can be in text only (.txt), rich text (.rtf) or Word (.doc) formats. (see Chapter 2).

1   Open NVivo7. Click on *New Project* button. Specify where to save it by choosing *Browse* or leave it in the default location of My Documents (this may change with different installations).
2   Select *Sources* in the Navigation pane. The List pane is always relevant to the function selected in the Navigation pane.
3   Creating document folders. You do not need to do this, but if it seems tidier, you can for instance create folders as containers for different types of data (but never a folder for each data file!) You could also create further subfolders within the first folders, but our advice is keep things simple and visible, so don't create too many (sub)folders!
4   Importing documents. Ensure the right document folder is selected. Right click in the blank area of the documents List pane: either create *New Document* (blank) or *Import Document* (e.g. transcribed data).
5   Code sources as cases. If the appropriate box is checked on import, sources can automatically be created as cases (i.e. coded at a *case node*: see detail in Figure 3.8). This is important since it relates to later interrogation across and within cases. If working with one-to-one interview data, this option is usually useful to tick at this stage (see Chapter 11).

(Continued)

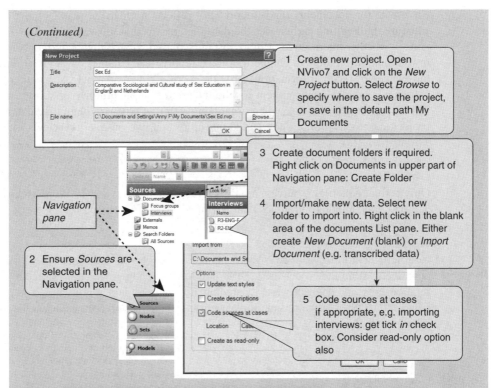

Figure 3.8 **Creating a project and importing data into NVivo7**
See additional step by step information in chapter sections – '**EXERCISE 3.1 NVivo7**' in which numbering of steps corresponds to numbers below

Exercise 3.10   NVivo7: exploring the user interface

The following suggestions are illustrated in Figure 3.9.

Experiment generally with functions and main menus in the three main views of the workspace:

- *Navigation View*: access and organize project items. Move between sources, nodes, sets, queries, models, links and classifications. Display related folders and create subfolders where necessary. Click the *Folders* navigation button to view all project items together.
- *List View*: selecting a folder in Navigation View shows its contents in List View. From here add new items to a folder, open and edit items. Summary information relating to each item is provided.
- *Detail View*: opening (double clicking) an item in the List View displays it in the Detail pane below. This is the main point of access to data for exploration, coding and retrieval and searching purposes (see Chapters 4, 7 and 8).

(Continued)

(Continued)

In addition:

- *Toolbars*: become familiar with different toolbars for shortcut icons to different functions. Toolbars can be changed and moved.
- *Menus*: all main functions can be accessed through main menus. Right clicking at a point reveals the corresponding context menu.
- *Undo button*: click on the spinner arrow to the immediate right of the *Undo* icon: the last five things you have done are listed and selectable (as generic operations). Selecting an earlier operation will undo subsequent actions. This only works until you save your work: this removes all undo operations from the list.

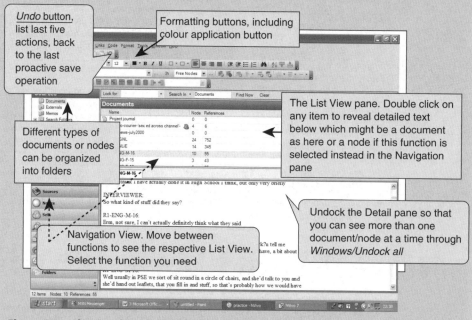

Figure 3.9   The user interface in NVivo7 (see Exercise 3.10)

Exercise 3.11   NVivo7: early handling of data in a project

The numbering of steps corresponds to Figure 3.10.

1   Open documents by double clicking on them in the List View. Opened documents appear in the Detail View and are tabbed to move between easily.

(Continued)

2   Edit text in the usual way, using colour and other marking features. Edit toolbar options are similar to those found in most word processing packages. To protect a document from edits, make it read-only from *Project/Document Properties.*

3   Create a memo linked to a document. Right click on a document in the List View, choose Memo *Link/Link To New Memo.* Name the memo. Write your early thoughts about the document this memo is linked to. Memos are standalone documents like any other, but are grouped in a separate folder. See how to create *annotations* in the next chapter, Exercise 4.7.

4   Get a printed output of a document with paragraphs numbered if it would be useful (see commentary at the end of this chapter). Ensure that the document you want printed is open in the Detail View. Then *File/Print.* See the options for inclusion in the report, and keep them in mind for later printouts.

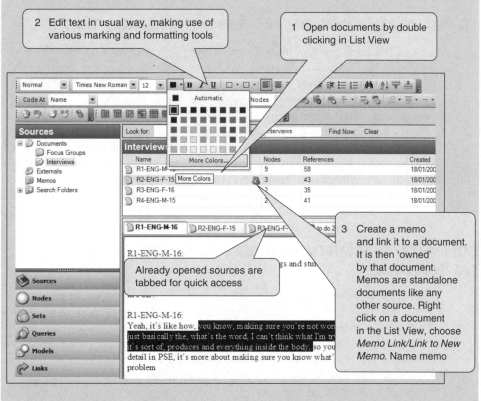

Figure 3.10   Early handling of data in NVivo7 (see Exercise 3.11)

Exercise 3.12   NVivo7: routine saving and backing up

The NVivo7 project is one file. It can therefore be saved, backed up and moved around like any other file on your computer. Use the *Copy Project* function in the File menu or simply copy and paste in Windows Explorer. It is very important to make regular backups which are thoughtfully named so that you can tell by the name when you saved it, and can then safely delete older versions. (See Chapter 2 and the advice notes in Task 3.1 earlier above about project and backup naming.)

Try to become a little aware now what the case structure that you may gradually build, as you import data, is doing (see Exercise 3.9) and how it is represented in the software. Look first at *Tools/Casebook*. Later these types of nodes may have attributes which organize your data and allow you to interrogate based on that organization. Also from the Navigation View, select *Nodes*, and then look at Case Nodes. If you have been coding a document at case nodes on import, these nodes will have been applied to the whole of that document.

SUMMARY: REVIEWING THE PROCESS OF FAMILIARIZATION

As a beginner, under-confidence can cause you to maintain a rather slavish adherence to menus, instructions and certain types of functionality without feeling certain about an overall picture in terms of your use of the software. This can interfere with your thinking about and reflection upon your project. Too much concern about using the software 'properly' can cloud your analytic direction and might even hinder your methodological approach. Teachers of software themselves must have some sensitivity about the individuals they are teaching. There is no one recommended way of using software, and, as with any piece of equipment, recipe or process, either you are the type of person who has the confidence to adjust the process from early on, or growing familiarity with it will increase your sense of independence. Work early and often at playing with software to become familiar with it in order to navigate it and apply its tools thoughtfully and easily.

COMPARATIVE COMMENTS ON GETTING STARTED WITH THE SOFTWARE

Familiarizing with and navigating around the interface

All three packages have intuitive user interfaces. The familiarity of the NVivo7 interface may be comforting to those used to working with MS Outlook. However, you can feel isolated from different aspects of work in this package because of the way the interface works. New NVivo users often enjoy the interface, whereas former NVivo2 users are more critical. The lack of line wrap in the text window increases a cramped feeling, and the inability to see more than one List View at a time reduces flexible movement between panes. ATLAS.ti5 and MAXqda2 allow any combination of functions to be open together. This adds to the fluidity with which you can flick between views and functions and to the slick interactivity between different objects and tasks. Whichever software package you are using, experiment to find ways of working which complement your methodology and style of working. MAXqda2 is the easiest of the three interfaces to become familiar with if self-taught.

Moving around the data

Qualitative researchers often need points of reference to work with, especially when relating printouts to original files. Line or paragraph numbers help in this respect. The former are usually not possible when using CAQDAS, but paragraph numbers are available in MAXqda2 and ATLAS.ti5. Although paragraphs can be numbered in output in NVivo7, there seems no concrete way to see where you are in the live detail document panes inside the software. Relatively simple information like this makes it easier to be systematic.

Saving, backing up and moving projects

It is very easy in MAXqda2 and NVivo7 to back up and move the project around because it is one file, just like any other on your computer. It can be disconcerting in MAXqda2 that you cannot proactively save the project and that instead the software is saving all the time. The backup and moving process in ATLAS.ti5 requires more planning, care and practice because of the 'external database' system. It is this aspect which produces the most requests for advice. However, it is precisely this aspect of software architecture which allows multimedia data to be directly assigned to the HU and treated (annotated, coded etc.) in similar ways as textual data. Generally, practice is needed, in all software, in backing up and moving projects around to become confident in a systematic process before you have done too much work.

NOTES

1 Coding reliability – in a team, how much you can rely on the consistency of each other's interpretations, code creation and code application. In some software programs (N6, CISAID), a mathematical reliability rating can be calculated when comparing identical coding schemata. In other software, the evaluation of the level of reliability may be more impressionistic and based on visual comparison and discussion. In NVivo7 you can generate a coding comparison report which will highlight differences in how the same document has been coded by different team members.

2 Merge – a function utilized by various software programs to enable the physical merging of two or more projects. This is because, to date, none of these programs except Transana enable simultaneous but separate inputting to one large project from different workstations (as per a bank or stock control type of database).

Chapter 4
Exploration and
Text-Level Work

In this chapter, we discuss data and *text-level* aspects of working with data to help you begin the process of situating your analytic work. Tasks covered in this chapter include marking and annotating text, note making, searching text for words and phrases, and hyperlinking between points in the text where possible in each software package. We continue to emphasize that working with software does not mean everything has to happen in front of the computer screen. We stay clear of coding tasks, though we suggest at times that you can use coding functionality just to mark interesting data in a relatively *non-labelling* way. This is one of the most important chapters of the book, since we feel the use of software itself can tend to conventionalize data and the expectations and assumptions of how to analyse qualitative data. We encourage independent application, critical and flexible use of software, and an awareness of the appropriateness of tools for certain types of data. The tools and possibilities discussed do not represent a discrete stage of analysis, nor are they specific to any methodological approach, but they do keep us within touching distance, throughout the analysis, with the fundamentals of information and data.

EARLY EXPLORATION OF TEXT

The process of becoming aware of what is interesting and significant in the information and data you have collected starts in the first moments of data collection. Reflection during and after data gathering and while transcribing forms part of the overall process of exploration, and for many this is an important phase of analysis. As the transcripts develop, your access to the data improves; as the files are incorporated within a qualitative software package, that access only increases. Now you need only open a single file (the project file) to have immediate access to any individual data file that has so far been imported or assigned. The data wait to be navigated, explored, thought about, searched and annotated. (See Table 4.1 for basic ideas of how text-level work is enabled in qualitative software.)

TECHNOLOGICAL DEVELOPMENTS AND METHODOLOGICAL DEBATES

The development of technology, the debate about methods, and initiatives to make creative use of software have widened methodological potential. One of the results of such initiatives is the idea that hyperlinking between data segments, as an alternative to coding, provides a different way to navigate around data. In this chapter, we try to stretch awareness of what is possible at the data level to emphasize what might be useful to more categories of user.

Then, there are the tools which allow an automatic or user-defined semi-automatic discovery of 'content'. They are part of the faster exploration of data enabled by software. They allow you to switch from the more careful vertical analysis, top to bottom, through an individual data file, to a horizontal process of flicking quickly through all the data files in order to discover recurrent words or phrases. The text searching tools discussed in this chapter are closely related to the auto coding tools discussed in Chapter 12 but they are dealt with separately since we distinguish the processes in several ways. Physically and philosophically, fast searching of content (without auto coding) and the use of specific annotating tools might be concerned with a closer level of work in the data. Auto coding, by contrast, implies a greater level of analytic reliance on possibly limited catchments of data, and, by implication, a lowering of the status of text left out of the auto coding process. The use of these tools is therefore more debatable, and what we do here is position the utility of the text searching tools within the context of more careful work with qualitative data. See Chapter 12 for discussion of using auto coding tools.

Table 4.1 *Exploration of textual data in software: tasks and uses of tools*

Task	Use – tips	Comments & comparison ATLAS.ti5, MAXqda2, and NVivo7
Read/mark/flag interesting data	Taking an inductive or a deductive approach, early on you may mark significance by underlining or emboldening without wanting to code. Use a non-committal code in any software to enable retrieval of 'interesting' passages MAXqda2 allows you to assign functional four colour-coding to text segments on basis of broad areas of interest, i.e. 'coding' without labelling.	These options resemble processes followed by more traditional techniques of analysis. ATLAS.ti5, MAXqda2 and NVivo7 allow such edits. ATLAS.ti5 allows the creation and listing of 'free quotations' of interest. Quotations are important objects in their own right in ATLAS.ti5 MAXqda2 has coding by colour option.
Comments and annotations	Note spontaneous thoughts linked to data segments to retrieve later. All methods would find useful.	Early notes taken while exploring data. All software supports this. For more on writing tools, see Chapter 9.
Linking interesting/relevant segments of data	Tracking a sequence of events that is talked about in a disorderly way throughout a narrative, as in a life history by using hyperlinks.	Enabled as described in ATLAS.ti5 MAXqda2 – pairs of links only, enabled NVivo7, no fast hyperlinks between text points.
Search text/'find' tools	Define searches for occurrence of individual words or phrases (or collections of topic-related words) and find them within source context. Search one file or search across the whole or selected parts of the dataset. Dip in and out of other tasks as you catch sight of an interesting word or phrase and use the search text tool to find out where else in the data it occurs and in what context.	If interested in eventual thematic coding, the findings might be a useful aid to building a coding frame. Essential if the researcher is concerned with use of language or terminology, e.g. when examining media discourse on a topic, but generally useful to gain quicker access to data, for most methods. All software has flexible text search tools enabled.
Frequency counts of words with/ without key Word in context (KWIC)	Provide overview of the word content of one several or all text files. Create stop lists to exclude certain words.	Only ATLAS.ti5 without KWIC and MAXqda2 (+MAXDictio) with KWIC support this. See resource sections for software which concentrates on statistical word/phrase content. NVivo7 – no word frequency tool

ANNOTATION TOOLS: THEIR *UNIVERSAL* UTILITY

Annotation involves applying a note or comment to other material. Software enables this in various ways. Such tools can be useful to anyone using software to manage any mass of data, to record spontaneous thinking processes and their connection to the data that instigated the thoughts. We see note taking as crucial to all types and approaches to analysis. Other functions such as coding, text searching, auto coding and modelling may be well used by particular approaches, but the annotation of data, documents and supporting material is indivisible from analysis generally. To that end, we encourage the use of software, and in particular annotation tools, for any type of research or day-to-day work which uses or generates any textual or qualitative material.

Note taking for continuity, neutrality, reflexivity and openness

Exploring the data will remind you that your role as researcher is not neutral. Managing the accrual of ideas and the analysis should be consciously reflexive. The tools discussed here provide convenient places for you to be explicit about any influences on the data and the analysis. Annotation tools allow you to connect spontaneous ideas with the data that produced the thought, and later in your iterative work, to be reminded of earlier thoughts and reasoning. This helps increase the transparency and continuity of the analysis. A crucial element of some methodologies, such as interpretive phenomenological analysis (IPA), is the development of a highly transparent audit trail comprising a log of all the processes followed and describing the small analytic leaps contributing to the analysis as a whole. This chapter provides an early look at annotating as a product of text-level exploration. We look at the broader topic of memo tools in Chapter 9.

TEXT SEARCH TOOLS: THEIR *UNIVERSAL* UTILITY

CAQDAS packages are generally useful in the management of multiple qualitative data files, whatever the methodology and discipline. Generally, text search tools are used to search for words or phrases that appear in the data, for example those stated by the respondent or interviewer. In addition, however, you may use these tools to search for words or phrases used in your own writing – in annotations or memos for example. There are two important general points to make about text search tools. First, software fairly consistently allows viewing of either all or some of the surrounding context where 'hits' of finds are made, though the ease with which this happens varies. Second, keep in mind that the use of the tool is initially deductive, based as it usually is on your choice of words to search for. Progressively such searches can become more inductive as you spot other words in the earlier result to include in more investigations.

Any researcher from any disciplinary background can make use of the record management potential of such software. The management of any collection of essays, abstracts, notes, lists, articles etc. would be enhanced by the ability to search for phrases or key words across a number of files. Seale (2000), for instance, describes how he used the NUD*IST database to help him manage book writing by supporting the process of collating and searching his notes and accumulated records on literature. You can use most CAQDAS software in such a way; you just need to know what tools are available and adapt them to your own needs.

The place of content-based searching tools

Technical competence with content-based tools can never replace the more thorough perusal of data and careful identification of meaning and significance. In their appropriate place, these tools may have multiple uses in the flexible toolkit of qualitative enquiry. Interpretive researchers often use these tools on the spur of the moment, while in careful reading and coding mode. A phrase or word in the text prompts a need to find out if this expression is used anywhere else in the data, and in what context. The ability to react in this manner to a sudden thought, and to gain direct access to all relevant areas in the data, is arguably one of the spontaneous aspects of computer use which has most changed the processes of interpretive analysis. This is not to say that it is a compulsory step in good analysis. Used as part of the process of seeing and understanding all the data, it changes the speed at which we delve into the data, and therefore makes us more ready to do so!

Text search, find and word frequency tools are useful for qualitative researchers from several traditions and may be applied in combination with other tools that help manage ideas, concepts and threads. This book focuses mainly on interpretive qualitative data analysis as supported by CAQDAS packages. However, it is useful to put content-based tools in a wider context since their utility, unlike coding tools, might reach researchers with quite different starting points.

Researchers who engage in content analysis, i.e. the statistical breakdown of text for constructionist approaches to analysis, are likely to use software which performs those mathematical tasks without providing other tools allowing thematic interpretation and annotation (for example, Concordance or TextQuest). It is worth noting that QDA Miner and the earlier CISAID were the first packages on the market to combine quite different epistemological starting points for their software, using a set of interpretive tools (with thematic coding) and also 'content analysis' or 'text mining' tools. The combination of QDA Miner and the add-on module WordStat provides both an elegant 'code and retrieve' module and a sophisticated statistical content analysis module (see Appendix C).

HYPERLINKING

The term *hyperlinking* is often used to describe the quick connection between objects of analysis, e.g. codes, annotations and their associated data. What we refer to here, however, are the tools which allow hyperlinking between points in the text. These tools vary in effectiveness in the main featured software packages. Weaver and Atkinson (1995), later expanded in Coffey et al. (1996), emphasize the need for a broader perception of what software could contribute to qualitative data analysis. They see fragmentation of the data by a computer-led predominance of code and retrieval strategy as restrictive and a less than ideal way to handle narrative or life history accounts. As one alternative they suggest hyperlinking between points in the text as a more flexible way to track routes through the data. In actuality, it is rare for those engaged in narrative analysis to use any customized software tool. This is not necessarily due to a lack of experimentation, but often results from the need to be deeply immersed in relatively small amounts of data. In the context of computer assistance, we should be open to the potential to manage diverse entry points and navigation paths through data and to fit the tools at our disposal to our specific needs rather than to fit the data and the method to the software.

 This chapter focuses on early exploration of textual data. When working with multimedia data, however, it will also be useful to consider how your chosen software allows the marking and exploration of audio/video. ATLAS.ti5 is the only software discussed in the main body of this book which allows the direct handling of graphic and audio/video files. The ability to segment audio/video into *quotations*, in particular, can facilitate the marking, annotating and subsequent retrieval of clips. These quotations can be retrieved, re-viewed, coded, and hyperlinked to text or to other clips or graphics.

GENERIC TASKS: EXPLORING DATA AND WORKING AT THE TEXT LEVEL IN SOFTWARE

Remember the non-linear and more flexible process of analysis made possible by CAQDAS packages. The functions listed below represent tasks that researchers from the whole range of social, health/medicine, arts, human and earth sciences might make productive use of while handling any mass of qualitative information or data.

TASK 4.1   USING COSMETIC TEXT MARKING AND FUNCTIONAL TEXT MARKING

Cosmetic text marking tools involve visually editing data for emphasis. For example, during an initial pass through data, it may be useful to colour, embolden, italicize or underline words or phrases which are salient in some way. Marking text in this way is cosmetic because it is usually not possible to retrieve text segments based on colour, boldness etc.

Functional text marking tools are those that not only allow you to flag interesting text, but enable you to list those segments, and work with them independently.

For example, you can:

- List interesting passages of text for further attention.
- Vary the way you mark data – to indicate different things, but to do so consistently.

TASK 4.2   ANNOTATING TEXT

Data segments can be annotated as well as marked, allowing you to note why the marked segment is interesting. There will usually be ways to later retrieve annotated segments within the software and to output them in a report format to view away from the computer. See the later software-specific exercises for notes about restrictions.

For example:

- You can annotate passages or anchor a note in the data. You may have insights as you are reading particular passages that are worth recording before you forget them.
- Occasionally, you may want to make a contextual remark about a particular happening in an interview in the body of the text.

TASK 4.3   FREQUENCY COUNTS, TEXT SEARCHING FOR WORDS OR PHRASES

Frequency counts

Software differs in its ability to run frequency checks across (subsets) of textual data, but most packages allow searching the content of files for words and/or phrases. Such tools may be useful in various methodologies, including interpretive social and ethnographic research, documentary analysis and discourse approaches.

For example, you can:

- Run a frequency check (where available) for words used in data to spot significant words and their usage level (remembering that some instances will include interviewers' own use of those words).
- Use a frequency check across one or all data files to get an overview of all words in the data – but focus attention on key words. Separating text by different speakers through auto coding before running a frequency check will help to isolate words used by respondents from those used by the interviewer or moderator.
- Search for one key word in one data file to find out the context in which it is used.
- Search for several related words in the same way. Will the findings be as expected, or will they test our previous assumptions?
- Use such a search to sensitize yourself to a topic – the who, how and why of the discussion – or to produce a rough idea of a topic's prevalence and relevance in one file, across a group of related files, or across the whole dataset. For instance in the Young People's Perceptions Project, a search for the following words/phrases/strings would enable a rapid overview of the tone of talk about 'precautions':[1]

preg*pregnancy test morning after pill pill contrace* precaution

(Continued)

- Use such a search to get an early comparison of how different groups talk about this topic – e.g. here to compare Dutch and British young people.
- Search for a range of words or phrases indicating a general attitude to see what topics are discussed, for example:

   don't care rubbish waste of time

Text searching for value-laden words

Researchers probing historical, legal or political documentation in machine readable format will benefit from the improved direct access to data that these tools offer.

For example, you can:

- Search for value-laden words, e.g. in documentary sources and secondary data in the Young People's Perceptions Project in *Government* [*UK*] *Guidelines for School Sex Education Provision*:
   inaprop|explicit|moral|value|corruptive
- Discover other loaded words in the searching process which allow you to expand the comprehensiveness of the previous search.
- Compare whether words used here differ from usage in earlier or later publications, or in publications from the different national governing bodies.
- Search for the mention of a particular event or personality.
- Search for words with a particular connotation, e.g. conciliatory terms:

   agree negotiat conciliat treaty compromis give and take conced concess

TASK 4.4   HYPERLINKING BETWEEN POINTS IN THE TEXT

Hyperlinking between points in the dataset by linking data segments to one another offers an alternative route through data, and a means of handling them. However, these tools differ greatly between software:

1   They are not available in every software in the same way.
2   They vary in ease of use.
3   They might be used for different reasons.

For example, you can:

- Link a trigger with a reaction.
- Link parts of an interaction or process together.
- Link contradictory statements.
- Associate one document with another or with several.
- Track a sequential route through the data based on narrative order or chronology (may allow the user to impose order of navigation backwards and forwards).
- Track logical reasoning.
- Link points in data where strong reactions are demonstrated, or very hesitant behaviour occurs.
- Link specific parts of different documents together.

SOFTWARE-SPECIFIC VARIATIONS: EXPLORING DATA AND WORKING AT THE TEXT LEVEL

Exercises in ATLAS.ti5

Exercise 4.1   ATLAS.ti5: marking/annotating interesting passages of text

The numbering of steps corresponds to Figure 4.1. See also the ideas in Tasks 4.1 and 4.2 earlier. The architecture of ATLAS.ti5 rests on the separate existence of quotations which the user can create, free of coding. Quotations, whether free or coded, are listed in the Quotes combo box (see Figure 4.1 for text, and Figure 4.2 for multimedia). When selected, they are highlighted in their full context. We do not include visual marking in this set of exercises, since ATLAS.ti5 is an external database and for beginners it might be better to avoid editing the data inside the software. If you have assigned .doc (MS Word) files to ATLAS.ti5 then you cannot edit them in any case, since only rich text files (.rtf) are editable in ATLAS.ti5. More importantly you should never edit the files you have assigned to the Hermeneutic Unit by opening them in another application, e.g. MS Word.

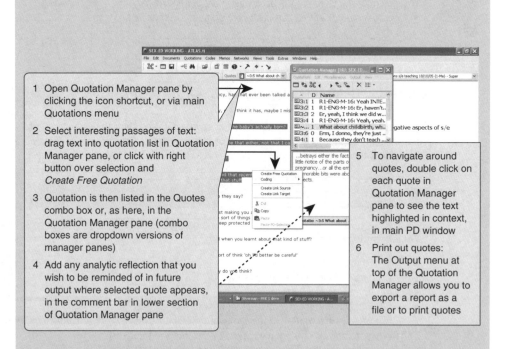

1 Open Quotation Manager pane by clicking the icon shortcut, or via main Quotations menu

2 Select interesting passages of text: drag text into quotation list in Quotation Manager pane, or click with right button over selection and *Create Free Quotation*

3 Quotation is then listed in the Quotes combo box or, as here, in the Quotation Manager pane (combo boxes are dropdown versions of manager panes)

4 Add any analytic reflection that you wish to be reminded of in future output where selected quote appears, in the comment bar in lower section of Quotation Manager pane

5 To navigate around quotes, double click on each quote in Quotation Manager pane to see the text highlighted in context, in main PD window

6 Print out quotes: The Output menu at top of the Quotation Manager allows you to export a report as a file or to print quotes

Figure 4.1   Marking and annotating text in ATLAS.ti5 (see Exercise 4.1)

(Continued)

1   Open the Quotation Manager pane via the main Quotations menu or by clicking the rectangular icon to the left of the Quotes combo box.
2   Select interesting passages of text: either drag text into the quotation list in the Quotation Manager pane; or click with right button (with cursor over selected text) to select Create Free Quotation option.
3   The quotation is then listed in the Quotes combo box or, as here, the Quotation Manager pane. (Combo boxes provide dropdown versions of manager panes.)
4   Add any analytic reflection you have in the Comment bar (the lower section of the pane) about the quote you now have selected in the Quotation Manager pane, so that in any future output where that quotation appears, you will be reminded of meaningful thoughts.
5   To navigate around quotes later, double click on each quote in the Quotation Manager pane and see the text highlighted in the main pane.
6   Export a file or print out interesting quotes by going to *Quotations/Output/All Quotations* and agree to 'Include quotations' comment, memos and hyperlinks content? File it or read it and annotate it. Do some thinking outside the software.

Note: optimize your contact with the whole context by keeping manager panes etc. clear of the main text window.

If you are working with multimedia data, you can experiment by squaring off parts of graphics and creating a free quotation, or marking the beginning and end of an interesting clip in audio/video data to create a free quotation (see Figure 4.2). Once created, multimedia

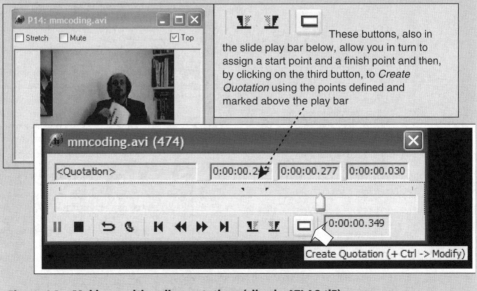

These buttons, also in the slide play bar below, allow you in turn to assign a start point and a finish point and then, by clicking on the third button, to *Create Quotation* using the points defined and marked above the play bar

Figure 4.2   **Making multimedia quotations (clips in ATLAS.ti5)**

(Continued)

(Continued)

quotations are listed alongside textual quotations and can be treated in the same way. You can rename quotations to make them describe explicitly what the image or clip is about. Playing or viewing multimedia clips happens in parallel with textual quotations, and can be accessed from all the different places where they are referenced or hyperlinked in the software.

Exercise 4.2   ATLAS.ti5: searching the text of documents and word frequency count

The numbering of steps corresponds to Figure 4.3. See also the ideas in Task 4.3 earlier. ATLAS.ti5 has a built-in word frequency checker, though the resultant list is not interactive with key word in context (KWIC) retrieval.

1   Build a search expression. To open the Text Search tool, choose the pink and green arrow from the vertical icons on the left of the primary document (PD) window, and fill in the box under *Enter or select Search Expression*. If you are searching for multiple words or phrases, the vertical slash or pipe character indicates 'or' to the software. On UK/US keyboards, this character is Shift+\(backslash, adjacent to left shift key), e.g. educate|inform (see also the note below). On other keyboards this will vary according to the alphabet system.

2   Open the required document. Make sure you have the first searchable text file open in the PD window. This ensures the search continues all the way through the list of documents.

3   See finds in context. Hit the *Next* button to examine the context around each highlighted find. Move through the remaining documents when prompted. See what prompted the use of the word or phrase you searched for.

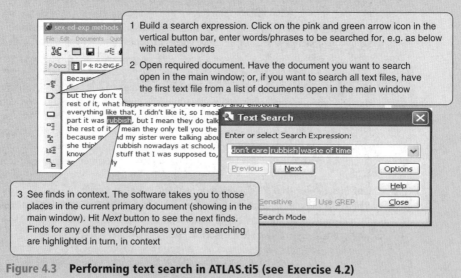

Figure 4.3   **Performing text search in ATLAS.ti5 (see Exercise 4.2)**

(Continued)

4   To perform a word frequency count (not illustrated). Go to *Documents/ Miscellaneous/Word Cruncher*. In the dialogue box, choose to run the count either to *Include Selected PD only* or on the whole dataset. If you choose the latter, a file save box appears, so give the file a name (keeping the .csv file extension). Click *OK*, then choose from *Do nothing, Run file or Run file and remove later*. If you choose to run the file, the word count will open in Excel. Each column will represent a P number (a primary document). If in the Word Cruncher dialogue box you opt to *Include Selected PD only* (i.e. the document appearing now in the main PD window) it will open the report in default format without going to Excel.

Note: if using the Text Search tool (steps 1–3 above), a good way to simplify the search but to uncover more related words is to insert the root of a word only. If searching for multiple root words, you additionally need the wild card character * placed before and/or after the word to catch the varying forms of the word, e.g. *educa* (educated, uneducated etc.).

Exercise 4.3   ATLAS.ti5: making and navigating hyperlinks in data

The numbering of steps corresponds to Figures 4.4 and 4.5. See also the ideas in Task 4.4 earlier.

Creating hyperlinks

The hyperlinking device in ATLAS.ti5 is the most flexible of similar tools provided by CAQDAS packages and could be used in a number of ways and for different reasons. It is advisable to attach a code or a memo to the beginning of a 'trail' clearly announcing the start point (see Chapters 7 and 9). Do not feel any compulsion to use this tool just because it exists. This is a tool to use because it will enhance your treatment and engagement with the text for particular purposes.

1   Would it be useful to hyperlink text passages together? Refer to Task 4.4. In the Quotation Manager pane you may have been creating free quotations by dragging selections of text from the main PD window into the manager pane.

2   Create hyperlinks between some of those quotations. In the Quotation Manager, drag one quotation onto another quotation to which you wish to link, at which point you can choose the appropriate type of hyperlink relationship, or experiment and create a new one by clicking on *Open Relation Editor*. (Refer to the online software manual for further help with this.) Note that this is just one way of many to create hyperlinks. You can create hyperlinks between quotations in a network (see Chapter 10); there are also icons in the vertical toolbar to the left of the main PD window which enable the links to be made concurrent with looking at full context.

3   Hyperlink quotations together in any direction and between/across any files.

(Continued)

(Continued)

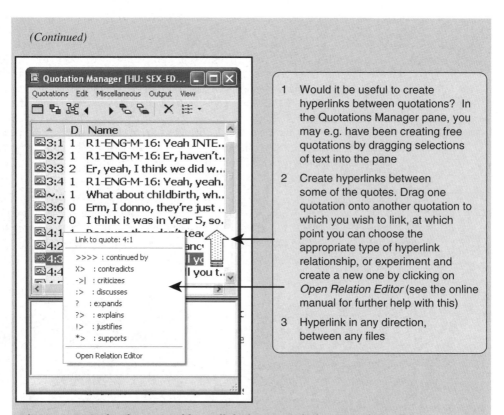

1 Would it be useful to create hyperlinks between quotations? In the Quotations Manager pane, you may e.g. have been creating free quotations by dragging selections of text into the pane

2 Create hyperlinks between some of the quotes. Drag one quotation onto another quotation to which you wish to link, at which point you can choose the appropriate type of hyperlink relationship, or experiment and create a new one by clicking on *Open Relation Editor* (see the online manual for further help with this)

3 Hyperlink in any direction, between any files

Figure 4.4   Navigating around hyperlinks in ATLAS.ti5 (see Exercise 4.3)

Navigating hyperlinks

4 Navigate hyperlinks. Experiment by double clicking on the hyperlink annotation in the margin. This will bring up the highlighted text in surrounding context to the left in the main window. It will also reveal a flag in the margin containing the onward linked quotation.

5 Flagged, linked text in margin. Click once on the flag containing the linked quote in the margin and you are then taken to that point in the data, with the relevant quote highlighted in context. An onward link *from* a point shows in the margin, e.g.:

   <Contradicts> 4:1

(i.e. the quote number after the <Relationship> refers *towards* the next link point in the text). A link point in the data which has been linked *to* has the quote number preceding the relationship, e.g.

   4.3 <Supports>

A link point which has a *to* and an *onwards* style annotation in the margin (one above the other) is part of an onward chain or star pattern of hyperlinks.

(Continued)

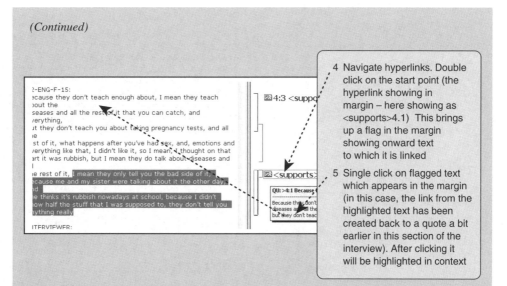

Figure 4.5 **Navigating around hyperlinks in ATLAS.ti5 (see Exercise 4.3)**

Note: take time to experiment with this device, to find out whether it will be useful to you. Do not use this tool heavily unless you are sure it will help and unless you work out an efficient way to manage the various different sets of linkages.

Multimedia quotations can also be hyperlinked, either to one another or to related or corresponding textual quotations. This can be a useful way to manage salient examples of audio/video where a textual transcript sits alongside.

Exercises in MAXqda2

Exercise 4.4 MAXqda2: marking/annotating interesting passages of text

The numbering of steps corresponds to Figure 4.6. See also the ideas in Tasks 4.1 and 4.2 earlier.

As with all software, you can simply use a coding device to mark interesting passages that you wish to remember in a non-committal way (e.g. a code called 'interesting'). MAXqda2, however, provides a quick dual-purpose colour-coding device, using four Colour codes, allowing the user to assign each colour for different reasons.

(Continued)

(Continued)

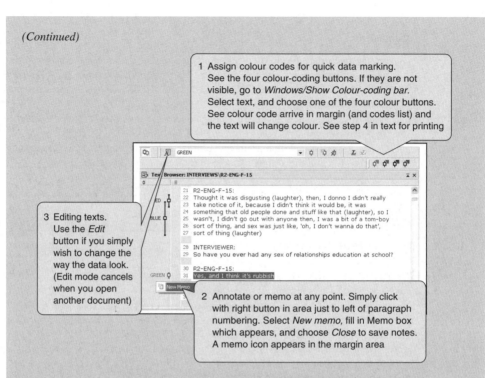

Figure 4.6   Annotating data in MAXqda2 (see Exercise 4.4)

1   Assign colour codes to data for quick data marking. See the four colour-coding buttons along the top button bar. If they are not visible, go to *Windows/ Show Colour Coding Bar*. Decide what the different colour codes will represent for you: e.g. *negative, positive, opinion, actions, questioning, hesitancy, interesting, uninteresting, follow-up, quotable*. Select text and click on the corresponding colour icon at top right. Note that the text changes accordingly and the coding bracket appears in the left-hand margin (adjust margin width if necessary). (See also step 4 below.) Note that colour codes do not have to be used: they are just an extra tool for managing data and provide an early sorting method. For retrieval of colour-coded segments, see Chapter 8.

2   Annotate, comment or memo at any point in text (without cluttering text). Right click in the area just to the left of the paragraph numbering and create a new memo. You need not fill in any of the fields apart from the main pane to write your comment. You could begin to devise your own system for using the different memo flags available in this window for different styles of memo/annotation. The chosen flag will appear in the margin. Double click on it to reopen the memo.

3   Mark or change the text by editing. You do not have to use the functional colour-coding device (see step 1) if you wish to simply colour segments for emphasis – although why not? It gives you retrieval options later, and colours the text as well. Alternatively, if you wish for instance to change the text, add underlines etc., click on the *Edit* icon to

(Continued)

get the open data file into edit mode. Once in edit mode, use the normal editing icons which will appear, or use the colour selector dropdown options (next to the underline icon) to change selected text. If you change the text file on view in the Text Browser, edit mode will switch off.

4   Print off a text which has been colour coded (not illustrated). With the text open in the Text Browser window, go to *Project/Print/Text Browser* and accept 'Display Memos and Codes?' A printout with margin coded information and memos will be a useful hard copy report to file and think about or take to a meeting and discuss.

Exercise 4.5   MAXqda2: searching the text of documents and the word frequency tool

The numbering of steps corresponds to Figures 4.7 and 4.8. See also the ideas in Task 4.3 earlier. Text searches are available in all referenced software, but a customized word frequency counting tool is not. In MAXqda2, you must also use the software MAXDictio in order for this tool to be enabled. (The MAXqda2 CD-ROM already has the software, but you need to purchase a licence number to authorize the installation of MAXDictio.) MAXDictio provides an interactive list of words (with KWIC).

Text search without MAXDictio
Refer to Figure 4.7. In MAXqda2 (without MAXDictio), a range of simple to complex text searches can be performed by following these steps:

1   Open Text Search tool: go to *TextSearch/Text Search / New*.
2   Enter search expression: overtype *Search String*. Enter the first single word or phrase you wish to search for.
3   Search widely about a topic: keep selecting *New* and overtyping *Search String* with additional words or phrases. If you need to save the search expression for future use on more data, select *Save* and name the search expression file sensibly. Note that you do not *have to* save any search expression.
4   Perform the search: click *Run Search* and see the list of finds in the Search Results window.
5   See finds in context: the results are listed. To see any word in the subsequent list in its full context, select it. Make sure you have the Text Browser pane open.

Word frequency using MAXDictio
Refer to Figure 4.8.

6   Choose the Word Frequency tool. Slide the cursor over the buttons shown at left, grouped together near the top of the screen. For a general word count on all the data, choose the first icon **Σ** (sigma). The next two icons refer to activated texts and may initially be greyed out.

(Continued)

(Continued)

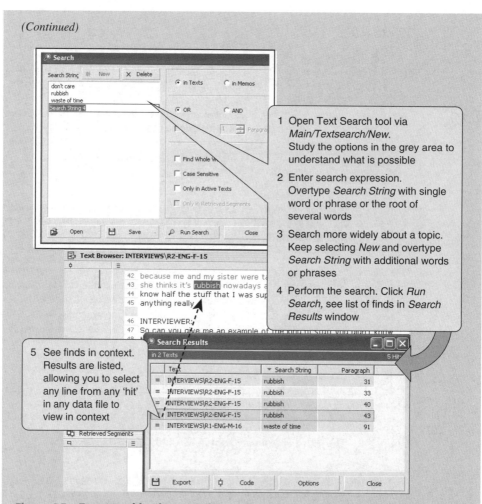

Figure 4.7 Text searching in MAXqda

Activated texts refers to selected texts on which you have chosen to *filter* searching or the Word Frequency tool. Activation can be arranged by right clicking when selecting a document, a whole text group of files, or a set of files, in the Document System pane.

7 Change the sort order. Clicking at the top of any column in the Word Frequency pane sorts the whole table by that factor; clicking again reverses the order. Alternatively, export to a statistical package for more manipulation if required by clicking on *Export*.

8 Create a stop list. Double click on any word you want added to the stop list. (You can opt to leave out such words from a count by choosing the relevant third icon in the group, next time.) Edit the stop list itself by choosing the fourth icon along (with 'no entry' symbol).

9 See key words in context (KWIC). Right click over a word in the Word Frequency list, and choose *Create Index*. The interactive listing will be the same as seen in Figure 4.7: just click

(Continued)

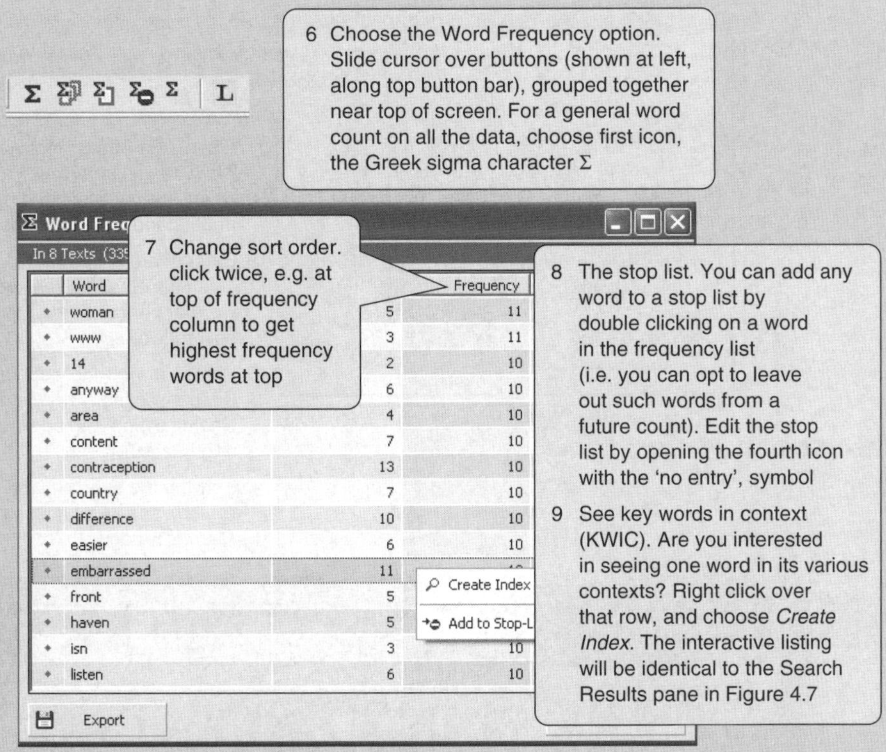

6 Choose the Word Frequency option. Slide cursor over buttons (shown at left, along top button bar), grouped together near top of screen. For a general word count on all the data, choose first icon, the Greek sigma character Σ

Σ 𝔉 Σ ϡ Σ   L

Word Freq

In 8 Texts (339

Word		Frequency
woman	5	11
www	3	11
14	2	10
anyway	6	10
area	4	10
content	7	10
contraception	13	10
country	7	10
difference	10	10
easier	6	10
embarrassed	11	
front	5	
haven	5	
isn	3	10
listen	6	10

🔍 Create Index

➕ Add to Stop-L

💾 Export

7 Change sort order. click twice, e.g. at top of frequency column to get highest frequency words at top

8 The stop list. You can add any word to a stop list by double clicking on a word in the frequency list (i.e. you can opt to leave out such words from a future count). Edit the stop list by opening the fourth icon with the 'no entry', symbol

9 See key words in context (KWIC). Are you interested in seeing one word in its various contexts? Right click over that row, and choose *Create Index*. The interactive listing will be identical to the Search Results pane in Figure 4.7

Figure 4.8 The Word Frequency tool in MAXqda2 (see Exercise 4.5)

on a line in the list to see its place in full context (provided you have the Text Browser pane open and have positioned frequency windows so that you can see the browser pane).

10 Any tables can be exported to other applications (e.g. Excel) and printed by clicking on the *Export* button at the lower edge of any table window.

Exercise 4.6   MAXqda2: making and navigating hyperlinks in data

This process (not illustrated) is simple because the software only allows discrete *pairs* of linked segments. It is ideal for pointing out contradictions or qualifications of a statement etc. Links can be made between different texts.

(Continued)

(Continued)

L **X** 1 Create the pair of hyperlinks. Select a phrase or segment you wish to link with another. Either hit the **L** icon along the top row of icons or use the keyboard shortcut Ctrl + L. Similarly with the second segment, which can be up or down from the first link or in another document.

2 Navigate backwards/forwards between links. Just click in the blue underlined area: you will be taken immediately to the second linked segment.

3 To remove the link: right click over the link and *Remove Link*.

Note: this tool is uncomplicated and yet restricted, because you can only make pairs of links. Consider the ways in which it is easily useful. For example, it could link a trigger and a reaction, or contradictory/confirmatory statements.

Exercises in NVivo7

Exercise 4.7   NVivo7: marking/annotating interesting passages of text

The numbering of steps corresponds to Figure 4.9. See also the ideas in Tasks 4.1 and 4.2 earlier. As with all software, you can simply use a coding device to mark interesting passages in a non-committal way (e.g. create a code called 'interesting' or 'check this out'). Apart from using such a coding device, you can physically edit the data to make segments stand out, but this is cosmetic only. There are times when it's necessary to avoid editing data, however, and optional read-only properties can be assigned to any document to prevent accidental editing. Read-only can be switched on and off as required: select the document in the List pane, go to *Document Properties* and uncheck the *Read only* option (you may have chosen this option on importing the document).

The annotation tool allows notes to be appended to the bottom of the document, which are then hyperlinked back to the annotated segments. These can be outputted via text and coding reports.

1 Create a new annotation: select a small passage of text which warrants a note, right click over the selected text to which you wish to 'link' an annotation, and choose *Links/ Annotation/New Annotation*. A footnote bar appears at the base of the document you are reading in which to type your entry.

(Continued)

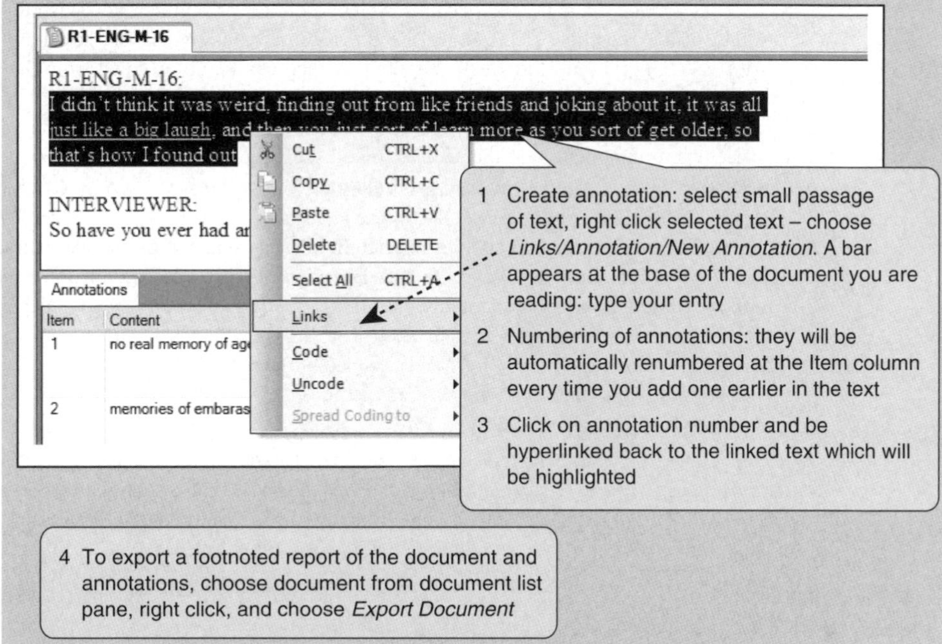

R1-ENG-M-16

R1-ENG-M-16:

I didn't think it was weird, finding out from like friends and joking about it, it was all just like a big laugh, and then you just sort of learn more as you sort of get older, so that's how I found out

INTERVIEWER:
So have you ever had an

	Cut	CTRL+X
	Copy	CTRL+C
	Paste	CTRL+V
	Delete	DELETE
	Select All	CTRL+A
	Links	▶
	Code	▶
	Uncode	▶
	Spread Coding to	▶

Annotations

Item	Content
1	no real memory of age
2	memories of embaras

1 Create annotation: select small passage of text, right click selected text – choose *Links/Annotation/New Annotation*. A bar appears at the base of the document you are reading: type your entry

2 Numbering of annotations: they will be automatically renumbered at the Item column every time you add one earlier in the text

3 Click on annotation number and be hyperlinked back to the linked text which will be highlighted

4 To export a footnoted report of the document and annotations, choose document from document list pane, right click, and choose *Export Document*

Figure 4.9   Marking and annotating text in NVivo7 (see Exercise 4.7)

2   Numbering of annotations: they will all be automatically renumbered at the Item column every time you add one earlier in the text. So '1' will always refer to the earliest (highest) text selection to which the annotation has been attached in each document.

3   Click in the annotation number to be hyperlinked back to the linked text, which is then highlighted. Annotated text will always appear with pale blue highlighting, to let you know there is an annotation attached.

4   To export a footnoted report of the document and annotations, choose the document from the document list, click with the right button, and choose *Export Document*. Save the file in a folder that you will remember! When opened in MS Word, the file will be highlighted at those passages and footnoted.

Note: the annotation tool is a good way to move around different parts of a document. Just making an empty annotation (but with a number) will allow you to click on that number to go to that point in the file. Use the tool in creative ways that suit your needs.

Exercise 4.8 NVivo7: searching the text of documents

The numbering of steps corresponds to Figure 4.10. See also the ideas in Task 4.3 earlier. Text searches are available in all the referenced software, but a word frequency counting tool is not available in NVivo7[2]. The Text Search tool is useful to explore data and to highlight occurrences of words within many files. Alternatively, use Edit/Find tools to search for one word or phrase within the currently selected document (not shown). The Text Search tool (across all or selected data) can be the precursor to other tasks, but here we demonstrate the preview (default) option.

1 Open the Queries function. Click once on the *Queries* option at the bottom left of the Navigation pane to make this the active function.

2 Create the text search query. Right click in the blank space of the Queries pane to select *New Query/Text Search*. In the Text Search Query pane, fill in the string/word or multiple words separated by OR. Check the *Stemmed Search* box to find alternative endings, shorter derivatives, plurals etc. Then *Run*.

3 See list of documents with finds. A list of documents with finds is generated. Double clicking in the list opens the chosen document.

4 See finds highlighted in context.

Note: this is a minimal use of the text search type of query. If you experiment with query options you may find that such queries can lead to the use of structures like sets in the software, as a way to organize data into analytically significant groups. See Chapter 12 for information on *compound queries* which allow words within coded data to be searched for.

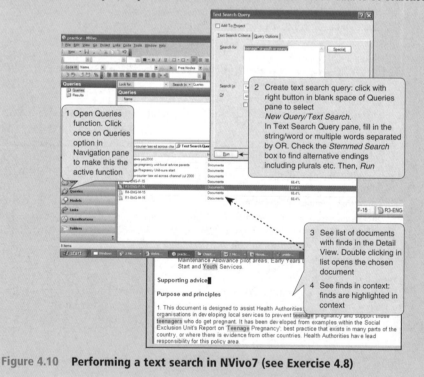

Figure 4.10   Performing a text search in NVivo7 (see Exercise 4.8)

Exercise 4.9   NVivo7: making and navigating links in data

The numbering of steps corresponds to Figure 4.11. See also the ideas in Task 4.4 earlier.

Passages of text can be linked to a number of different project items using *See Also* links. A passage of text can be linked to related data within the same source or in another source. A passage can also be linked to whole existing or new project items, e.g. sources, nodes etc. Note though that these are not *hyperlinked* together since navigating between them involves many menu and dialogue box selections. The term *hyperlink* in NVivo7 refers to links made to web-page URLs or to external files. We do not include this process here, but the starting point is similar to that described as follows:

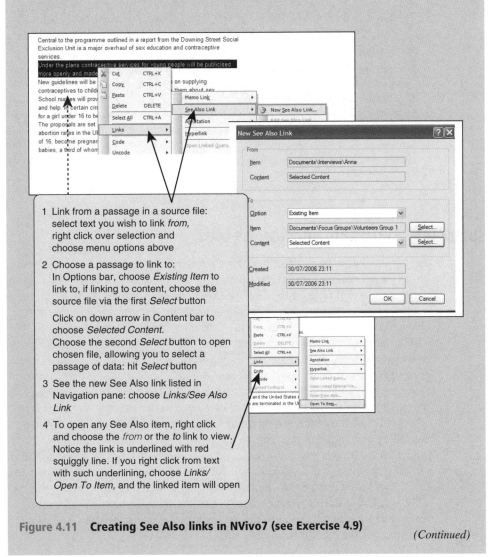

Figure 4.11   Creating See Also links in NVivo7 (see Exercise 4.9)

(Continued)

1   To link *from* a passage in a source file. Select the text you wish to link *from*. Right click over the selection and choose from the menu options.

2   To choose a passage to link *to*. In the Options bar, choose *Existing Item* to link *to*; if linking to content, choose e.g. the source file via the first *Select* button. Click on the down arrow in the Content bar to choose e.g. *Selected Content*. Choose the second *Select* button to open the chosen file, allowing you to select a passage of data; hit the *Select* button to confirm the selection of data.

3   To see the new *See Also* link listed. Go to the Navigation pane, choose *Links/See Also Link*

4   To open any *See Also* item. Right click over the item and choose to view the *from* or the *to* link. Notice that the link in e.g. text is underlined with a red squiggly line. If you right click from text with such underlining, choose *Links/Open To Item*, and the linked item will open.

Note: the passage at which a *See Also* link is created is underlined with a red squiggly line (as misspelled words are in MS Word), but the passage to which it is linked is not marked in any way. A *See Also* link can be created back to the original passage to enable navigating the link both ways, but the user must do this manually if required. Think carefully why this tool might be useful. Make it a rule not to use a tool just because it is there. If it adds to your ability to track ideas and connections between different aspects of the data, then it will serve a purpose. If it just becomes something you have done and then forget about, perhaps the process was not productive.

SUMMARY: EARLY EXPLORATION OF DATA

The precise anchoring of text-based hyperlinking may appeal to certain researchers wanting to track processes or different paths through data, after much intense thought about a narrative. Careful note taking and speedy skimming through the data, on the other hand, might be of use to most researchers or administrators. For the interpretive researcher, this chapter's tasks might seem to be more to do with earlier exploration. In fact, they can enrich the work processes at all phases of analysis. The timing of and reasons for using any of these tools depend on the spontaneous needs of the individual researcher. They encompass a text-level vertical process through an individual data file to a horizontal process of flicking quickly through the data. With all such tools, however, it is advisable to remain aware of their limitations. Notes have to be retrieved and reread. If that process is too difficult, important insights may be overlooked. Text searches will miss useful data not falling exactly within the parameters of the search expression. Conversely, text searching will miss what is *not* in the data, and an absence may be the really important thing. So our message is to stay conscious, self-reliant and sceptical, and at all times use the annotation tools imaginatively to write reflexively and reflectively about what you find and what is missing during your exploration of the data. In particular, it is important not to perform text searching tasks to the exclusion of viewing the data as a whole; there is no substitute for the careful reading of texts.

COMPARATIVE COMMENTS ON EXPLORING DATA

Annotation (i.e. anchoring notes to text)

NVivo7's annotation tool is useful since its footnotes are hyperlinked to the data that prompted the thought. Footnoted output can be generated later but, as always when notes are dispersed, care should be taken that they are retrieved and become part of the coherent process of analysis. ATLAS.ti5 provides many different ways to annotate, including attaching 'comments' to any object, i.e. quotations, documents, codes or networks. Such notes can be usefully output together with the object(s) they belong to. Additionally, memos (centrally listed) can be anchored to quotes in text with an interactive icon visible in the margin display and with right click to edit functionality. Again there is a need to maintain some control of all the places that useful notes have been created in ATLAS.ti5. MAXqda2's annotation device is the memoing tool. When memos are created at specific points in the margin of text, they are flagged like post-it notes. The natural links that memos have to the text and documents and groups of documents that they belong to, and the proactive links you can include to topics and codes in the process of making the memo, mean that retrieval of all notes according to any of these different aspects of the data is the easiest and most systematic of the three software packages.

Word frequency tools

MAXqda2 and ATLAS.ti5 provide word frequency tools; NVivo7 does not.[3] MAXqda2 provides a fully integrated key word in context (KWIC) facility. ATLAS.ti5 outputs the information in a table or Excel file only with no KWIC.

Hyperlinking

By hyperlinking we mean the point-to-point jumping around the dataset at text level. ATLAS.ti5 enables this very effectively for both text and multimedia, e.g. audiovisual data. In text the hyperlinks flagged in the margin view are easily navigated by clicking. MAXqda2 allows the linking of pairs of discrete segments only (i.e. you cannot follow an extensive path through the data as yet). NVivo7 allows linkages between pairs of different project items via *See Also* links, but these are not hyperlinks. The process of creating the links (up to eight separate actions), navigating between them and visualizing them in the text is cumbersome. The purpose of the *See Also* links is in any case rather different to the other software, and is a way of managing connections between objects rather than providing fast movement between them. A better aspect of these links is the listing of *See Also* which remind you of all the links made per document and enable contact to the elements of each linkage. Hyperlinks as described in NVivo7 are specific links from places in a document to URLs or external files, which can be opened (Ctrl + click) from the link, but not annotated or handled directly in any way inside the software.

Exploring multimedia data

ATLAS.ti5 allows quotations to be created in multimedia and textual documents, whereas MAXqda2 and NVivo7 do not. This makes ATLAS.ti5 the better tool for the management and analysis of various forms of qualitative data and information. The ability to annotate multimedia quotations, and to hyperlink between them and textual data files, enables flexible integration of different aspects of work. This is because multimedia files can be assigned like textual files to ATLAS.ti5 as standalone documents. In MAXqda2 and NVivo7 this is not possible, although embedded objects are possible in textual data in both software.

NOTES

1   In some software (ATLAS.ti5) a 'wild card' such as * has to be inserted before/after a string of characters, e.g. before/after the root of a word, but where you want all words with alternative endings or prefixes to be found. Other software may not require the wild card or the vertical pipe character separating strings.
2   At the time of writing. Later Service Pack 3 will include this tool.
3   As note 2, above.

Chapter 5
Qualitative Coding in Software: Principles and Processes

This chapter discusses principles and processes in coding textual data using qualitative software (although much of it is also relevant to coding multimedia data). We illustrate what qualitative coding is and how it works in software, discussing theoretical and practical approaches to coding and the possibilities software provides in supporting and integrating them.

Underpinning the development of CAQDAS programs are code and retrieve capabilities (see Chapter 1), but software does not specify whether or how to generate codes or apply them to data. While specific coding functionality varies, packages allow a similar degree of flexibility and a range of different ways to apply and combine coding techniques.

WHAT IS QUALITATIVE CODING?

Qualitative coding is the process by which segments of data are identified as relating to, or being an example of, a more general idea, instance, theme or category. Segments of data from across the whole dataset are placed together in order to be retrieved together at a later stage. Whether coding manually or using software, you will build up a system to organize data and your ideas about it (see Chapter 6 on developing coding schemes). Coding therefore manages and orders qualitative data. It enables easier searching of data for similarities, differences, patterns and relationships. As such coding is often an integral part of the analytic process, but it is not analysis in itself.

HOW CODING WORKS IN QUALITATIVE SOFTWARE

When a code is applied to a data segment in a CAQDAS package, a link is created between the segment and the code. Software packages comprise two elements of a database system. The first holds the data files, and the second houses the codes (see Chapter 3). When a link is created between the code sitting on one side of the database and the data segment on the other, the quick retrieval of coded text has been enabled. Any number of codes can be applied to a single segment of text of any size and to overlapping/embedded segments. Codes can be defined and analytic memos attached (see Chapters 4 and 9). For graphic illustrations of coding in different software see Chapter 7 and the software reviews in Appendix C. Coded data can be retrieved in different ways. Chapter 8 considers basic methods of retrieval and Chapter 12 illustrates retrieval based on the position of codes in the data and combinations of conceptual coding and known data characteristics (e.g. socio-demographics) (see Chapter 11).

APPROACHES TO CODING

Coding is often seen to be central to the 'qualitative method'. We reflect on various different terms used to describe coding processes. For example, authors refer variously to:

- open, axial and selective coding (Strauss and Corbin, 1998)
- descriptive, topic and analytical coding (Richards, 2005)
- provisional, core and satellite codes (Layder, 1998)
- literal, interpretive and reflexive indexing (Mason, 2002)
- descriptive, interpretive and pattern coding (Miles and Huberman, 1994)
- objectivist and heuristic codes (Seidel, 1998).

Some approaches, such as forms of narrative analysis, resist organizing and categorizing data through coding. In such cases the need is to retain the inherent structure of the data rather than to compare themes across data files. Coding may therefore be seen to fracture the data too much (see for example Mason, 2002). In this context some have criticized qualitative software, suggesting for example that it encourages coding at the expense of other analytic processes, or that it is biased towards Grounded Theory, thereby promoting orthodoxy in qualitative methods (see for example Coffey et al., 1996). Such comments are refuted by Fielding and Lee (1998) who argue that any link between Grounded Theory and CAQDAS is overdrawn and that the availability of CAQDAS does not imply an orthodoxy in methodology or in software use. Similarly, we argue that CAQDAS packages are not methods of analysis but provide a range of tools which can be used to facilitate various analytic processes. As highlighted in Chapter 1, these tools continue to increase as software develops. We encourage researchers to take a critical view of these tools and make an informed decision as to whether particular tools within a software package are appropriate to the research project and whether they will suit their needs.

Generating and using codes

There are two main issues to think about in coding:

- the most appropriate means by which to generate codes
- how different types of codes and coding techniques help at different times in the analysis.

Whilst no qualitative software program will, on its own, solve either issue, it can support different approaches to both.

The overriding aim of coding is to facilitate developing a detailed understanding of the phenomena which the data are seen as representing. This may involve gaining an insight into the underlying meaning respondents attribute to a social situation or particular experience, identifying patterns in attitudes, or investigating processes of social interaction. Employing a systematic coding strategy will allow you to revisit significant instances and to produce further insights. Be clear how the codes you use are helping you make sense of the data.

The codes you develop may be influenced by a number of factors, including:

- research aims
- methodology and analytic approach
- amount, kinds and sources of data
- level and depth of analysis
- constraints
- research audience.

A code may represent a deeply theoretical or analytical concept; it could be completely practical or descriptive; or it could simply represent 'interesting stuff' or 'data I need to think about more' (see Chapter 4). A project will usually consist of different types of codes. As the analysis proceeds, their purpose and use will usually change and you may collect them together in different ways. Above all, codes provide access to those parts of the data which are making you think about the phenomena you want to examine (see Chapter 6 for more on making the most of your coding schemes).

As well as having multiple functions, codes may be generated in a number of ways. For example, they may be based on:

1 *themes or topics* – initially derived from an interview or identified within the data
2 *ideas or concepts* – derived from existing literature in the research area or developed from close reading and thinking about the data

3 *language or terminology* used in the data – whether that be words or phrases used by respondents or documentary evidence, or (un)conventional structures in discourse or narrative.

Codes can be generated inductively (from salient aspects identified in the data) or deductively (according to predefined areas of interest). Labels and definitions need to be *meaningful* in the sense that they indicate the nature of the data grouped at that code in some way. This may have a descriptive or more analytic purpose, which in turn may vary according to the approach to and stage of analysis.

Inductive approaches to coding

The general principle underlying inductive approaches to coding is a desire to prevent existing theoretical concepts from over-defining the analysis and obscuring the possibility of identifying and developing new concepts and theories. As Abrahamson states:

> an inductive approach begins with the researchers 'immersing' themselves in the documents (that is, the various messages) in order to identify the dimensions or *themes* that seem meaningful to the producers of each message. (1983: 286)

'Grounded Theory' (originated by Glaser and Strauss 1967) is a well known and frequently discussed form of inductive qualitative research. It comprises a methodological approach to qualitative research rather than simply being an analytic or coding strategy. It is not our purpose to describe or discuss grounded theory in detail (this has been done extensively elsewhere). However, proponents suggest that grounded coding is an iterative process, distinguishing between open, axial and selective coding procedures. In our experience many researchers work in grounded ways, without necessarily strictly adhering to the processes of Grounded Theory as they have been described. It is nevertheless useful to briefly discuss open, axial and selective coding procedures and indicate ways software tools can facilitate them.

- *Open coding* refers to the first coding phase in which small segments of data (perhaps a word, line, sentence or paragraph) are considered in detail and compared with one another. This process usually generates large numbers of codes from the data level, which encapsulate what is seen to be 'going on'. These codes may be descriptive or more conceptual in nature. They may be very precise, or more generally specified. Often terminology found in the data is used as code labels, termed *in vivo* coding. Open coding fragments the data, 'opening' them up into all the possible ways in which they can be understood.
- *Axial coding* is a more abstract process. It refers to the second pass through the data when the codes generated by open coding are reconsidered. Code labels and the data linked to them are rethought in terms of similarity and difference. Similar codes may be grouped together, merged into higher-level categories, or subdivided into more detailed ones. Data are revisited and compared continually as the way codes represent

the data is examined. Axial coding thus brings back together the fragmented data segments identified in the open coding phase by exploring the relationships identified between the codes which represent them.

- *Selective coding* refers to a third stage of coding when the researcher again revisits the data and the codes. Instances in the data which most pertinently illustrate themes, concepts, relationships etc. are identified. Conclusions are validated by illustrating instances represented by and grounded in the data. Identified patterns are tested and core categories in the developing theory illustrated. This process will lead to segments of data being chosen to quote and discuss in the final written product of the research project.

See Strauss and Corbin (1998) for a detailed discussion of coding in Grounded Theory.

Software tasks supporting inductive approaches to coding

All the packages discussed here provide flexible means by which to generate codes and analyse qualitative data in an inductive way. These include the following specific tasks:

- creating codes grounded in the data (open coding) or based on language used in the data (*in vivo* coding)
- retrieving data segments based on how they have been coded
- grouping similar codes together and viewing the data coded at them together (within or outside the software)
- defining codes, printing lists of codes, renaming codes
- increasing and decreasing the amount of data coded, uncoding
- recoding data
- commenting upon and writing about what is seen.

See Chapter 7 for step-by-step instructions for these tasks in software, and see Chapter 8 for memo writing tools and ways they can be used at different stages.

Working inductively is characterized by careful and detailed inspection of the data on a number of levels. This 'bottom-up' approach starts at the detailed level and moves through recoding, regrouping, rethinking, towards a higher level of abstraction. The aim may often be to generate theory from the data.

Deductive approaches to coding

Deductive approaches to coding are more explicit about the themes or categories to be considered at the outset of the coding process. There may be many reasons for taking such an approach, for example, where the intention is to test an existing theory or hypothesis on newly collected data or to investigate its transferability to a different social context. You may not be testing a theory or a hypothesis, but may simply know what you are looking for. This is often the approach taken in non-academic research settings, where the focus may be a more applied and practical understanding for a specific and fairly immediate objective, or a set of specifically identified outcomes. In academic settings, as Berg notes, a theoretical framework may guide code development and application (see Chapter 6):

> In a deductive approach, researchers use some categorical scheme suggested by a theoretical perspective, and the documents provide the means for assessing the hypothesis. (2001: 6)

Miles and Huberman (1994) describe a deductive method of coding. They suggest that a variety of factors (e.g. the conceptual framework, research questions, hypotheses, problem areas etc.) inform the generation of a provisional list of codes prior to commencing fieldwork. They illustrate how a segment of text can be read on different levels, suggesting that (re)consideration of data in the following terms leads to the identification and explanation of themes and patterns:

- *Descriptive codes* are fairly objective and self-explanatory in nature; they are used at the outset of the coding process when considering a segment of text for the first time. They allow the organization of data according to what it is descriptively about. They are based on predefined areas of interest, whether factual, thematic or theoretical in nature.
- *Interpretive codes* are subsequently used to add a more detailed layer of meaning to the data coded descriptively. Coded data are revisited in relation to the broad areas of interest and considered in more detail. Similar aspects may be recoded where they exemplify a meaningful concept or relationship. Existing concepts or themes may be deconstructed into more detailed aspects. Elements of a particular theme may be seen as relating to other aspects of different themes, and perhaps linked to one another.
- *Pattern codes* are used in the third stage, which moves to a more inferential and explanatory level. It involves considering how the themes, concepts, behaviours or processes identified through descriptive and interpretive coding occur within or are relevant across the dataset. This could be within an individual account. It could also be across subsets of data, for example amongst respondents with certain similar characteristics. Similarity, difference, contradiction etc. are investigated, the aim being to identify meaningful and illustrative patterns in the data.

In many ways, therefore, deductive approaches are similar to more inductive ones. They are also iterative and cyclical, involving close and repeated consideration of the data. The main difference is that the process starts with at least some predefined, higher-level areas of interest which are explicitly looked for in the data. There are many different reasons for adopting a deductive approach. Here we briefly describe two.

Theoretical coding

In projects which directly use or apply existing theoretical ideas, the coding process will be inherently deductive. Speller (2000) provides a good example of such an approach using software in her study of residents' attachments to place when their mining village had to be relocated because of methane seepage (see Appendix A for a fuller account of this project). Major elements of the theoretical framework underpinning the study were place attachment theory (Brown and Perkins, 1992) and identity process theory (Breakwell, 1986; 1992), but little empirical research had been conducted using either. Speller was therefore aiming to contribute to the theoretical area by empirically testing their applicability. Core principles of each theory were incorporated into a hierarchical coding schema which was built before coding of the text began (see Chapter 6 for information on the way Speller developed and used the coding schema to help with this, and Appendix A for project information). Gulati's (2006) project 'Understanding Knowledge construction in online courses' is another example of a theoretical approach to coding and is discussed in Chapter 6 and Appendix A.

Question-based coding

In applied research settings, analysis may be based around respondents' answers to particular questions, perhaps derived from a structured interview or open-ended questions to survey data. In such cases it will be useful to code all the answers to each question across the dataset separately in order to view and analyse the answers in isolation. This can usually be achieved semi-automatically if the data are formatted in a particular way (see Chapter 12).

An example of such an approach comes from a workshop programme evaluation conducted with the Centre for the Development of Healthcare Policy and Practice (CDHPP) at the University of Leeds, UK (see Appendix A). This project aimed to gain an insight into participants' experience of the workshop, and to explore the transference of techniques to workplace situations. The purpose was to inform CDHPP's understanding of the effectiveness of its programme in order to make improvements where necessary. The analysis and report were therefore in large part based around the questions asked, which were closely related to the stated aims, objectives and intended outcomes of the programme. One part of the analysis focused on how respondents had answered each question and the sense in which this information comprised evidence of the effectiveness of that aspect of the programme. This allowed easy identification of findings such as which aspects of the workshop were most useful to participants in their professional roles, and the enablers and inhibitors for applying learned techniques into those workplace situations (see Chapter 8). Another aspect of the analysis was more explorative, cutting across the question structure to consider, for example, the enablers and barriers to creativity and innovation in the workplace.

Question-based analysis is often required by commissioned research in various applied settings, for example, public consultations, service evaluations and some forms of government research. Sometimes, though, coding *only* in this way can restrict your flexibility and ability to think outside the question structure, and we discuss these issues more fully in Chapter 6.

Software tasks supporting deductive approaches to coding

In all software packages, codes can be generated independently of data – perhaps even before data are collected, transcribed and assigned to the software project.

- Codes can be generated at any point in the process independently of data.
- A mature and complex coding schema which represents an existing theory or hypothesis may already exist and be applied to data about a different topic.

- Broadly specified codes can be revisited in order to consider, for example, patterns in the way respondents talk about that issue; the serious theoretical thinking therefore may happen at a later stage than in inductive approaches.
- Deductive approaches tend to start off coding in a fairly descriptive way – but that is not necessarily very different from inductive approaches.

See Chapter 7 for step-by-step instructions for these tasks in software, and see Chapter 9 for memo tools.

COMBINING APPROACHES: THE PRACTICE OF CODING USING SOFTWARE

The above discussions concerning inductive and deductive approaches to coding are necessarily simplistic and the two methods should not be viewed as dichotomously opposed or mutually exclusive. We present them separately to begin illustrating the ways software tools can support very different approaches to coding. However, as Gibbs states, 'you do not have to do either one or the other or even one and then the other' (2002: 59).

Some authors have developed particular approaches to qualitative research and analysis which formally advocate a combination of approaches to coding. Layder's (1998) 'adaptive theory', for example, is a multi-strategy approach to the whole process of analysis in which he argues that particular aspects cannot be viewed in isolation. In coding data this approach takes account of both existing theoretical ideas and those which develop directly from the data under consideration.

One of the basic tenets underlying this book is that whatever the approach, using software can help to encourage the cyclical and iterative nature of qualitative research. The structure and functionality of CAQDAS packages do not promote in themselves a linear progression of tasks. Coding qualitative data is part of a flexible process, and coding using software can also be cyclical and iterative in nature, regardless of the approach(es) employed.

Many researchers who use software combine grounded approaches to coding with more deductive processes. Even those who are following a prescribed method, or working within a particular paradigm, often want to be able to incorporate an element of flexibility for working in other ways. For example, where a project is commissioned and the brief specifies certain outcomes, a fairly mature coding schema may be identified at an early stage. In such cases, however, researchers usually also want to allow for the identification and analysis of 'surprising' or contradictory aspects. CAQDAS packages support this very well (see also Chapter 6 on developing and managing coding schemes).

The Young People's Perceptions Project provides an example of how software can effectively integrate different approaches to interpretation through complementary coding strategies. An inductive approach was employed in the initial wave of primary data collected through focus groups. The purpose was to explore participants' perceptions of the similarities and differences between the Netherlands and England and Wales. Having identified factors, participants discussed and prioritized them. The findings shaped the subsequent direction of inquiry, grounding the project in a young person's perspective. The coding of these data initially took the form of an 'open coding' process whereby many *in vivo* codes were generated. Codes were often very detailed and specific (e.g. 'social segregation'; 'moved with the times'), but others were more general (e.g. 'laws'; 'tolerance') or descriptive (e.g. 'public transport'; 'fashion') in nature. After the initial coding phase around 175 codes had been generated. The codes were then grouped together in order to deconstruct the nature of the similarities and differences identified, the participants' thoughts about why they existed, and the ways in which they discussed and characterized them.

The schedule for interviewing young people about their experiences and evaluations of sex education was informed by concepts developed from the focus-group data and existing literature. Codes identified from literature included 'marginalization of young men', 'integration within broader curriculum', 'teaching environment'. They were used to consider how pre-existing theoretical conceptualizations were relevant to the data, particularly in terms of the differences in policy, practice and experience between the two countries. Amongst those developed from careful reading and reconsideration of the data and the codes themselves were 'non-engagement' and 'empowered learning'.

Documentary analysis of government policy documents and newspaper articles included a focus on the language and terminology used. This was partly informed by the accounts provided by focus group respondents to explain the differences they identified between the two countries. These included the terms 'liberalism' and 'tolerance'. These concepts were considered in relation to discourses of government policy and print media and were compared with how the young people had articulated them.

The direction of the analysis was therefore influenced by both theoretic conceptualizations and empirical identifications. A flexible approach to coding maintained a grounding in the young person's perspective whilst being open to and looking for the new and contradictory. At different phases in the project, codes needed to be developed in different ways and used for different purposes. The project was identifying cultural, political and practical influences. It was necessary to be able to keep these aspects separate, and analyse the various forms of data independently, but also to be able to combine them to make linkages and comparisons in order to build a holistic comparative interpretation. Employing a multifaceted approach supported by software facilitated this.

SUMMARY: USING SOFTWARE TO SUPPORT YOUR APPROACH TO CODING

There are many ways in which to organize qualitative data through coding. The processes and sequences you go through may be influenced by a range of factors, including:

- the amount and type(s) of data you are collecting
- the purpose of the research
- the pressures on time
- whether you are working individually or as part of a team
- your methodology (if you have one) and analytic approach.

However codes are generated and applied to data, their purpose is to enable you to revisit the data and to carry on thinking about them. As such, codes function as 'heuristic devices for discovery' (Seidel and Kelle, 1995: 58). Coding is not about perfectly capturing an instance or concept. Codes act as signposts to remind you to go back and think about an issue and the data linked to it again. Using software offers flexible ways to code and supports discrete and combined approaches. This flexibility, however, requires being clear about how and why different codes are generated, applied and used. There are various ways of achieving this including consistent and meaningful code definition (see Chapter 7), the use of integrated memo tools (see Chapter 9) and modelling ideas and relationships (see Chapter 10).

We are not advocating adherence to a particular methodology, process or strategy. Conversely, we would argue that different coding strategies are suitable in different situations rather than that there is a 'right or wrong' way of coding. It may be appropriate to follow different procedures and processes for coding different types of data within the same project as well as in different projects.

It is important to be aware of the ways your chosen software handles coding processes and to develop your own strategy of coding within your project efficiently. A balance needs to be found between your analytic needs *vis-à-vis* coding and the ways in which your chosen software will support you during the various coding phases. The following chapters have been written to help you reach such a balance.

Chapter 6
Coding Schemes, Coding Frames

In this chapter we talk about coding schemes. We discuss how they develop, what they mean to different researchers and how they can be variously represented and refined inside the software. Coding scheme structures and what you make of them have a great effect on how you work. They are handled rather differently in each of the three packages. We discuss the distinctions carefully, especially since full step-by-step procedures are not included here. The chapter was difficult to place. For some researchers, thinking about coding schemes might be about getting started with the theory or ideas that inform the project, embodied somehow within a coding scheme. Whether you are working in that way, or in a more grounded, bottom-up way, this chapter is written to assist in the 'moving on' phases of analysis. It is well documented that the end of a first-pass coding process can produce a 'block': where to go next, what to do with it all? We often find that the way forward involves moving beyond the structures of the coding scheme. Consequently we see other ways of grouping codes as critical to thoughtful progress. You can reorganize codes without affecting the main code structures and have codes appear in new collections for different purposes. Although tools to enable this vary in name and effectiveness in each software package, we illustrate that whatever constraints you perceive in a coding scheme there are simple strategies which will help you move on in theoretical and practical directions. Though full step-by-step support is not included in this chapter, there are many indications of processes in accompanying figures and tables. We also cross-reference to step-by-step processes in other chapters, though you may well find sufficient information here to make use of our suggestions.

BREAKING DOWN THE DATA, PUTTING THEM BACK TOGETHER

Qualitative data analysis often involves initially breaking data down into many different significant aspects (see the descriptions of coding in Chapters 5 and 7). The later processes of analysis often necessitate bringing those fragments back together into different collections and for different purposes (for relevant step-by-step exercises see Chapters 8 and 12). This may help you to see the data in different ways and to arrive at multiple levels of understanding about the nature of connectivity between themes, emotions, actions, outcomes etc. Such processes often do not have to change the way your main coding scheme is structured. Some of these strategies also provide ways to recover from perceived coding scheme problems but, at the same time, preserve what you have done already. Everything achieved so far will have value.

We have two more subliminal objectives with this chapter. We want to encourage a confidence in various tools as early as possible, so that you can avoid the constraints of over-caution which can stop you playing with ideas and using the tools available. We also want to convey in a constructive sense that, although it may seem natural for your coding scheme to begin or end as a reflection of the way your theory is modelled, or how you perceive the framework of your final analysis or write-up, it does not have to be any of these things. Together with the Young People's Perceptions exemplar, we discuss five other projects which use different coding scheme structures to suggest ways to 'move on'.

STRUCTURES OF CODING SCHEMES IN SOFTWARE

In Chapter 5, we covered some methodologically specific aspects of coding and more pragmatic (and common) combination methods. However codes are generated, and whatever methodological approach, if any, underpins this process, what we mean by the 'coding scheme' in terms of software is the manifestation of the way codes are listed or organized within the software program. Researchers often discuss the benefits and limits of hierarchical and non-hierarchical coding schemes. However, practical distinctions between coding schemes in terms of hierarchy and how this is manifested in different CAQDAS packages are not predictable. One cannot make logical assumptions about what is enabled by the coding schemes provided by particular packages. For example, in hierarchical schemes, software users often assume that higher-level codes automatically contain all the data coded by all of their subcodes. This is not always the case. In terms of simple retrieval, therefore, hierarchy does not always serve a functional purpose within the software (see Chapter 8).

Hierarchical systems

Some packages, including MAXqda2 and NVivo7, encourage an inherently hierarchical organization of the coding scheme. Within them, however, you can be as non-hierarchical as you like. It is up to you to choose how the structures at your disposal best fit your purpose.

The functioning of hierarchies in software

MAXqda2 is the only package discussed in the main body of this book which provides a simple *functional* coding scheme hierarchy. It functions as a retrieval engine as well as a way to organize the listing of codes. Switching on or 'activating' the top or an intermediate level of a coding hierarchy activates everything below that point (although individual subcodes can be activated separately). Relevant text segments are retrieved from activated text files in the adjacent window. We discuss two projects using MAXqda (versions 1 and 2) to discuss the ways the software can be utilized for contrasting approaches to developing and using coding schemes.

In QSR software (NUD*IST, NVivo2 and NVivo7), the hierarchical structure provides a way of organizing codes rather than enabling simple retrieval on this basis (see Chapter 8). Later we use project examples to discuss two quite different approaches in using QSR software (NUD*IST and NVivo2) which make use of hierarchical and non-hierarchical structures.

Non-hierarchical systems

In ATLAS.ti5 the default structure of the coding scheme is not hierarchical. Functional hierarchies[1] or the cosmetic appearance of hierarchies or collections of codes can be created or imposed in some windows, but in the main Code Manager all codes will be listed at the same level. To make any cosmetic[2] grouping of codes (e.g. prefixing code labels) work, retrieval on that basis happens by using the Ctrl key and selecting adjacent or non-adjacent codes and requesting output on them. In a cosmetic hierarchy such as this, the visibility of all the codes (rather than being hidden under clickable upper levels) can be just as effective as the more hierarchical structures in MAXqda2 and NVivo7. Codes can also be grouped in ATLAS.ti5 either by creating shortcut code groupings (*code families*) or by specifying links between codes (expressed as relationships). These are not visualized in the main code listing, though they can affect the way retrieval happens in later searches (see Chapters 8 and 12). Both the ATLAS.ti5 example projects discussed here (ESHA 2000; Gulati, 2006) use code families as effective ways to manage codes.

Note: NVivo7 allows the creation of shortcut groupings of codes (sets), which function in a similar way as families in ATLAS.ti5. MAXqda2 does not provide shortcut groupings of codes visually within the coding scheme, but combinations of activated codes can be saved and reloaded, enabling similar functionality (see Chapter 12). This chapter does not discuss linking codes in ATLAS.ti5 via relationships, but it is worth noting at this point that links made between codes in ATLAS.ti5 are different from those you might create in MAXqda2 or NVivo7 (see Chapters 10 and 12).

WHAT ARE THE BENEFITS AND DISADVANTAGES OF DIFFERENT STRUCTURES?

A hierarchy can make you feel more organized, though it can also present dilemmas – as we illustrate in the Young People's Perceptions Project later. You may have a fairly deductive approach, using theories to inform the way you are looking at data. Aspects of a theory can fit well into hierarchical structures: see the Speller (2000) project example. On the other hand, even when you work inductively, creating codes bottom-up, you might also use hierarchies to develop higher-level categories and concepts from earlier grounded coding: see the Silver (2002), ESHA (2000) and Gulati (2006) project examples. Hierarchical coding schemes can also be usefully employed to manage team projects: see the Rich et al. (2006) and Taggart et al. (2004) project examples. If nothing else a hierarchy is often a way to tidy up (see Chapter 5 for discussion on methodological approaches to coding).

 In team projects, coding schemes often have to be planned at the outset to provide some agreed commonality and consistency. Teams often begin with simple hierarchical structures, having identified key areas of interest, but may also construct the coding scheme to allow space for emergent codes to be incorporated.

We discuss two team projects in this chapter, both using hierarchical systems. Taggart et al. (2004) for the National Foundation for Educational Research (NFER), in their 'Curriculum progression in the arts' project, used a simple question-based hierarchical structure (see also Appendix A, Example 5). These very often work well, especially in applied situations where the brief from a client is very specific (see also Chapter 5). There are other ways that hierarchical coding structures can work for teams. For example, in the 'Video intervention/prevention assessment-Transitions (VIA)' (Rich et al. 1994 in progress) project, the research team used an unusual and successful approach to manage emerging coding by multiple individuals and the handling of negotiated and agreed codes (see later and see Appendix A, Example 3). Although the team projects we discuss in this chapter both made use of hierarchy, team projects can also be effectively managed by non-hierarchical systems.

The attractions of organization via hierarchies can be exaggerated. A common problem can be that in structures involving more than three or so layers, codes can become concealed and forgotten under layers of intermediate levels.

Despite the structures of hierarchical systems, some researchers are immediately attracted to non-hierarchical systems. For example, some researchers are very clear in their minds about their methodological requirements, and their focus is entirely on the nature of the relationships they can build between codes. They see hierarchies as a distracting irrelevance. Others have subjective reactions which place the coding scheme structure as only one very small part of the overall attractions of a user interface or software package. In any case, as we explain later, there are always several ways to achieve organized, hierarchical structures even when they are not immediately obvious. In turn, if hierarchical structures are available you do not have to use them at all (see also Table 6.1).

However you make use of coding scheme structures, what you very often need later is a way to escape the structures of the main code listing, in order to combine codes and express connections between them in ways which are not exclusively hierarchical. As discussed above, this can usually be achieved regardless of the coding scheme structures provided by software. In a very real sense then, it is advisable when considering the usefulness of a software package to focus on how it might be possible to step back from structures in the coding scheme later on (see Table 6.2 and Chapter 10 on mapping and linking).

FACTORS WHICH INFLUENCE APPROACHES TO THE DEVELOPMENT OF CODING SCHEMES

As discussed in Chapter 5, there are many factors which can influence the development and use of codes and coding schemes, including research questions, methodology, style of working and research context. It is useful to give some thought to this early on, although remember that there are many ways to rename codes, recode data and reorganize structures and code groupings as you progress. Factors which may contribute to the way the coding scheme develops include:

- The process of creating a coding scheme may be a reflection of your own preferred way of working.
- Researchers using Grounded Theory, or pragmatic derivatives of grounded theory, may generate most of the coding frame 'bottom-up' as 'things' are identified in the data, later using inductive reasoning to combine codes to create higher concepts, themes or categories.
- Many researchers, particularly in applied contexts, will use an *a priori* coding frame, embodying a clear set of objectives which help to govern and inform thinking at the outset (i.e. a deductive approach).

- Some researchers, who work with theoretical frameworks or who are testing models of theory, will stick quite firmly to the elements of the framework in coding the data deductively.
- Others look to expand on existing theories, and will use the coding scheme as a guide to building the coding frame and the coding process, but will be open (although in a very focused way) to new issues and themes arising from the text.
- Team projects may create and use a less flexible coding scheme after much early negotiation and agreement.

Is 'coding scheme' the same as 'theoretical framework'?

Not all researchers will have theoretical frameworks at the outset, or at all. Working in a grounded, inductive way, your analysis may be working towards a theory or an explanation. Alternatively, your whole project (or the qualitative element) might be designed around a theoretical framework. In either case, there are no hard and fast rules about the relationship between the coding scheme in the software and the theoretical framework of your project. There are, however, some questions which you could ask yourself:

- Do the principles and concepts of a theory *represented as codes* allow enough room for manoeuvre?
- Are some of the concepts likely to be fed by themes or issues which 'feed' more than one concept?
- Are you ready to define how a concept is broken down into other elements?

We illustrate how we deal with some of these dilemmas using the project examples later (see in particular Speller, 2000; Silver, 2002; ESHA, 2000; Gulati, 2006).

The way you learn software can also affect your use of coding schemes. Teachers themselves develop preferred ways of working and may promote an ideal way to use a software package. We often meet with researchers at later stages of their work, and are always comforted when we see innovative uses of coding schemes and software tools in general. Without suggesting that 'anything goes' what is important is that you can independently justify the way you are working, and that this fits in with your chosen methodological approach, if you have one. We would suggest that a so-called ideal way to work in a software package should be the last consideration.

Drilling down, or building up?

There will be ways that software can help manage the process of drilling down through broadly coded segments of data to undertake a more detailed deconstruction of the topic. Conversely if you have begun at a very detailed or grounded coding level, you can build collections of codes into higher concepts and categories (see Figure 6.2, and see Chapters 8 and 12). The drilling down and building up does not have to stop there.

Seeing beyond the coding scheme: grouping and combining codes

You may have a very clear idea of how a coding scheme structure works in terms of your project and how it relates to what you are looking for and what you find. How the coding scheme works in the software adds another dimension. In Table 6.1 we summarize some of the routine tasks associated with codes lists and coding scheme structure. In Table 6.2 we summarize how hierarchy itself, and other simple grouping devices allowing you to group codes in other ways, can help go beyond the structures of the coding scheme. Remember that the structure of your coding scheme may be simply about efficient organization rather than the explanation or theory that you are developing. As we illustrate in example projects, grouping codes in different ways without changing the coding scheme is an ideal way to approach this idea collecting process.

We further illustrate some of the simple grouping/combining features in later chapters: see Figure 7.6 in ATLAS.ti5, Figure 8.4 in MAXqda2 and Figure 7.18 in NVivo7.

CODING SCHEME PREDICAMENTS

We now provide some practical solutions to the two most common problems with coding schemes that we have experienced ourselves and seen others grapple with.

Working top-down, feeling stuck between tramlines?

Sometimes researchers feel constrained by hierarchical structures. We have made reference to several escape routes already in terms of combining codes in other ways. Here are reminders and other options:

• Codes which appear to have linkages beyond the theme which is being deconstructed could either come out of the hierarchical structure, or be collected elsewhere using another parallel collecting/grouping device. (See references to sets and families in Tables 6.1 and 6.2.)
• Write memos about your concerns about the linkages beyond the hierarchy – and/or use mapping tools in the software or scrawl on wallpaper to express the connections (see Chapter 9).
• Build searches (and save the way you did them) to act as pointers to what you need to check out later – but only if you feel ready to try them out (see Chapter 12 on searching, queries and supercodes).

Table 6.1 *Grouping devices for easy retrieval in software (excluding complex searches and queries)*

Easy devices for grouping codes and retrieval	ATLAS.ti5	MAXqda2	QSR NVivo7
Hierarchies	Main codes list, not hierarchical. Can add useful cosmetic hierarchy by prefixing codes, e.g. 'Attit-suspicious' 'Attit-optimistic' (for default alphabetic sorting)	Main codes lists hierarchical if required	Two areas, Free Nodes (not hierarchical) or Tree Nodes (hierarchical if required)
How *functional* is the main codes hierarchy? How does it help you retrieve everything within a hierarchy, if you require this?	If using cosmetic hierarchy as above, select all required adjacent codes with cursor, sitting close together (e.g. as above, prefixed in same way). Choose *Output/Selected Codes*, clearly labelled output in same file	*Activating* (switching on) a code at any level switches on all codes below, and retrieves respective coded data on activated texts	Can select multiple codes one-by-one by holding Ctrl key down; can't easily get clearly labelled combined output on them. Exports each code into separate Word files …
How can you make new groups of codes without changing the coding schema (or existing hierarchies where applicable)? (Those with fairly fixed theoretical coding schema may not need these options. Those who have worked in a combination of grounded (inductive) and theoretical (deductive) will often use them. Fully grounded approaches where many codes have been created, and dilemmas have been met with the coding schema, would definitely find them useful)	Easy to make *Code families*, and quick output on that basis. Codes can belong in any number of families Print, export or send to editor. All coded segments clearly labelled for each code in one output Or select miscellaneous codes from anywhere and ask for output *for selected codes*: codes plus data will be clearly labelled in one file	If other collections of codes required for retrieval, just cherry pick from anywhere and *Activate*, or copy codes and hang under new/different hierarchies. *Activate* top level to activate subcodes, to get retrieval on all. Apply new code to all contents of any Retrieved Segments window if useful. Easy export, clearly labelled, code, source file etc., print etc. into one file	…select multiple codes (Ctrl key, click one each), put into a new Set, and browse each node separately as usual or export set contents. Each code occupies its own MS Word file Easy option on a set of nodes, create new node (one code) from all in set

Note: value the work you have already done. Try not to feel compelled to make the schema into a perfect bullet pointed reflection of your theoretical framework or how you will write up. The other grouping devices above enable you to think outside apparently restrictive coding schema structures

Table 6.2 *Coding scheme and flexibility*

Coding scheme tasks and functionality	Comment	Software notes
Coding can begin in a broad-brush way	Top down, deductive	All
Codes can begin as detailed codes and be collected into broad-brush categories	Grounded, bottom up, inductive method emerging from the data	All
Label/relabel codes	Define and describe, stay on top of development of thinking	All
Add prefixes to impose structure to codes list (or to clearly label subcodes)	Prefixes keep codes you want to see together adjacent to each other in codes list. Subcode prefixes are helpful to remind of the hierarchical association when seeing out of context subcodes	All
Copy codes into temporary (or permanent) different hierarchies, serving e.g. another analytic function to main coding schema	Good for reminders, easy retrieval

Not advisable on a large scale (too much duplication and muddle) | NVivo7, MAXqda2 |
Move codes around (if hierarchical schema)	Change your mind about whether a code belongs where it is	MAXqda2, NVivo7
Put codes into any number of sets or families (only moving shortcuts of actual codes into groupings)	Collections of shortcuts to codes means codes are not multiplied by inclusion in sets or code families – a good way to manage ideas and potential focus	ATLAS.ti5, NVivo7
Merge codes to create higher concepts or categories	Analytic task in which you can lose the original detailed codes: make sure you want this	ATLAS.ti5, NVivo7, MAXqda2
Colour codes to indicate a particular status code or relevance for a code for e.g. a work session or team member	Activate (retrieve) on the basis of colour code	MAXqda2
Change sort order of the codes listing, or tabular views	Useful for seeing most frequently used?	All – though functionality varies

The 'large' coding scheme: moving on, refining?

Large coding schemes may often be intuitively and thoughtfully created and may present no problem at all to the researcher. Sometimes they are large because they have very many detailed descriptive codes. Sometimes though, they can become unwieldy. You can become aware that you have an *overly* difficult coding scheme with the realization that data and ideas about them are over-fragmented. Even if you have 'filed' ideas efficiently, they may be dispersed and possibly duplicated over the coding scheme (whether hierarchically arranged or not). It can then become difficult to move on, to 'analyse' at a deeper or more abstract level. You can become very engaged in navigating around parts of the coding scheme. In fact, a deep hierarchical coding scheme can exacerbate the sense of lost contact with previous work, because codes become buried at the lower levels. Time is wasted: what to do next, how to pull everything together to form a coherent explanation? We generally suggest that when you have more than three levels of hierarchy you can usefully ask yourself: why? Is this helping? If so, then how? Just be sure it is actually helping you. There may be several ways to approach the problem.

 This is an opportunity to come out of the software and use markers to annotate a printed codes list. Sometimes it is easier to rationalize the whole of a coding scheme on paper, to see where there are empty levels which are not really performing any function. Use highlighter markers to indicate what you want to do. Back in the software you can do any of these things if they seem relevant:

- Merge codes which really do represent the same thing.
- Move little-used codes aside into a special hierarchy or group called 'marginal codes' *or* 'redundant codes'.
- If the codes list is not hierarchically structured, prefix each of your little-used codes with e.g. '*zz-*' to ensure they drop down to the bottom of the codes list, to stop them cluttering up the important codes.
- Experiment with the combining or grouping functions listed in Tables 6.1 and 6.2, and read and review the coded output retrieved from the new combination. You might see something new.
- Use search/query tools to make new combination codes or to save queries and searches which you will want to perform again and again to bring your regrouped combinations up to date (see Chapter 12).
- Draw a map to visualize your current thinking about how codes are grouped and related to one another (see Chapter 10).
- Write a memo about what you are thinking and how reorganizing the coding scheme is helping (see Chapter 9).

CODING SCHEME STRUCTURES IN CAQDAS PACKAGES: PROJECT EXAMPLES

As discussed above, ATLAS.ti5, MAXqda2 and NVivo7 provide different coding scheme structures. The options available in your chosen software may affect the way you work, although all can be manipulated to support various approaches to coding and analysis. To illustrate this, we discuss six projects using software, and outline how researchers managed differing methodological and practical requirements. Appendix A contains slightly fuller accounts of the six projects (and one other project) all of which are used to illustrate various approaches to analysis at moments throughout the book. It was difficult to include an example project in NVivo7, since the software was too new at the time of writing. We therefore provide one example using NUD*IST and another using NVivo2, but where tools in NVivo7 are similar and enable similar actions we refer to this. Although the purposes and dynamics of each project are quite different, they share a flexible approach to addressing common coding dilemmas using software. In each case, researchers found ways to manipulate the tools at their disposal to suit their particular purposes. As with many projects using software, approaches to coding were combined to good effect and these examples provide useful tips for others using CAQDAS packages. Table 6.1 summarizes the coding scheme tools provided by ATLAS.ti5, MAXqda2 and NVivo7 and comments on some of their analytic and practical uses.

Speller (2000): 'The relocation of Arkwright'

(see Appendix A, Example 2, for more information about this project)

In the first example we illustrate how Speller (2000) used the hierarchical coding scheme in NUD*IST 4 to support a theoretically driven project. Within the same software project Speller was able to both isolate and combine inductive and deductive approaches to coding to support theory generation and confirmation. This example also illustrates the place of printed output in the analytic process.

Project background and methodology

Arkwright was a north Derbyshire coal mining village which narrowly avoided a major explosion in 1988 when methane gas seeped into houses from the local disused coal mine. The 100-year-old village of 177 households was blighted. In 1990 British Coal Opencast put forward a plan to opencast mine the area. Together with the North East Derbyshire District Council a plan was agreed to build a new village nearby at a cost of £15 million in exchange for planning permission to opencast, thereby also providing a solution to the ongoing methane problem.

This longitudinal study concerned the relocation of Arkwright coal mining village over a six-year period (1992–8). A total of 259 in-depth interviews took place at five points in time. They were transcribed and imported into NUD*IST 4. The main purposes of the study were to identify the psychosocial processes involved in detaching oneself from a place and forming new attachments to a future place, and to explore the relationship to individual and community identity. The theoretical concept informing Speller's work was *place attachment* (the emotional bond with place), clearly linked to identity theories within social psychology. The overall theoretical framework was provided by Breakwell's (1986; 1992) *identity process theory* (IPT) as it integrates change and dynamic temporal processes. The development of the coding scheme fell into two different methodological elements: an inductive and a deductive element.

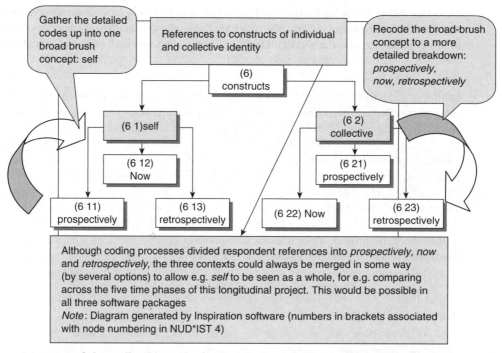

Figure 6.1 Part of the coding hierarchy for 'Relocation of Arkwright' (Speller, 2000): working 'bottom-up' or 'top down'

Inductive element

There was little previous empirical work on place attachment and the first coding phase was therefore grounded and exploratory, resulting in the creation of many codes. The next analytic stage involved printing out participants' responses in a concentrated form according to the codes generated. This highlighted complexities within a category, including nuances or differences which frequently resulted in splitting the category through recoding or merging codes with one another (see Chapter 8). Through the process of scrutiny and comparison, codes were categorized as feeding into five main categories for place attachment: 'sense of security'; 'sense of autonomy'; 'desire and ability to engage in appropriation'; 'optimal levels of internal and external stimulation'; and 'place congruence'.

Deductive element

The other part of the coding process was theoretical and confirmatory, informed by the intention to investigate the presence of the IPT principles and whether the change of place was associated with a change in the salience of the following key principles for each respondent: 'distinctiveness for the person'; 'continuity across time and situation'; 'self-esteem'; and 'self-efficacy'. In Figure 6.1, part of Speller's coding scheme focused on the ways that individual reflections on *individual identity* and *collective identity* were located, retrospectively, prospectively etc. The diagram also suggests that there are two ways to work in this context (see also the section 'Drilling down, or building up?' earlier in this chapter).

Summary

Speller's inductive, grounded coding and subsequent development of five analytic categories reflected major variations in participants' behaviour which were not envisaged before the completion of the analysis. This part of her analysis refined and enriched ideas about place attachment. This laid the groundwork for combining the results of the inductive coding on place with the more deductively coded identity process elements of her analysis, while being able to compare all elements of both over time. By using search (or query) tools she was able to test coding across time phase information (earlier applied to each interview). Thus, the theoretical background of identity process theory, having been the overall framework of her project, also informed the way Speller created part of her coding scheme. Within the same project, alongside the same coding scheme but somewhat separately, the concept of place attachment was used as a lens through which she coded inductively and created new codes to produce an empirically based exploration of the concept.

Note: Chapters 11 and 12 discuss how qualitative cross-tabulations and comparisons might be performed to produce such breakdowns across time.

Rich, Chalfen, Polvinen, Szymczak and Patashnick (2006): 'Video intervention/ prevention assessment-Transitions (VIA)'

(see Appendix A, Example 3, for more information about this project)

The Video Intervention/Prevention Assessment (VIA) Project at Childrens Hospital Boston conduct research into a range of issues experienced by adolescents with chronic illnesses.

As mentioned earlier, VIA's use of the non-hierarchical and hierarchical areas of the NVivo2 coding scheme is quite different from Speller's example above and to the way many team projects use hierarchical scheme. We use an example VIA project to further illustrate that the researcher is in control of how to use hierarchical systems and that these structures can support a combination of coding strategies. This example also illustrates that hierarchical coding schemes can be effective ways of managing and combining the work of different team members. It also demonstrates the role of memo writing and note taking in the incremental analytic process.

Project background and methodology

Informed by ethnography, participant observation and visual anthropology, VIA's analysis process draws on principles of Grounded Theory to generate themes which unify participants' illness experiences. In one VIA study, participants aged 16 years and older with cystic fibrosis (CF) were given video camcorders and asked to 'teach your doctor'what it is like to live with CF. Participants were asked to video their everyday life but were otherwise not directed as to aspects of their lives with CF in which the research team were particularly interested. Until recently CF has been a condition which proved fatal in childhood. With medical developments and increasingly effective interventions, many adolescents now survive into adulthood. The analysis team was therefore particularly interested in the way participants experienced the transition from childhood to adulthood in their lives generally and, in terms of their medical care, from paediatrics to adult medical care.

VIA-Transitions coding scheme

The wide brief given to participants in generating video data necessitated the inductive generation of codes as the video logs were read in detail and initially coded (see Chapter 5 for discussion of inductive coding). Since VIA conducts analysis in teams it was also necessary to find a workable way to handle the analytic contribution of several researchers. In meeting these requirements, they combined inductive and deductive coding processes in NVivo2 using both the *free nodes* (non-hierarchical) area and the *tree nodes* (hierarchical) area of the coding scheme.

They broke new ground at several levels. In this project, hierarchical 'trees' act as 'filing cabinets' which house each individual team member's grounded codes. The non-hierarchical free nodes are only used for agreed, negotiated concepts (see Figure 6.2). At the outset a number of free nodes were deductively created which represent some key areas of interest (e.g. health, cystic fibrosis, transition etc.). Codes generated through inductive open coding processes (see Chapter 5) were only moved from team members' individual hierarchies after team meetings. Whilst coding, team members noted thoughts, insights, questions etc. in memos which are read and discussed by other team members. At the team meetings, researchers discuss the analysis and negotiate which codes generated separately are similar, and whether they should be 'promoted' to a core category in the free nodes area. The coding scheme is reorganized incrementally as the researchers synchronically code the same documents.

Summary

The coding process used by the VIA team provides a working example of using a hierarchical coding scheme in two key innovative ways. First, they were able to effectively and efficiently combine inductive and deductive coding strategies in order to reflect the methodological needs of the project. Second, they made unusual but effective use of the non-hierarchical and hierarchical areas in the NVivo2 coding scheme structure in order to efficiently and logically manage the analytic contributions of several research team members.

In our view this is a useful exemplar for other researchers seeking ways to combine coding strategies, or those who see hierarchies as limiting in some way. It also provides useful insights into issues to consider when planning team-based projects using hierarchical coding schemes.

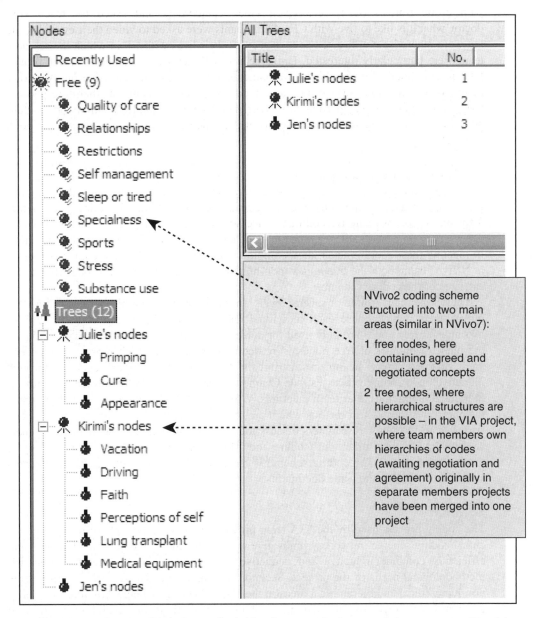

Figure 6.2 **Part of the coding scheme for 'Video intervention/prevention assessment-Transition (Rich et al., 2006) project: using hierarchies to manage work of different team members**

Taggart, Whitby and Sharp (2004): 'Curriculum progression in the arts' (NFER)

(see Appendix A, Example 5, for more information about this project)

The National Foundation for Educational Research (NFER) is the largest independent educational research institution in Europe. It is a not-for-profit organization and a registered charity. The majority of the Foundation's work is funded through securing research, evaluation, test development and information service contracts from government departments, charitable organizations and public agencies in the UK and abroad. The project discussed here used MAXqda because of its ease of use for researchers and accessibility to sponsors who wished to contribute to the analysis. Set in an applied rather than an academic setting, this example illustrates simple but effective use of a selection of tools to enable collaboration and rigorous analysis within a tight time-frame.

Project background and methodology

'Curriculum progression in the arts' is a thematic probe commissioned by the Qualifications and Curriculum Authority (QCA) as part of the International Review of Curriculum and Assessment Frameworks Archive (INCA). Thematic probes are comparative education reports providing snapshot cross-national data on specific subject areas and themes of interest across the INCA countries. The project aimed to define the content, progression and assessment of the arts curriculum in the compulsory phase of education from an international perspective. In order to gather data, a questionnaire was emailed to 41 educational specialists in 23 countries/states. Twenty-one countries/states replied electronically and the data were imported directly into MAXqda. Electronic versions of curriculum documentation were also incorporated in the software.

Analysis was initially directed by the six questions from the questionnaire, each of which was created as a top-level code in the hierarchical coding scheme. In addition there was a code for references and another for mentions of culture in order to capture the international dimension. MAXqda's colour attribute tool was used to tag the different types of code: blue for questions, pink for references and yellow for culture. We do not include a graphic illustrating this project due to the heavy reliance of the code colour attribute function (see Chapter 4).

In this format, the research team (one researcher, one senior researcher and one principal researcher) were all able to access the project data and contribute to the coding.

After top-level coding was completed, the research team met with the sponsors. At this meeting the research team explained the basics of MAXqda, presented the interim findings using the software and discussed the coding and analysis. By the end of the meeting, the sponsors themselves were able to contribute to labelling and coding the data.

Summary

This project clearly illustrates that focused use of simple tools can be effective. The creation of a simple hierarchical coding scheme enabled the analysis to be clearly focused around specific questions according to the research brief. The vexed notion of rigour is particularly relevant in team research where subjective ideas and priorities, different ways of applying codes and misunderstandings can lead to a lack of consistent work. The use of colour-attributed codes to encourage rigour at the outset among coders illustrates exactly what this particular software can offer at a basic level to improve collective understandings. The simplicity of the design of the project's coding scheme is itself designed to make everyone's involvement in it easier. The research team were able to illustrate their progress to the research sponsors, enabling them to actively contribute to the process in team meetings without the need for prior software knowledge. This project provides useful tips for team-based projects; those which require easy access to data by a range of stakeholders; and those in which software is used as a means of dissemination.

Silver (2002): 'Young People's Perceptions Project'

(see Appendix A, Example 1, for more information about this project)

The original coding scheme developed for the Young People's Perceptions Project used both the free (non-hierarchical) and tree (hierarchical) areas of the NUD*IST 4 database. For the purposes of this chapter, we have reworked the initial phase of the project using MAXqda2. In so doing we illustrate how functional hierarchies can be used to help manage inductively generated codes and explore the linkages between them in developing a useful coding scheme. We also discuss how this early exploratory work informed the direction of subsequent data collection and was integrated with the more deductive approach to later analyses.

Project background and methodology

The project comprised a comparative exploration of the historical development, provision and experience of school-based sex education in England and Wales and the Netherlands. Initially three focus groups were held to help define the framework and analytic objectives of the interviews. Previous (comparative) research largely considered the effectiveness of school-based sex education in terms of specific aspects, including content, timing and teaching environment, knowledge attained and the inclusion of young men's needs. Here the focus was on the role of wider social, cultural and political influences in understanding historical approaches towards school-based sex education. The project was broad in scope and exploratory in nature and did not adhere to any formal set of empirical or analytic guidelines, and the research design evolved as the project proceeded.[3] Large amounts of various forms of primary and secondary data were used, including primary data collected through questionnaires, focus groups and interviews, and secondary data derived from various forms of documentary evidence (see Chapter 2).

Integrating codes developed inductively and deductively

The variety and nature of the data necessitated a flexible and open approach to the analysis. The focus-group data were initially coded using an inductive approach in order to ensure the categories developed were grounded in a young person's perspective (see Chapter 5). From this analysis, several key themes were identified to be explored further in the interview data. As well as throwing up concepts to explore, the focus-group data informed the development of the interview guide. Data were formatted to facilitate comparison in terms of respondents' responses to questions and auto coded accordingly (see

Chapter 11). Later there was a need to integrate this more deductive approach with the rest of the coding scheme, so that data derived from different sources could be viewed together. Often it seems logical to keep codes generated in different ways and from different data sources separate in a coding scheme. Many researchers may create different software projects for different types of data or stages of a longitudinal project. As discussed in Chapter 11, this is usually not advisable as the software provides flexible ways to isolate parts of a dataset. In the Young People's Perceptions Project it was important to find ways of integrating the more deductive approach to coding the interview data with the more inductive approach already employed for the focus-group data, whilst maintaining the ability to consider them in isolation from one another.

Handling codes which feed several concepts

Concepts identified from the analysis of the focus-group data included 'transition to adulthood' and 'perceptions of sex education'. Both of these were top-level codes in a hierarchical coding scheme. 'Taking responsibility', 'thinking about sexual health', and 'changes in direction' were amongst the various more detailed codes contributing to the 'transition to adulthood' codes. While 'taking responsibility' was a clear element of 'transition to adulthood', it also needed to be connected to many other concepts and issues. With some uncertainty at the outset about how to manage the concept and what it would throw up, this general theme was dealt with as a separate and broad-based structure in the coding scheme, quite separate from the structure of 'transition to adulthood'. Figure 6.3 illustrates how this part of the coding scheme was organized to incorporate aspects of 'responsibility' separately, but that at some later date these coded data would be recoded where it was appropriate to new codes under e.g. 'transition to adulthood' and 'perceptions of sex education'.

This allowed for all aspects of responsibility as they were identified in the data to be coded simply. Later the 'responsibility' data could be revisited, deconstructed and coded in more detail (some of it in the light of 'transition to adulthood'). The functional hierarchy in MAXqda2 allows for easy retrieval of data coded at and below a top-level code; therefore the issue of 'where to code' became less problematic during the first-pass coding phase. This type of approach allows for inductive coding within a predefined structure and is replicated in many projects. As projects progress, however, further core categories are often identified which may not be best handled by further reorganization of the main coding scheme. This was illustrated by the need to explore the concept of 'autonomy' later in the Young People's Perceptions Project. It became clear that societal perceptions of young people as entities seemed to underlie many concerns about young people's sexual behaviour – evidenced in official documentation, media representations and legislation. Primary data collected from young people and teachers also provided an insight into these issues. In considering the coding scheme again, it did not seem appropriate to create another hierarchy for 'autonomy' as this concept cut across many existing hierarchies. In ATLAS.ti5 and NVivo7 this could be handled by creating shortcut groupings of codes, i.e. families or sets (see for example the projects by ESHA, 2000 and Gulati, 2006 later). The principle of 'activation' in Maxqda2, however, can act in a similar way, allowing for quick

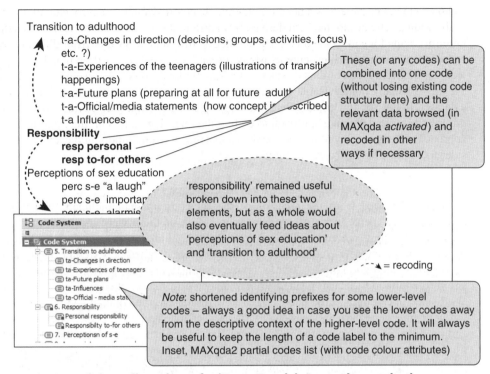

Figure 6.3   Part of the coding scheme for 'Young People's Perceptions project'
(Silver, 2002): finding ways to 'move on'

retrieval of data coded at codes from different hierarchies together, in order to be recoded or outputted as necessary. States of activation can be marked using the colour attribute facility, and saved to load subsequently.

Summary

This example shows how the structures that can be made in a coding scheme cannot replicate exactly how a topic is unfolding. It did not matter in this case that 'responsibility' was a topic on its own in the coding scheme and not included under 'transition to adulthood'. 'Autonomy' was a similar 'standalone but cutting across many aspects' code. For 'responsibility', the researcher could also recode in order to track which parts needed to be considered as subcodes, e.g. under 'transition to adulthood' if she needed to have the whole picture coded in each place. What really mattered however was that the researcher was aware that these were areas to be addressed, when writing about 'responsibility' and 'transition'. Far more important then, at these stages of dilemma about the coding scheme structure, was the need to be writing full notes systematically in an analytic diary or in appropriate memos, and to be constantly revisiting these notes (see Chapter 9). The coding frame certainly accounted for some major areas of discussion. Importantly though it provided access points to the data and was used to provide evidence to back up assertions, or to point out the exceptions and variations. It could not, though, entirely reflect the complex and interwoven structure of her account .

ESHA (2000) 'Older people's needs assessment exercise: focus groups'

(see Appendix A, Example 4, for more information about this project)

This project was chosen to illustrate ways to manage unwieldy coding schemes, or to move on from a bottom-up coding exercise. We discuss these issues in an example using a non-hierarchical coding scheme, but they may also be relevant to working in hierarchical structures. We discuss different but related issues as raised earlier in relation to the Young People's Perceptions Project, Speller's (2000) example and the VIA programme. We include this example to illustrate some practical resolutions to a common dilemma, usually connected with grounded or bottom-up approaches to coding: what 'level' do you need to be working at? At what stage do you begin to code the data in a more analytical way?

Project background and methodology
East Surrey Health Authority (ESHA) aimed to find out the present and future health and social care needs of people aged over 50 living in an affluent area where many older people have unmet needs. The research was based on postal questionnaires, one-to-one interviews and three focus groups, one with health and social care professionals and two with representatives of the community and community organizations. Lewins was commissioned (post data collection) to conduct the analysis but no explicit theoretical framework or methodological approach to the analysis was specified. The client wanted dominant themes from the focus-group transcripts to be identified and, since the research manager had some knowledge of the software, requested that ATLAS.ti (version 4)[4] be used to assist in the process. Delivery of the results was to be in the form of an awareness raising presentation of both the software and the output.

ESHA coding scheme
Lewins, who was not familiar with the data, decided that an inductive, grounded approach should be taken to initially code the data. This resulted in about 150 codes. Figure 6.4 illustrates some typical themes identified, showing in the margin area next to the text. The coding scheme in ATLAS.ti is initially non-hierarchical; codes are listed in the default alphabetic order but usefully can be sorted in different ways according to frequency, creation order, recent usage etc. (see Chapter 7).
  It was quickly obvious during the early coding processes that one of the key themes would be 'resistance' (i.e. to day centre services) amongst the clients. In generating the list

of non-hierarchical codes, it became clear that some codes were fairly generally conceived, others were descriptive, others were detailed and specific. Some were related to one another in certain ways. This led to a dilemma about where to code quotations which embodied multiple interpretations.

The dilemma

1   Progressively Lewins realized that since she was unfamiliar with the data, what she wanted from the coding exercise was to carry out detailed open coding. She did not want to overlook any nuance about older people's sensitivities.
2   Lewins became concerned that she was inconsistently coding. Sometimes she double coded, for example at the detailed code 'don't want to feel rejected' and the general code 'resistance', and sometimes she coded only at the detailed code. Sometimes she knew that she chose the general code because it was a very general remark about resistance. The role of 'resistance' as a code thereby became bothersome during this first-pass coding process.
3   Another problem was that some detailed codes were beginning to be partly about 'resistance' but also about other broad categories: so how far to take the double coding process?
4   Another and subtler factor in generating codes was that having created some broader categories she did not want to be thinking in a purely hierarchical way about detailed codes which were contributing to higher concepts. Clearly, quite a number of the detailed open codes had connections with 'resistance', but had other potential connections as well. For example, 'connotations' (of day centres) contributed to 'resistance' but was also linked to another broad category 'information' (and who delivered it), itself another key factor in the general take-up of services. The exploration of 'information' issues on the other hand was key to many other aspects of services: 'care', 'support of carers' and clients' 'comprehension' and 'take-up' of services.

The solutions

It is possible in ATLAS.ti to have all of these codes contributing to many different collections (code families). Because families are not mutually exclusive, one code can belong in many families, since it is only creating a *shortcut* to codes. The actual code is still in its original location in the main codes list. Families can be broad collections and in this project some families were used as broad and descriptive categories, for example 'carers' codes', 'transport issues', 'care issues', 'GP associations', 'access issues', 'Information' etc. Code families can also be much more tightly and theoretically focused. For instance 'resistance' became a small family of codes, instead of the unsatisfactory and uncertain broad-brush code it started out as in the open coding process (see Figure 6.5 for illustrations in another example showing how code families can be visualized). 'Independence' was another small code family; its member codes, e.g. 'not old enough', 'connotations of day centres', inevitably overlapped in the 'resistance' family (ESHA, 2000).

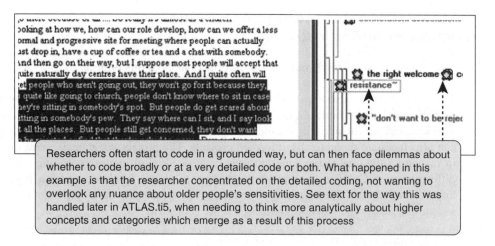

Researchers often start to code in a grounded way, but can then face dilemmas about whether to code broadly or at a very detailed code or both. What happened in this example is that the researcher concentrated on the detailed coding, not wanting to overlook any nuance about older people's sensitivities. See text for the way this was handled later in ATLAS.ti5, when needing to think more analytically about higher concepts and categories which emerge as a result of this process

Figure 6.4   Part of the coding scheme for 'Older people's needs assessment exercise' focus group's (ESHA, 2000): Dilemmas about coding – what level are you working at?

Code families facilitate several processes: they allow quick, clearly labelled output of all relevant coded segments; they can be viewed in a network; they can be put into a query (search) and combined with other codes (see Chapters 10 and 12). Creating a code family in ATLAS.ti5 does not change the coding scheme. It does not commit the researcher to using it or relying on it. What it did do in this case was to free the researcher from her dilemma. It offered a way of catering for the possibility that 'resistance' was important, without having to physically code the data to a broad-brush concept as well as the detailed topics and issues being discussed. (See Figure 6.5 in the Gulati, 2006 project example to follow.)

Summary

The ESHA project illustrates a common dilemma encountered when coding with software. Deciding which 'level' to code at can be an issue in both hierarchical and non-hierarchical systems (see the earlier project by Silver, 2002). In the absence of (cosmetic or functional) hierarchy in the main code lists, this project used code families in ATLAS.ti to collect and think about related codes. Other CAQDAS packages, including NVivo7 and MAXqda3 (see Appendix C), allow grouping of codes using shortcuts (sets) in similar ways as can be achieved in ATLAS.ti5 using code families.

The ESHA project is a useful exemplar for thinking about ways to escape coding scheme structure to move on in the analytic process. Here the need was to make sense of concepts, patterns and relationships when following a non-theoretical but grounded approach to coding. The next example by contrast illustrates a combined approach to coding using ATLAS.ti5 which is underpinned by a theoretical framework and a clear analytic strategy.

Gulati (2006): 'Understanding knowledge construction in online courses'

(see Appendix A, Example 6, for more information about this project)

This final example also uses ATLAS.ti5 but begins from a rather different starting point than the previous example. Gulati's (2006) project, like Speller's (2000), was theoretically directed, and we include this example to illustrate how non-hierarchical coding systems can also facilitate theoretically informed projects. The project integrates several methods in managing the qualitative data and uses creative ideas to manage a coding scheme in different ways. Gulati uses constructivist ideas to shape, label and order a large non-hierarchical scheme. She then uses code families to manage the development of her analysis, cutting across the labelled groupings in the codes list.

Project background and methodology

Gulati's doctorate research investigated how postgraduate learners constructed meaning in online and blended courses. The research questions and methodology were situated in the constructivist paradigm. The method used George Kelly's (1970) repertory grid technique to elicit 29 learners' construction processes during online and blended courses. Data collected included audiotaped interviews, repertory (numerical) grids saved in Excel, factor analysis correlation data output (quantitative analysis results), graphical representation of learning dimensions saved in PowerPoint, and metaphorical pictorial representation of individual learning spaces.

The aim was to explore individual differences in learning constructions and to identify emerging themes using the grounded theory principles from Strauss and Corbin (1998). The textual, numerical and visual data (including graphical representations and learning metaphoric representations) were imported into ATLAS.ti (version 5.0) and assigned as primary documents.

Grounding theoretical coding and the organizing of concepts

What we focus on here is the researcher's use of a constructivist lens through which she generated codes (grounded in the data) and how she organized her coding scheme. Gulati used the least hierarchically structured software, ATLAS.ti5, but used two devices to counteract this:

1 Codes have been prefixed in a way to assign a cosmetic sense of structure to the codes list (the default sort order is alphabetic: see Figure 6.5).
2 Code families have been created to organize codes and provide output, networks etc. in different collections and for other analytic reasons. At times similar prefixed codes are together in families; sometimes Gulati gathered codes from different prefixed areas. Remember that code families are 'shortcuts' to groups of codes. The following is an example of a code family report generated in ATLAS.ti5, listing codes in the 'informal learning with others' family. Note that the family cuts across several labelled groupings within Gulati's codes list.

Code family: informal learning with others
Created: 09/02/05
Comment: learning informally with others in the course or outside the course

Codes (6)
-[(IT) Using email/phone/text(instead)]
 [(relate) Socialising informally]
 [(share) Learning from others' experiences]
 [(share) Sharing informally to learn/bounce ideas off others]
 [(share) Sharing my ideas with others]
 [(share/des) Informal]

Quotation(s): 296

See also Figure 6.5 showing a segment of Gulati's codes list, organized by construct prefixing, and also how the code families can be visualized in different ways.

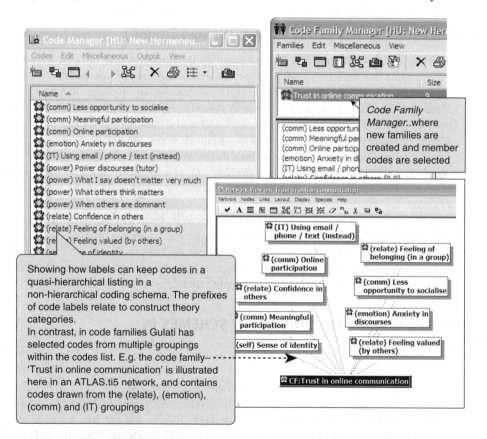

Figure 6.5 **Part of the coding scheme for 'Understanding knowledge construction in online courses' (Gulati, 2006): Prefixes, code families, and a network view of one code family**

Summary

Gulati's project illustrates an acknowledgement that what was required was to see some structure in her codes list. She had a good overall conception of how software could generally support her needs at the outset. This, together with ideas about how to mould software tools to her needs, is key to her creative use of ATLAS.ti5. She was particularly in need of structure because of the different types of construct theory codes she had generated. Though she coded in a grounded way, she needed to stay analytically and methodologically in control as she created codes and identified data which fitted. There is no doubt that the code prefixing in this context worked very well as an aid to see collections that were essentially hierarchical, but were not hidden from view in the way that hierarchical structures in software can tend to become. This was clearly differentiated from a later stage of identifying analytic concepts which sometimes cut across those construct-prefixed categories of code by using code families, which did not spoil the structure of the codes list. She used the tools available in a very practical, creative and systematic way which was absolutely appropriate for her methodological approach.

SUMMARY: MAKING THE MOST OF A CODING SCHEME

There is a fairly clear underlying message in this chapter. Use devices, some that you invent, some that are provided by each software package, to control how you wish to work. The example projects illustrate that CAQDAS packages can facilitate the management of ideas, represented in a coding scheme in various ways, and that tools can be effectively used to facilitate different methodological and analytical approaches and practical needs. This is the case whether working in a hierarchical or non-hierarchical software system. In particular, the examples demonstrate how different approaches can be integrated by manipulating coding scheme structures themselves, and by using tools to escape the main listing of codes. This allows you to step back from the coding scheme to view and reconsider individual codes, the data coded by them and groups of similar issues in alternative ways. Your coding scheme will evolve, and the list of codes as it appears in the software is just a small part of the overall system that helps you manage your thinking processes and developing analysis. Refer to other chapters for complementary tasks and tools which may be useful at times: in particular, Chapter 4 on exploring text, Chapter 5 on approaches to coding, Chapter 9 on memos, Chapter 10 on mapping and Chapter 12 on searching.

COMPARATIVE COMMENTS ON CODING SCHEMES IN CAQDAS PACKAGES

Hierarchical nature of coding scheme structure

NVivo7 and MAXdqa2 are structurally hierarchical in terms of the main codes listing, though you can be as non-hierarchical as you like in any of the software packages. MAXqda2 has an easily functional hierarchical coding scheme for simple retrieval purposes, whereas the hierarchical coding scheme in NVivo7 is not functional in the same way. ATLAS.ti5 provides other ways outside the main codes list to create hierarchies (see linking devices in Chapter 10). However, cosmetic prefixing indicating hierarchy can in the end be more effective in terms of easy retrieval for 'subcodes' than NVivo7. Additionally in ATLAS.ti5 the Object Explorer, a separate clickable tool lists all work and connections in turn between documents and their quotes and then codes assigned to quotes. It also shows connections of every code with every other code and so provides not exactly a hierachical view of the coding scheme, but all the interconnections within it.

Grouping codes

All the software packages offer alternative ways of grouping codes (i.e. without using hierarchies). ATLAS.ti5 and NVivo7 provide combining methods (families and sets) which store shortcuts only at the groups, saving the coding scheme itself from duplications. This option will be available in MAXqda3, although in MAXqda2 activated codes can be saved and reloaded and codes can be visually grouped across the main coding scheme using the colour attribute function (see Chapters 7 and 8).[5] NVivo7 has the most instant and useful device for creating one larger code out of several selected, though this is possible in both the other packages by slightly lengthier processes.

Combining codes in retrieval

We discuss this in other chapters, but it is relevant when thinking about constraints of coding scheme structure. MAXqda2 provides the most interactive and immediate live (recodable) device for getting grouped retrieval, via selective activation of codes anywhere in the coding scheme. In ATLAS.ti5 such grouped output is easily achieved into one new file in a number of ways, but is not live and interactive and therefore not recodeable at this point. In NVivo7 grouped coded output is exported to separate output files for each code which will mean separate printing operations and again not live and recodeable from this point.

NOTES

1 A *functional hierarchy* has other purposes in software, e.g. for retrieval of all data associated within a hierarchy or collection, i.e. it is more than just the cosmetic appearance of hierarchical structure.
2 *Cosmetic hierarchy*: prefix codes to keep those you want to appear together in the main listing. This does not link codes, but may make it easier to think about similar codes, perhaps as a precursor to creating hierarchies or relationships or groupings.
3 It did not take place in a theoretical vacuum, however. For example, the areas of interest and the nature of the initial research questions reflect a social or cultural constructionist perspective in that an underlying assumption was that the analysis of a country's social, cultural and political history can add to the understanding of one particular area of policy development, implementation and effectiveness.
4 ATLAS.ti 4, is identical in basic architecture to ATLAS.ti5 with respect to code families.
5 Where we are given information about forthcoming versions we provide it. Some software producers however will not release such information very early.

Chapter 7
Coding Tasks in Software

This chapter builds on previous chapters about coding to provide step-by-step instructions for basic coding tasks in ATLAS.ti5, MAXqda2 and NVivo7. It leads into Chapter 8 on basic retrieval of coded data and Chapter 12 on interrogating the dataset. Chapter 8 concludes with a comparison of coding possibilities.

From a software point of view, there is no 'right' or 'wrong' way or prescribed sequence to generate or apply codes. As we discussed in Chapters 5 and 6, researchers use a combination of coding and coding scheme strategies. Tasks and exercises presented here build on these previous discussions. We first list various coding tasks supported by software, and note how they may be useful. We then provide step-by-step support in ATLAS.ti5, MAXqda2 and NVivo7. The range of coding options available will support, reflect and encourage an iterative and cyclical process, but *you* the user remain in control of how to proceed.

GENERIC TASKS: GENERATING AND APPLYING CODES

TASK 7.1   GENERATING CODES

As discussed in Chapters 3 and 5, you may already have predefined areas of interest and have begun to think about and create codes. Alternatively you may be waiting until most data have been accumulated in order to generate codes from the text level as you read through the data.

*   *Create a* priori *codes.* Any key issues or themes you know you will be interested in can be generated independently of data at any stage. They may be fairly broadly specified and/or identified from existing literature and theory.
*   *Create codes grounded in the data.* Whether descriptive or interpretive, new codes can always be created whilst reading through textual data, and linked immediately to the precise segment which prompted that new idea, concept or category.
*   *Create* in vivo *codes.* If you are particularly interested in the language used in the data, or if a term is identified which neatly encapsulates an idea or theme, you can create codes *in vivo*. Many packages allow words and phrases used in the data to be quickly and automatically turned into a code label. Be aware though that if you use this tool widely, it has methodological implications. It may seem very useful as a shortcut to code generation, but if working interpretively you should use it critically, being aware that it only has a temporary role to play in the whole process of producing more analytic ideas about the data.

TASK 7.2   APPLYING EXISTING CODES TO TEXT

Your chosen software may provide many different ways to code text, so become familiar with options and how they may be useful (see software-specific sections below).

*   *Define the amount of text to be coded.* Whether it is the word, phrase, sentence, paragraph or whole document, the researcher specifies the relevant unit of context.
*   *Apply codes as relevant.* Apply as many codes to a text segment or to overlapping segments as relevant, if this seems methodologically appropriate.
*   *View codes appearing in the margin.* ATLAS.ti5 and MAXqda2 allow you to view codes appearing in the margin pane while coding. NVivo7 also allows you to view codes in the margin, but this view has to be switched on and off to keep up to date. Viewing codes this way is useful because it allows you to see co-occurring codes and identify interesting patterns and relationships as you proceed.

TASK 7.3   DEFINING AND LISTING CODES

*   *Define the meaning, scope and intended application of codes.* It makes sense to do this as codes are generated. Therefore, consider the function and impetus for generating the code and revisit and refine definitions. Date any changes in definition so you can track developments in thinking. Small leaps in reasoning are important, and increasing the transparency of your work in this way will add to the potential quality of your work.

(Continued)

- *Generate code reports.* Listing codes and their definitions is useful for analytic and practical reasons. Generating a code list can help at various stages, for example, when thinking about grouping codes, generating higher-level categories, reorganizing the coding schemes etc. Retaining these reports can provide a useful 'snapshot' of the various stages of the analytic process.

 Do not underestimate the value of 'thinking outside the software'. Printing a list of codes and thinking about their definitions and how they may be related to each other at an abstract level on paper can be just as useful as revisiting data coded at one code within the software.

 Team situations call for well understood code definitions to ensure as much consistency as possible. Hard-copy printouts are useful here where the main structure of the coding schemes has been developed prior to the coding process (see Chapter 6).

TASK 7.4   CHANGING YOUR MIND ABOUT HOW DATA ARE CODED

One of the advantages of using software is the ability to change your mind at any stage and reconsider the data in light of how they have previously been coded. It also allows you to refine coding, to deconstruct broad issues into more detailed and precise concepts and so on (see Chapter 6).

- *Increase or decrease the amount of text coded.* Refining the coding in this way may be useful when considering themes or concepts in more detail and moving on beyond the first pass through the data.
- *Unlink a code from a point in the data.* It is just as easy to uncode data as to code it if you change your mind about the need for a code at a point in the data.

TASK 7.5   REORGANIZING THE CODING SCHEMES

As you proceed through different coding phases you will probably feel inclined to reorganize the coding schemes to more accurately reflect the development of your thinking. As we saw in Chapter 6, your coding schemes is not likely to be a neat encapsulation of theoretical ideas (whether preconceived or emerging from the data); however, it is unusual not to reorganize the coding schemes at some point. Software provides several useful tools to facilitate this.

- *Rename codes.* Renaming codes can indicate more precisely the phenomena they represent.
- *Merge codes.* You might merge codes either because the difference between them is not as meaningful as you first thought, or because a broader theme is more appropriate.
- *Group codes.* For example, if you started coding in an inductive way you might later want to collect similar codes together – perhaps into a hierarchy where this is supported, or a looser collection of codes (see Chapter 6 and the software-specific sections below).

(Continued)

(Continued)

- *Move codes.* For example, if you began with a more deductive coding schemes, you might want to reorganize the structure in light of growing interpretations or reconceptualizations.
- *Delete codes.* You may want to delete codes because they have become redundant. Doing so, however, will remove all the references the codes have to data across your whole dataset, and it will not usually be possible to retrieve that coding at a later stage. Consider therefore isolating redundant codes from the main coding schemes by grouping them, rather than deleting them, unless of course you are sure they really are no longer relevant.

Any *output report* generated from software is a snapshot of that moment in time. Reports are fully editable, and you can save them as files (see Chapter 9). Always print a codes list report before and after making major changes to the coding schemes. There will always be an easy way to do this from the export functions associated with the project or main menus.

Integrating the different aspects of your work

In coding textual data you will notice interesting aspects, patterns and relationships. Note insights and questions in your mind as you progress, so as not to forget them. As discussed in Chapters 4 and 9 you can mark interesting data, comment about specific segments and write broader memos. The flexibility of software allows use of these tools in tandem with the coding procedures illustrated here. For example, it is usually possible to link your writing to the data which prompted a train of thought. Consider the most useful ways to use the writing tools provided by your chosen software at various points. Also consider how visually mapping ideas and relationships (Chapter 10) and testing ideas and hunches using search tools (Chapter 12) can facilitate the iterative coding process.

SOFTWARE-SPECIFIC VARIATIONS: CODING PROCESSES IN SOFTWARE

Exercises in ATLAS.ti5

Coding in ATLAS.ti5 is simple yet flexible. You have the ability to arrange the interface so that you can see the documents, margin and Code Manager simultaneously. The floating Code Manager window enables easy drag and drop coding.

Exercise 7.1   ATLAS.ti5: generating codes

The numbering of steps corresponds to Figure 7.1.

1   Open the Code Manager pane via the main Codes menu or by clicking the rectangular icon to the left of the Codes combo box.
2   To create *a priori* codes: use the New Item icon at the top left of the Code Manager.
3   Type the new code name in the Free Code(s) dialogue box. You can create several codes at once in this window by using the pipe character | (Shift+backslash on UK/US keyboards) between code labels.
4   To create codes from text level: select a passage of text to code in the main document window. Right click over the blue text selection, choose Coding/Open Coding. Type the new code label(s) as required and click *OK*.
5   To create *in vivo* codes: select a word or short passage in the data that you wish to use as a code label. Drag the selection with the left mouse button depressed and drop in the Code Manager. Or with text selected, click on the *In Vivo* shortcut icon on the left of the main user interface.

Note: however you generate codes in ATLAS.ti5, they will appear listed in the Code Manager. The default is to list them alphabetically, but practise changing the sort order using the Codes menu and the appearance using the View menu in the Code Manager.

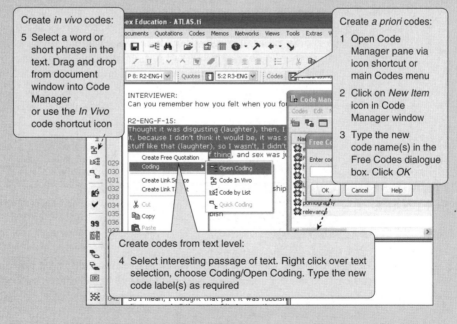

Figure 7.1   Generating codes in ATLAS.ti5

Exercise 7.2   ATLAS.ti5: applying existing codes to text

The numbering of steps corresponds to Figure 7.2.

1   Open the Code Manager pane.
2   Select the amount of text you want to code.
3   Drag and drop codes from the Code Manager onto the data.
4   View the codes appearing in the margin as *quotations* are created and coded.

Note: the colour of the codes appearing in the margin relates to the relative size of quotations at that point in the text. You cannot alter their colour and a code may change in colour as you continue coding.

ATLAS.ti5 provides many different ways to code data. Experiment with the different options to find those which suit your style of working best. For example, *Coding/Code by List* is useful for coding the same quotation to several already existing codes. Look in the main Codes menu, or right click over selected text, or use the shortcut icons down the left of the main interface.

If working directly with multimedia documents in ATLAS.ti5, the processes of coding are very similar to those described here. Parts of a graphic file can be selected and coded, and audio/video can be segmented into quotations which can be treated in the same way as textual quotations (see Chapter 4).

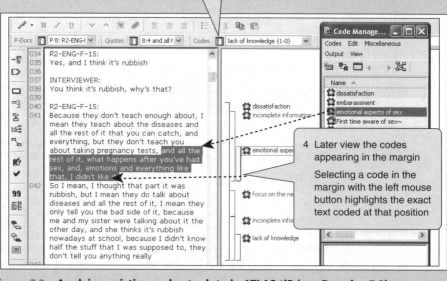

Figure 7.2   Applying existing codes to data in ATLAS.ti5 (see Exercise 7.2)

Exercise 7.3   ATLAS.ti5: defining and listing codes

The numbering of steps corresponds to Figure 7.3.

1   To define a code: in Code Manager, select a code to define. Put the cursor in the Comment bar and type a definition. Consider dating these entries using *Edit/Insert/Insert Date/Time* from the Code Manager menu.
2   To generate a list of codes including any attached comments, go to the Output menu in Code Manager (or the Codes main menu) and choose *Print Codes with Comments*.

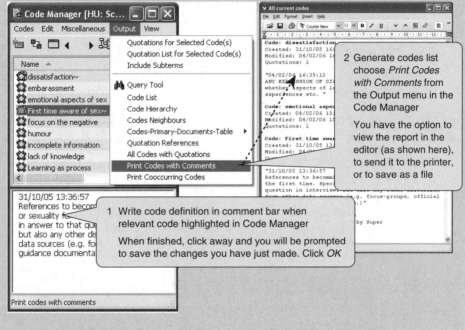

Figure 7.3   **Defining and listing codes in ATLAS.ti5 (see Exercise 7.3)**

Exercise 7.4   ATLAS.ti5: changing your mind about how data are coded

The numbering of steps corresponds to Figure. 7.4.

1   To increase or decrease the amount of text coded at a particular point: select the coded quotation by clicking on the code in the margin. Reselect the new quotation. Click on the tick icon ✓ in the left vertical shortcut icon bar. The quotation will be resized accordingly.

(Continued)

(Continued)

Note: if exactly the same quotation was coded by another code, the corresponding change in size will also happen for that code. In other words, the quotation is an independent object, and its reduction in size is relevant to every other object it is linked to.

2 To remove a code from a position in the data: select the code in the margin you wish to remove. Right click over it and choose *Unlink*. The code will be removed but the quotation will still exist. If you also want to remove the quotation, right click over the quotation bracket in the margin and choose *Delete*. This will remove the quotation and any comment attached to it.

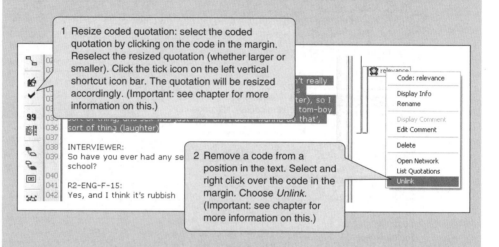

1 Resize coded quotation: select the coded quotation by clicking on the code in the margin. Reselect the resized quotation (whether larger or smaller). Click the tick icon on the left vertical shortcut icon bar. The quotation will be resized accordingly. (Important: see chapter for more information on this.)

2 Remove a code from a position in the text. Select and right click over the code in the margin. Choose *Unlink*. (Important: see chapter for more information on this.)

Figure 7.4 Changing your mind about how data is coded in ATLAS.ti5 (see Exercise 7.4)

Reviewing Coding: navigate around coded data and recode if appropriate (Chapter 8).

Exercise 7.5 ATLAS.ti5: reorganizing the coding schemes

The numbering of steps corresponds to Figures 7.5 and 7.6.

Renaming, merging and deleting codes

1 To rename codes: in Code Manager, choose the code to rename. Either click once with the left mouse button and wait until the code label goes into renaming mode, then rename the code; or right click over the code and choose *Rename*.

(Continued)

2 To merge codes: choose the code from the Code Manager to merge into another (i.e. the one whose name will be lost). Right click over the code, choose *Miscellaneous/Merge Codes* and select the code to merge into. Click OK.

3 To delete a code: choose the code from the Code Manager to delete. Right click over it, choose *Delete*. This will also delete all links (references) attached to it across the whole dataset. You will be reminded how many quotations the code is linked to. Click *Yes* to delete the code. You are then asked if you wish to 'remove all quotations which have no further references' (i.e. no other codes linked). Click *Yes* or *No* accordingly.

Prefixing codes

Prefixing codes may be a useful way to group together codes as they appear in the Code Manager list. Doing so is only cosmetic, but it can help to have similar codes listed as a precursor to grouping codes into families (see below).

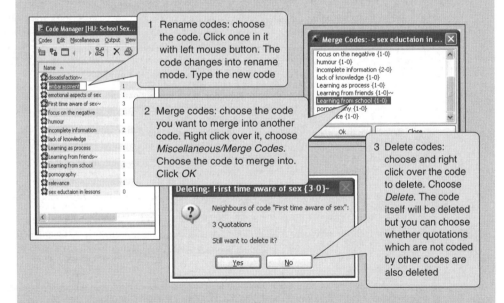

Figure 7.5   Renaming, merging and deleting codes in ATLAS.ti5 (see Exercise 7.5)

Grouping and moving codes

Refer to Figure 7.6. See also Chapter 6, the projects by ESHA (2000) and Gulati (2006), for ideas about grouping codes into code families in ATLAS.ti5.

(Continued)

(Continued)

4 Create code families. Open the Code Family Manager either via *Codes/Edit Families/ Open Family Manager,* or by clicking on the shortcut icon at the top right of the Code Manager. Use the *New Family* icon at the top left of the Code Family Manager to create and name the new code family.

5 Select the relevant code family to assign codes to. Move codes from the right side (non-members) to the left side (members) by double clicking or using the left arrow. As you do this the size of the code family increases, indicating the number of codes which belong to it. Choose the following code family and continue.

6 Move codes out of families at any time in the Code Family Manager by double clicking on member codes or using the right arrow.

Note: code families contain only shortcuts to codes and any code can belong to any number of code families. They can be created for multiple purposes at any stage. They do not affect the main listing of codes in the Code Manager (unless you are filtered to a code family: see Chapter 8). Code families can perform any number of tasks for you, e.g. small analytic groupings of related codes, broad collections of codes about a topic, all the codes that might be somehow relevant to Chapter 10 of your thesis, all codes except certain categories, and so on. Code families can start empty, but act as markers for future analytic direction. When creating code families it is useful to note why you are doing so. Use the Comment bar in the Code Family Manager. Date the comment and include information on how you intend to use the family.

Combining code families

 Experiment with combining code families using the Super Family Tool. Access this in Code Family Manager via *Families/Open Super Family Tool*, or use the icon. Combine families using Boolean operators such as AND, OR and NOT (see Chapter 12).

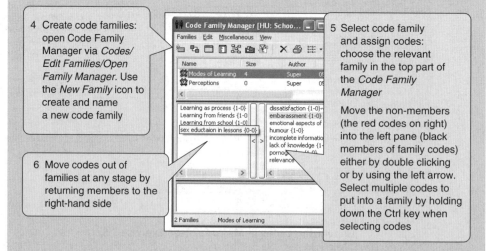

4 Create code families: open Code Family Manager via *Codes/ Edit Families/Open Family Manager.* Use the *New Family* icon to create and name a new code family

6 Move codes out of families at any stage by returning members to the right-hand side

5 Select code family and assign codes: choose the relevant family in the top part of the *Code Family Manager*

Move the non-members (the red codes on right) into the left pane (black members of family codes) either by double clicking or by using the left arrow. Select multiple codes to put into a family by holding down the Ctrl key when selecting codes

Figure 7.6 Grouping and Moving codes in ATLAS.ti5 (see Exercise 7.5)

(Continued)

Visualize code families in a network (Chapter 10). Filter to code families to focus in on an area of your coding schemes (Chapter 8). Get focused retrieval/output based on quotations linked to codes belonging to a family (Chapter 8).

Exercises in MAXqda2

The MAXqda2 coding schemes can be as hierarchical or non-hierarchical as you wish. It is worth having in mind that (in Chapter 8) you will see that retrieval of coded data in MAXqda2 happens by *activating* or switching on individual selections of codes, or whole code hierarchies.

Exercise 7.6   MAXqda2: generating codes

The numbering of steps corresponds to Figure 7.7.

1   To create codes listed at the same level: codes in MAXqda2 are created in the Code System. Right click on the top level of the Code System and choose *New Code*. Type the name of the new code.

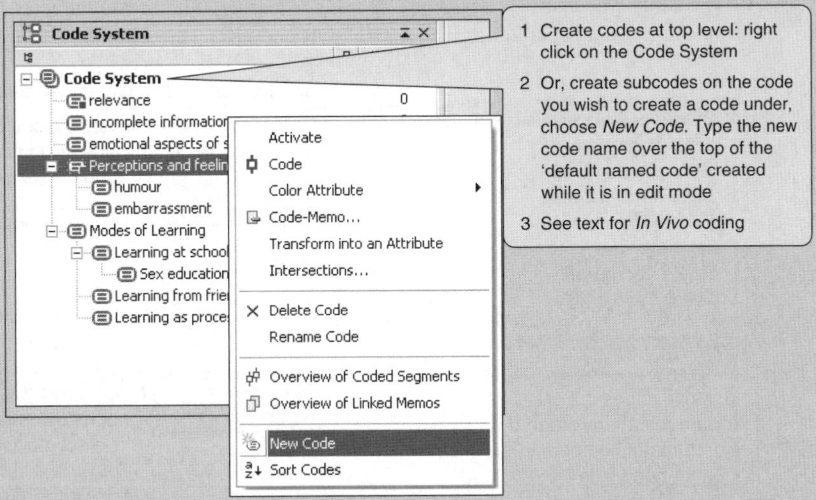

> **Code System**
>
> - Code System
>   - relevance   0
>   - incomplete information
>   - emotional aspects of s
>   - Perceptions and feelin
>   - humour
>   - embarrassment
>   - Modes of Learning
>   - Learning at school
>   - Sex education
>   - Learning from frie
>   - Learning as proce
>
> Menu:
> - Activate
> - Code
> - Color Attribute ▶
> - Code-Memo...
> - Transform into an Attribute
> - Intersections...
> - ✕ Delete Code
> - Rename Code
> - Overview of Coded Segments
> - Overview of Linked Memos
> - New Code
> - Sort Codes
>
> 1 Create codes at top level: right click on the Code System
> 2 Or, create subcodes on the code you wish to create a code under, choose *New Code*. Type the new code name over the top of the 'default named code' created while it is in edit mode
> 3 See text for *In Vivo* coding

Figure 7.7   Generating codes in MAXqda2 (see Exercise 7.6)

(Continued)

(Continued)

2 To create subcodes: right click on the code you wish to create a code under and choose *New Code*. Type the name of the new code.

3 To code *in vivo*: select the short phrase or word you wish to use as a code label, and click on the *In Vivo* shortcut icon along the top button bar. The code is created and the data are coded.

You can also give codes a colour attribute (11 colours to choose from). The colour appears on the codes in the Code System and in the margin view when you begin coding (see below). There are also four default colour codes which can simply be assigned to data: these change the colour of the text as well. To use this specific tool, see the MAXdqa2 exercises in Chapter 4.

Exercise 7.7   MAXqda2: applying existing codes to text

The numbering of steps corresponds to Figure 7.8.

1 To assign codes to text: make sure the Code System *and* Text Browser windows are open. Select the amount of text you want to code.
2 Choose the relevant code in the Code System: that code appears in the coding toolbar at the top of the window.

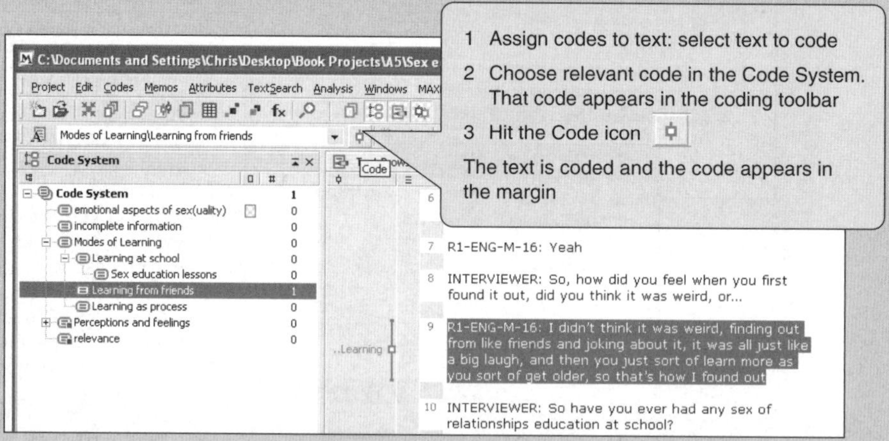

Figure 7.8   Applying existing codes in MAXqda2 (see Exercise 7.7)

(Continued)

 3   Click on the Code icon along the top button bar. The text is coded and the code appears in the margin of the Text Browser. Codes will appear in green in the margin unless you have given codes a different colour attribute.

 Try dragging and dropping selected text onto codes and using the recently used dropdown menu in the coding toolbar.

You can *weight* coded segments or codes. This is a good way to enable variable retrieval according to weight (it is also a way to cut down on codes providing some idea of measure, i.e. 'very', 'not very' etc.). The software assumes you have used 100% weight on all codes unless you use this tool. It would only be appropriate to use weight in certain circumstances.

If you are working with multimedia objects embedded into MAXqda2 texts, the processes of coding are very similar to those described here. But you can only code whole objects, not parts of a graphic or audio/video files.

Exercise 7.8   MAXqda2: defining and listing codes

The numbering of steps corresponds to Figure 7.9.

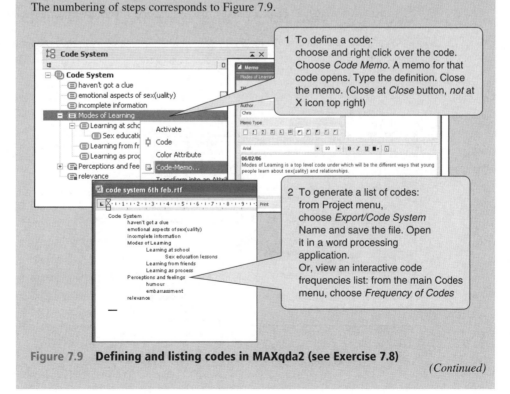

Figure 7.9   Defining and listing codes in MAXqda2 (see Exercise 7.8)

(Continued)

(Continued)

1   To define a code: choose the code to define in the Code System. Right click over it and choose *Code Memo*. Type the definition in the Memo window. Date the entry manually. Close the Memo window. A yellow post-it note flag appears next to the code in the Code System. To reopen the memo, double click on the yellow flag.

2   To generate a list of codes: from the main Project menu, choose either *Print/Code System* or *Export/Code System*. This will print or export the entire Code System to a file, illustrating its (hierarchical) structure.

You could also see the interactive code frequencies list: from the main Codes menu choose *Frequency of Codes*. This table can be sorted in various ways by clicking once or twice at the top of each column.

Memos: the MAXqda2 Memo System (see Memos menu) is simple, flexible and powerful, allowing a range of options for retrieving your writing (see Chapters 4 and 9).

Exercise 7.9   MAXqda2: changing your mind about how data are coded

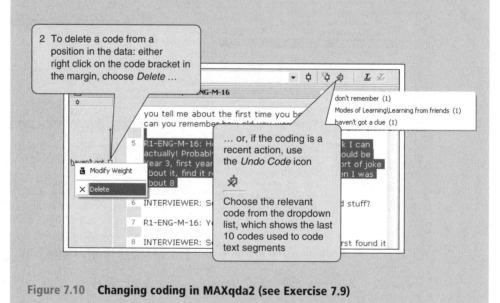

Figure 7.10   Changing coding in MAXqda2 (see Exercise 7.9)

(Continued)

The numbering of steps corresponds to Figure 7.10.

1   To increase or decrease the amount of text coded: select the new text segment (whether smaller or larger than original). Choose the code from the Code System or the recently used dropdown menu in the coding toolbar. Hit the *Code* icon in the usual way. The size of the coded text segment will be altered accordingly (illustrated in Figure 7.8).
2   To delete a code from a point in the data. *Either* select and right click on the code in the margin (at the centre point of the code bracket), choose *Delete,* then Delete again. The code will be unlinked from the text segment.

Or, if it is a recent action, use the *Undo Code* shortcut icon in the coding toolbar. A dropdown list appears, showing the last 10 codes applied. The last code assigned is at the top of the list. Choose the relevant code and it will uncode the last text segment coded with it.

Exercise 7.10   MAXqda2: reorganizing the coding schemes

Renaming, merging and deleting codes

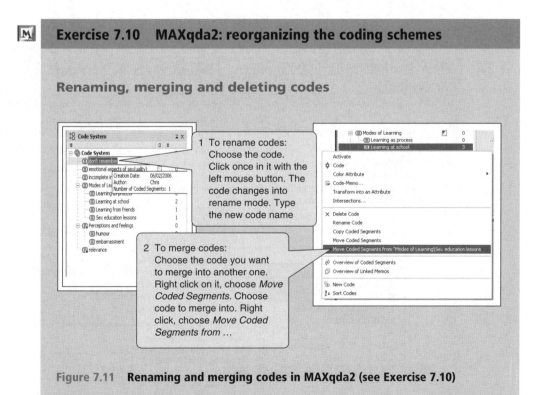

Figure 7.11   Renaming and merging codes in MAXqda2 (see Exercise 7.10)

(Continued)

(Continued)

The numbering of steps corresponds to Figures. 7.11 and 7.12.

1 To rename codes: in the Code System, choose the code to rename. Either click once with the left mouse button and wait until the code label goes into renaming mode; or right click over the code, choose *Rename Code,* and the code will go into renaming mode. Then rename the code.

2 To merge codes: choose and right click on the code in the Code System to merge into another. Select either *Copy Coded Segments* (leaving the original code in place, as well as merging the codings into the target code) or *Move Coded Segments* (moving the codings from the original code into the target code). Choose and right click on the target code. Choose either *Insert Coded Segments from {name of original code}* or *Move Coded Segments from {name of original code}.* If you move segments the codings will move from the original code to the target code, but the original code will still appear in the Code System.

3 To delete a code: select the code in the Code System. Right click over it, choose *Delete Code* and confirm *Delete*. The code and all its references to text segments across the whole dataset are deleted.

Grouping and moving codes

Codes can only be grouped into hierarchies inside MAXqda2. These can be created upfront as described above in Exercise 7.6 and Figure 7.7. Moving codes around the Code System is very easy, as illustrated by the following. Refer to Figure 7.12.

4 To move codes around the Code System: choose the code to move. Hold the left mouse button down and drag and drop the code towards its new position. You may also need to hold down a Shift key, simultaneously with the drag and drop, if moving a code into a hierarchical position; this varies according to the state of the coding schemes. The black line indicates where the code will be moved to when you drop it.

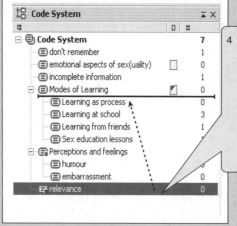

4 Choose the code to move. Hold the left mouse button down and drag and drop the code into its new position. You may also need to hold down a Shift key simultaneously with the drag and drop if moving a code into a hierarchical position. This varies according to the state of the coding schema

The black line indicates where the code will be moved to when you drop it

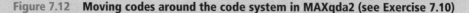

Figure 7.12 Moving codes around the code system in MAXqda2 (see Exercise 7.10)

(Continued)

Code hierarchies: retrieving coded data in MAXqda2 is based on the principle of activation; therefore activating the top or intermediate level of a hierarchy of codes can be useful ways of retrieving a group of similar codes (Chapter 8). In this way, code hierarchies are functional objects in MAXqda2. Whatever codes are activated, and whatever segments of data subsequently appear in the Retrieved Segments window, you always have the option of recoding them to e.g. a higher concept or category. You can manufacture groups of codes which cut across hierarchies by saving activations (see Chapter 12).

Exercises in NVivo7

Exercise 7.11   NVivo7: generating codes

The numbering of steps corresponds to Figures 7.13 and 7.14.

The terminology of NVivo7 refers to *nodes* as specific locations in the database which reference parts of documents. For our purposes, the node label becomes the code label. In NVivo7 nodes refer also to aspects of organization of the data, i.e. *case nodes*; while *relationship nodes* refer to various codings of connections you might see between project items. In terms of interpretively coding the data though, we generally make use of *free nodes* and *tree nodes*: you can just use free nodes, and you can just use tree nodes or use both. In Chapter 6, the VIA project (Rich et al., 2006) used them quite differently to many researchers. Free nodes are often used for emergent codes, and tree codes for a more organized arrangement of developing concepts and codes.

Generating codes independent of data: free nodes and tree nodes
Refer to Figure 7.13.

 1   To create *a priori* or up front codes: click on the *Nodes* option (bottom left of Navigation pane) to make this the active function.
2   Where to place nodes? Choose either the Free Nodes folder (if creating a list of unorganized, maybe emergent/grounded codes) or the Tree Nodes folder (if creating a hierarchical structure).
3   Create a node/code: right click in the clear white space in the List View and choose *New Free Node* or *New Tree Node* (depending which List View you are in).
4   Name the code and describe /define it in the dialogue box which appears. Click *OK*.
5   To create a subcode of an existing code: right click over the higher-level code in the Tree Nodes view and choose *New Tree Node*. Type the new code label and click *OK*. It will appear hanging below the higher-level code.

(Continued)

(Continued)

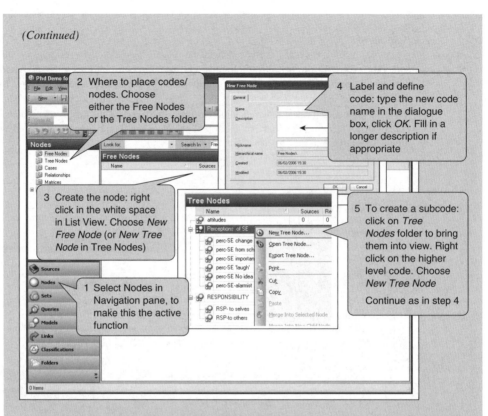

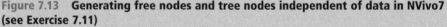

Figure 7.13 Generating free nodes and tree nodes independent of data in NVivo7 (see Exercise 7.11)

Generating codes from text level

Steps correspond to Figure 7.14

6 To create codes from text level: with the relevant document in the Detail pane (see Chapter 3) select the text to code. Right click over selected text, choose *Code / Code Selection at New Node* (compare Figure 7.15). Type the new code label in the dialogue box which appears. Click *OK. Note*: the default for new codes is a free node. If you want the new code to be a tree node, hit the *Select* button and navigate through the next window to create the code within the hierarchical structure.

7 Use the Coding bar to type in new nodes (see Figure 7.14): select text to be coded, type in name of new code in the Code at Bar – in the figure, 'Responsibilities'. Decide if you want the code in Free Nodes or Tree Nodes in the next bar along. Hit the green tick icon to create code and assign to text.

8 To create *in vivo* codes: choose the word or short phrase you want to use as a code label. Right click over the selected text and choose *Code / In Vivo*. This creates the code and

(Continued)

codes the word/phrase to it, (see below for coding more surrounding context). Alternatively, with text selected, click on the *In Vivo* shortcut icon on the coding toolbar.

Note: to view free nodes and tree nodes at the same time in the List View, choose *Search Folders/All Nodes* in the nodes Navigation View. Note that you cannot move codes around in this view, however.

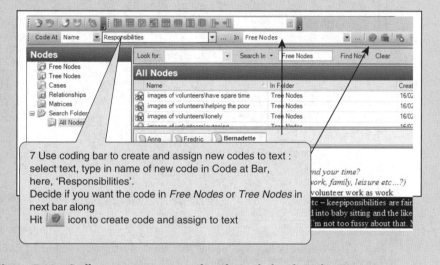

7 Use coding bar to create and assign new codes to text :
select text, type in name of new code in Code at Bar,
here, 'Responsibilities'.
Decide if you want the code in *Free Nodes* or *Tree Nodes* in next bar along
Hit icon to create code and assign to text

Figure 7.14   Coding text on screen using the code bar in NVivo7 (see Exercise 7.11)

Exercise 7.12   NVivo7: applying existing codes to text

The numbering of steps corresponds to Figure 7.15.
Note: You may find it easier to code in NVivo7 if you alter the way the different panes are displayed. From the View main menu, *Detail View / Right* allows you to see more data in the Document pane (see Chapter 3 for other aspects of customizing the interface).

1   Select the text to code and right click over it. Choose *Code/Code Selection at Existing Nodes.*
2   Select the code /node: in the Select Project Items window that appears, navigate through the coding schemes to find the relevant code. Put a tick in the check box next to the code (you can choose several codes in this way). Click *OK*.

(Continued)

(Continued)

Coding stripes (not illustrated)

3   See in margin area how codes have been applied: after coding, turn on the Coding Stripes View occasionally, so you can see confirmation that codings have been executed. Choose *Coding Stripes* from View main menu. Choose the basis upon which to view coding stripes. Try out some of the available options.

4   To make the All selection, ensure your cursor is in the Document detail pane, go to *View/ Coding Stripes/Show Nodes coding item* (i.e. the whole document) *or Show Nodes coding selection* (selected data). In dialogue box check the *All* box.

5   Updating coding stripes: note though that the margin area does not keep up to date with coding actions as you do them unless the code being applied was already showing in that document. To update, close it down by going to *View/ Coding Stripes/None* and reopen as above.

Note: after the installation of Service Pack 2 or later for NVivo7, you can view all codes in the margin view if that is what is required (as opposed to seven codes only in earlier versions of NVivo7).

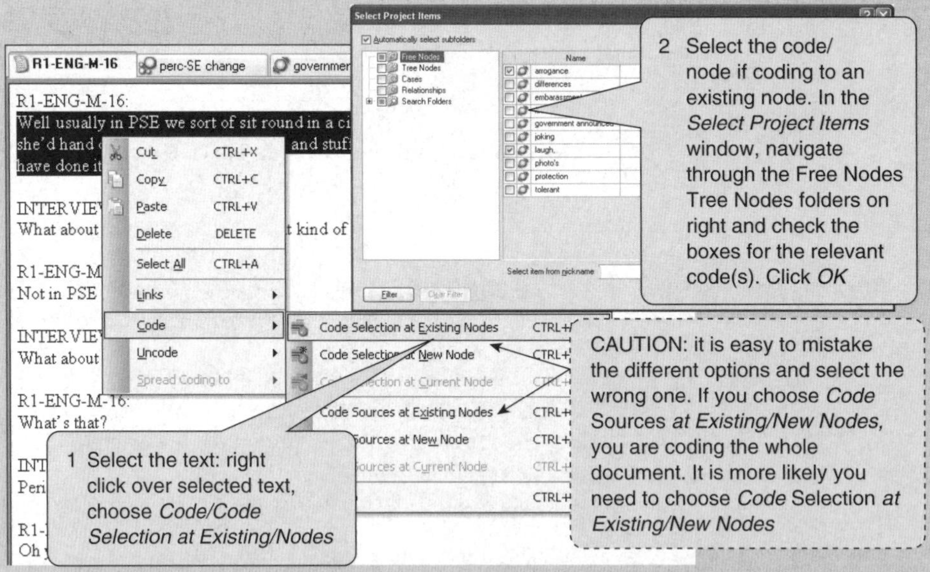

Figure 7.15   Coding to existing codes in NVivo7 (see Exercise 7.11)

(Continued)

If working with graphic objects embedded into NVivo7 documents, the processes of coding are very similar to those described here. You can only code whole objects, not parts of a graphic. Audiovisual files cannot be embedded.

NVivo7 provides many different ways of coding data. Experiment with different options to find those which best suit you. Try dragging and dropping selected text onto codes. Note this can be confusing as you cannot always see with certainty that the text has been coded correctly.

Exercise 7.13   NVivo7: defining and listing codes

This exercise is not illustrated.

1 To define a code: define codes in the Node Property dialogue box. If the code already exists, right click on the code in the List View and choose *Free Node Properties* (or *Tree Node Properties*). This opens the corresponding Node Property dialogue box. Type the definition and click *OK*.
2 To generate a list of codes: from the Tools main menu choose *Reports/ Node Summary*.

Exercise 7.14   NVivo7: changing your mind about how data are coded

Steps correspond to Figure 7.16

1 To increase the amount of text coded: you will need coding stripes or highlighting (from View main menu) on view in order to know exactly how much text is coded at any point (see Exercise 7.12 on coding stripes). Select the new larger text segment, code it by dragging the segment on to the code; or right click and choose Code to Existing Code etc. (see Exercise 7.12 steps 1 and 2).
2 To decrease the amount of text coded: the easiest way to perform this action in a document is to have coding stripes open. Select the coding stripe at the position required; select the text to be uncoded.
Choose the *Uncode* icon along the Coding bar.
3 To unlink a code from a whole coded passage in the data: right click on the relevant coding stripe in the margin and *Uncode* (see Figure 7.16).

Note: in practice you may find it easier to alter the way text is coded when opening a node in Detail View rather than a document (see Chapter 8).   *(Continued)*

(Continued)

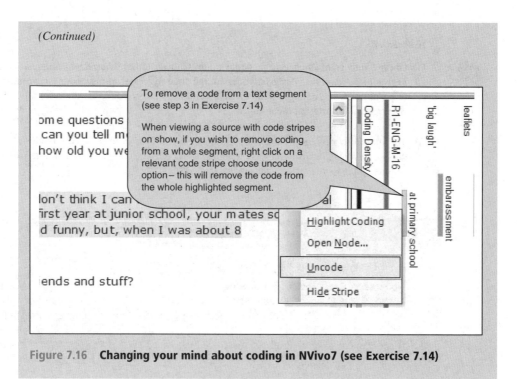

Figure 7.16   **Changing your mind about coding in NVivo7 (see Exercise 7.14)**

Exercise 7.15   NVivo7 reorganizing the coding scheme

The numbering of steps corresponds to Figures 7.17 and 7.18.

Renaming, merging and deleting codes
Refer to Figure 7.17.

1   To rename codes: click on *Nodes* option (see Figure 7.13). In the Free Nodes or Tree Nodes view, choose the code to rename. Either click once with the left mouse button and wait until the code label goes into renaming mode, then rename the code; or right click over the code, choose *Free* or *Tree Node Properties*, when the Node Property dialogue window will open, and rename the code.

2   To merge codes: choose and right click on the code you wish to merge in the Free Nodes or Tree Nodes view. Select either *Copy* or *Cut*.

(Continued)

Choose and right click on the target code. Choose either *Merge Into Selected Node* or *Merge Into New Child Node* (if you want the code to appear as a subcode). If you copy the original code, the codings will be merged into the target code, but the original code will still exist in its original location.

3   To delete a code: right click over the code in the Free Nodes or Tree Nodes view and choose *Delete*. Confirm you wish to delete the code. The code and all its references to text segments across the whole dataset are deleted.

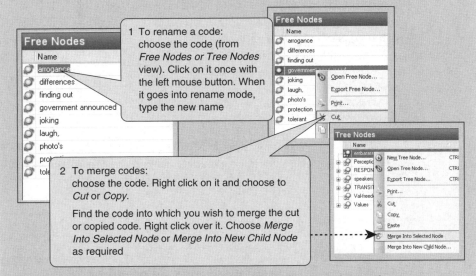

Figure 7.17   **Rename and merge codes in NVivo7 (see Exercise 7.15)**

Moving codes in NVivo7 (not illustrated)

4   To copy or move codes from Free Nodes to Tree Nodes (or vice versa): click on *Nodes* option to make this the active function (see Figure 7.13). Choose the relevant folder (Free Nodes or Tree Nodes). Select the code from the relevant node List View, right click over it and *Copy* or *Cut*. Select the folder you want to copy or move it to (either Free Nodes or Tree Nodes). If moving or copying to Free Nodes, right click in the white space below the list of codes, choose *Paste*. If moving or copying to Tree Nodes, choose the higher-level code you wish to hang the code from, right click, choose *Paste*.

(Continued)

(Continued)

5   To move codes between hierarchies in Tree Nodes view: choose the code to move, hold the left mouse button down and drag and drop the code onto the higher-level code you want it to hang underneath. If you want the code to be a top-level code itself, right click in the white space below the list of codes, choose *Paste*.

Note: when reorganizing your coding schemes in NVivo7 you cannot easily see Free Nodes *and* Tree Nodes simultaneously. If your coding schemes is large you may therefore find it useful to have a hard copy printout next to you whilst you move codes around. Alternatively, restructure your coding schemes initially on paper, then return to the software and reorganize accordingly.

Grouping codes: creating sets of codes as an alternative way of grouping in NVivo7

Steps correspond to Figure 7.18.
Sets are shortcuts to original project items.

6   To create sets: in the navigation pane, click on *Sets* option to make this the active function. Right click on Sets folder and choose *New Set*. In the New Set dialogue box, name the new set (and define if necessary).

7   Add codes to a set: return to the relevant nodes view, select the code(s) (select multiple codes within the Free Nodes or Tree Nodes view by holding the Ctrl key down whilst selecting codes with the left mouse button). Right click over selected code(s), choose *Add To Set*. Choose relevant set in the Select Set dialogue box, click *OK*.

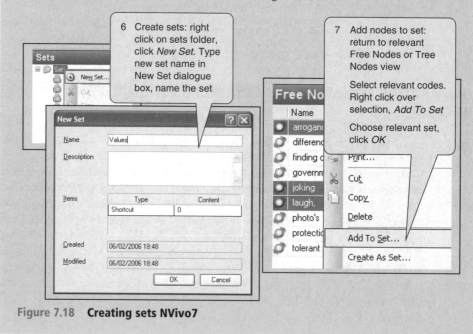

Figure 7.18   Creating sets NVivo7

(Continued)

8 Create a new set out of codes: select codes as described above. Then this time, right click over selected code(s). Choose *Create As Set*. Type the new set name (and definition?) in the New Set dialogue box, click *OK*.

Sets can contain any combination of nodes and sources. Experiment with creating sets for different reasons and think about how this may be useful for the different aspects of your project, and the way you like to work.

Sets: select several nodes, then right click to create output files on each or create a set or a new node. Visualize sets in a model (Chapter 10). Work on a focused aspect of the project by using sets (Chapter 12). Use sets as markers for future analytic groupings; they do not have to contain anything until it becomes relevant.

SUMMARY: GETTING STARTED WITH CODING IN SOFTWARE

ATLAS.ti5, MAXqda2 and NVivo7 provide many different ways to create, use and group codes. In comparing software in terms of coding functionality and processes it may be subtle differences, and particularly the ease of flicking between options, views and processes, which affect the flexibility of use. Coding devices are always just tools. They can be used in ways which are very analytical, just descriptive, or merely as connections to certain points in a file. You as the user need to make use of coding processes in a way that reinforces your contact with the data. Find ways to adjust coding processes to fit your methodological approach and as a way to move backwards and forwards in an iterative journey towards analysis which is transparent and robust.

COMPARATIVE COMMENTS ON CODING FUNCTIONALITY AND PROCESSES

Getting started with coding

Coding in ATLAS.ti5 and MAXqda2 is very interactive and flexible. It is easy to see immediately how codes are building up at the document level as you proceed, and drag and drop works well in both packages. In NVivo7 it is not so easy to see your coding procedures working. This may be uncomfortable as you cannot always see with certainty that the text has been coded as you wished. The ability to sort codes in multiple ways in ATLAS.ti5 – aided by the simplicity of the code structure – adds flexibility to the ways information about progress and frequency can be produced. MAXqda2 also provides an interactive table of codes in its Frequencies of Codes function, which can be sorted in various ways. NVivo7 lists the frequency of code application in the List Views, but only the Free Codes listing can be variably sorted.

Modifying coding

All three programs have a normal range of code adjustment devices. NVivo7 and MAXqda2 provide particularly easy ways to create one new code out of several selected – good for moving to more abstract concepts (without losing detailed codes). This obviates the need for more complicated OR type searches/queries. Unique to MAXqda2 is the ability to assign weight to codes or coded segments, which adds another dimension to coding and filtered retrieval according to weight.

Viewing codes in the margin as you code

Many researchers new to using software find the margin view in MAXqda2 and ATLAS.ti5 helpful as it is always on view and is useful, allowing you to see codes appearing simultaneously as you code. The NVivo7 margin view (coding stripes) has one exclusive feature, the coding density stripe, which provides a relative idea of how many codes have been applied at any point. However, in other respects it is cumbersome. Each time you view a different source you have to ask again for the coding stripes which is tedious. Printing of transcripts showing coding stripes in NVivo7 is possible, but the stripes are printed on a separate page, so two printouts have to be stuck together (even when printed in landscape). Of the three software packages, MAXqda2 has the easiest printing out options.

The coding schemes: grouping codes

NVivo7 free nodes and tree nodes are never visible with all functionality and structure at the same time: this is difficult. However, NVivo7 has a good ability to easily create sets. Unlike the other two programs, several different types of project items can be included in sets. They are good for overall management and reconstructions of ideas and processes and storing the things relevant to them without changing other structures like the coding scheme. ATLAS.ti5 similarly has ways to group codes without changing the coding scheme. The simple to use code families (shortcuts to codes) replicate processes for making families of documents, memos etc. MAXqda2 has the only hierarchical coding schemes in which the subcodes are automatically incorporated in the higher-level code at retrieval if this is required – though this can be a problem when you only want the top level. MAXqda2 as yet does not provide a code sets device, like ATLAS.ti5 and NVivo7, but this is expected in MAXqda3.

Chapter 8
Basic Retrieval of Coded Data

This chapter builds on the tasks discussed in Chapters 5–7 to introduce some basic retrieval options. Whatever your purpose in coding, you will inevitably want to retrieve data based on that work at various moments. 'Code and retrieve' functionality is the basic tenet underlying the packages we discuss in this book (see Chapter 1). Retrieval will be a useful part of the analytic process whatever your methodology or analytic approach. This chapter is practical in orientation, considering ways and reasons to retrieve data based on how they have been coded without using the search tools discussed in Chapter 12.

We illustrate tasks *within* the software and how to generate reports to get information *out* of the software by providing step-by-step exercises in ATLAS.ti5, MAXqda2 and NVivo7. Despite the placing of this chapter, retrieval is not necessarily a task you will conduct *only* *after* a particular coding phase has been completed. Just as you continually reflect on how you are coding as you proceed, you will see interesting patterns, relationships, contradictions etc. whilst retrieving coded data. As always, we encourage you to capture these thoughts as they enter your mind by noting them down (see Chapters 4 and 9).

Be critical in how you think about and use tools. Consider how they may support your analytic approach and style of working. Be flexible in integrating them into other aspects of work. Above all, experiment. Retrieving coded data is about reviewing your progress so far. It is about cutting across your dataset in different ways, to gather together similar data, to think about them again, to work on more conceptual and abstract levels. You may subsequently continue coding – perhaps as you identify gaps or inconsistencies. Always be alert to what is not showing up in the data. Code and retrieve inevitably reinforces what is in the data. Write about what you are not seeing, what people are not talking about, that might have been expected. Write memos about what you do see. Coding is a way of managing your ideas about your data, and retrieval allows you to consider how this process is helping your developing interpretations.

PURPOSES AND VALUES OF BASIC RETRIEVAL

There are benefits to sophisticated searching tools which provide retrieval in different ways. However, these should not distract from the usefulness of more simple forms of retrieval. Many researchers do not make use of complex search tools – perhaps because their project does not require this level of interrogation, because they feel intimidated by the search tool's capabilities or user interface, or simply because they 'run out of time'. Chapter 12 on interrogating the dataset addresses some of these issues.

We illustrate ways in which using basic retrieval can contribute to the process of 'moving on', perhaps from description to a more abstract level of analysis. As illustrated in Chapter 7, it is easy to change your mind about how data have been coded. You may be doing this as you look through one document. Retrieving coded data across (parts of) the dataset, however, can further support the cyclical and iterative processes of conducting analysis when using software.

Where did I get to last time?

Perhaps the most practical reason for basic retrieval is to check what and how much has been coded so far. This may seem very basic, but it is a useful exercise upon starting a software session when you are in 'serious coding mode'. Remember the ways in which software can act as a project management device (see Chapters 9 and 11). Revisiting key components of your coding scheme through basic retrieval will aid your continuity. Similarly, it can also be very useful to reread the last entry in your project process journal at the beginning of each software session (see Chapter 9). These tasks are invaluable in getting your mind back into the project.

Reflexivity and rigour

As discussed in Chapters 5 and 6, coding processes are not straightforward, uncomplicated or easy from a theoretical or analytical point of view. Coding is a cumulative rather than a one-stage process, and the meaning and application of codes will change over time, as will the development of the coding scheme (see Chapter 6). Using software will not automatically resolve any of these issues. Neither will software ensure reflexivity or rigour in itself. Some tools, however, when used systematically, can help illustrate the processes you have gone through. However, you remain accountable. Reviewing all the data so far coded at a code, for example, can help you decide whether the code label adequately captures the concept, theme or category. Does the code label need refining? Should all data currently coded there remain there? Are there subtle or key differences in the way respondents talk about the same issue? Does the code need deconstructing into more precise concepts, or perhaps combining into broader ones? We introduced these issues in Chapter 7. Now we encourage you to think more deeply about them.

GENERIC TASKS: RETRIEVING CODED DATA

CAQDAS packages provide many ways to retrieve data based on earlier tasks. We now present generic retrieval tasks supported by ATLAS.ti5, MAXqda2 and NVivo7, focusing on what can be achieved *within* the software and how to get information *out* of the software.

TASK 8.1   RETRIEVE ALL DATA CODED SO FAR

Software packages vary in the ways they provide retrieval. One aspect to consider, in comparing packages, is how 'close' you remain to the original source data when in retrieval mode.

- *Within the software.* You can retrieve coded data based on any individual code, or based on different groups of codes. Whatever stage you are at, retrieval will help you to think about one issue exclusively, in isolation from other aspects. You will also be able to see these coded segments in their original source context and to continue coding where necessary.
- *Generating output reports.* As well as reviewing coding within the software it is always possible to pull this information out of the software by printing or saving to view in other applications, such as MS Word.

TASK 8.2   VIEW ALL CODES APPEARING IN ONE DOCUMENT

It can be useful to view how one document has been coded in its entirety. This can usually be achieved in a number of ways. (For retrieval based on groups of documents see Chapter 12.)

(Continued)

(Continued)

Inside software

- *The margin view.* You can usually see within the software how a document has been coded in its entirety. All three packages discussed here also allow you to filter the margin view to different groups of codes.
- *Code listings per document.* Generate a simple list of codes appearing in a document, to gain an overview, without necessarily viewing the data.

Generating output

- *Print a document with margin view.* This can be useful for many different reasons. Software packages vary, however, in terms of the presentation and 'readability' of such output.
- *Report on all codes for one document.* Output how one document has been coded according to 'all codes' or selections of them.

TASK 8.3   RECODE DATA

In Chapter 7 we suggested that you are likely to change your mind about how data are coded as you proceed. Similarly, as you retrieve coded data you may see them in a new light and identify additional aspects of significance. As well as altering the amount of data linked to a particular code and reorganizing your coding scheme, you will probably want to recode. If taking an inductive approach, this may involve thinking about how more detailed codes are related, whereas a more deductive approach may necessitate the deconstruction of broader concepts into more precise ones (see Chapter 5).

- *Recode while in retrieval mode.* Software provides flexible means by which to recode data, whether into related categories or subcategories, or into codes which are completely unrelated.
- *Recode while considering how a document has been coded in its entirety.* You will also find it useful at times to view how one document has been coded in its entirety, either within the software or by printing a document with its margin view showing codes.

TASK 8.4   OVERVIEW CURRENT CODING STATUS

Qualitative software provides up-to-date frequency information concerning the status of your coding, showing, for example, how many times across your whole dataset a code has been applied to discrete segments of data.

- *View coded references building up as you code.* Seeing code frequencies increase whilst you code serves to reassure you at the same time as provide you with a useful and immediate guide as to which themes, categories and concepts are occurring more than others across the dataset. Some lists can be organized by frequency.

(Continued)

- *Generate output.* Various types of output report can be generated which reflect frequency information relating to the application of coding. In some cases this type of tabular summary information is also fully integrated with your project (see MAXqda2 software-specific exercises later).

It is useful to save copies of reports as snapshots of progress, perhaps at significant analytic stages. When thinking about whether and how to recode, for example, consider printing out coded data and code frequency reports as well as viewing data within the software.

Quantitative information about qualitative data, however, should always be viewed in context. Qualitative samples are often not random or representative, and this needs to be accounted for when manipulating frequency information in a statistics package. Treated appropriately, however, summaries can add another dimension to qualitative work. When writing up a final report, consider whether some forms of frequency information will be useful to present. If you have a large dataset and are conducting a mixed-methods project then outputted frequency information can be further manipulated in a statistical package, if appropriate.

Teams often find it useful to share basic output at various stages, especially when not all team members are using the software. A group session to 'brainstorm' coded output can be a very rewarding and productive experience. The pooling and exchange of ideas in such a way can help inexperienced team members gain insights from the more experienced researchers, while the different perspectives each brings to the discussion help the team arrive at optimum agreements. Such sessions, scheduled early on, around coded output are especially useful.

SOFTWARE-SPECIFIC VARIATIONS: DATA RETRIEVAL

Exercises in ATLAS.ti5

Retrieving data in ATLAS.ti5 is very easy, achieved by navigating around the dataset, viewing coded quotations within their original source context. This keeps you very *close* to the data. It is only when generating *output* that data is lifted out of its source context. The independence of the quotation means that data need not only be retrieved on the basis of how it has been coded. Quotations linked to one another via *hyperlinks* or quotations linked to memos for example, can also be easily retrieved (see Chapters 4 and 9).

Coding of multimedia data is treated in the same way as described here in relation to text. Navigating around quotations linked to an individual or group of codes (see below) will take you to a highlighted part of a graphic or play back the corresponding quotation in audio/video. ATLAS.ti5 is not video editing software, however, so any output generated which relates to multi-media data will be referenced by listing information (e.g. the co-ordinates of a graphic quotation, or the time counts for audio/video quotation).

Exercise 8.1   ATLAS.ti5: retrieve all data coded so far

The numbering of steps corresponds to Figure 8.1.

1   Open the Code Manager pane (not illustrated).

To retrieve data coded at one code:

2   *Either* choose a code. Use the left and right navigation icons at the top of the Code Manager to navigate between quotations ◀ ▶ (not illustrated).

3   *Or* choose the code and double click on
it. This opens a window listing the quotations for that code. Choose the quotation you are interested in. Flick between quotations using the up and down arrows on your keyboard.

To retrieve data coded at a group of codes:

4   🖼 Open the Code Family Manager window using the shortcut icon in the Code Manager.

5   Double click on the relevant code family. The codes available in the Code Manager, drop-down combo box and margin view are now filtered to members of that code family only. Navigate around coded quotations as described above.

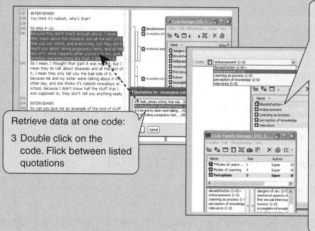

Retrieve data at one code:

3 Double click on the code. Flick between listed quotations

Retrieve data coded at group of codes:

5 Double click on family in *Code Family Manager*. Code list and dropdown Codes Combo box is filtered to the family members. Navigate around quotations

Or, in Code Manager, choose a number of codes by holding down the Ctrl key when selecting codes. Then from the Output menu you can output *Quotations for Selected Code(s)*

Figure 8.1   Retrieving coded data in ATLAS.ti5 (see Exercise 8.1)

Generate output based on coded data (not illustrated)

Select the relevant code(s). Holding the Ctrl key down will allow you to select more than one code. From the Output menu in the Code Manager, choose *Quotations for Selected Code(s)*. Choose whether to send the output to the editor (to view immediately), straight to the printer, or to save as a file. You can choose to include attached comments, memos or hyperlinks (see Chapters 4 and 9) in the output. In the report, any other codes which apply to *exactly* the same quotations are also listed, in brackets above the quotations.

(Continued)

Note: generating output from the Code Manager or the Codes main menu will sort the output by code (i.e. a horizontal coded retrieval across data files). When you do so from the Codes Family Manager or the Query Tool (see Chapter 12), the output is sorted by document (i.e. a vertical retrieval of all codes in one document, then the next document, and so on).

Exercise 8.2 ATLAS.ti5: view all codes appearing in one document

The numbering of steps corresponds to Figure 8.2.

1 The *margin view*: the default is for the margin to always be visible (although you can remove it from view through the View main menu). Scrolling down through a document provides a clear overview of the current coding status of the document. The colour of codes appearing in the margin relates to the size of quotations in relation to each other at that point (a code may therefore appear in different colours through a document). The margin is fully interactive: clicking on a code in the margin highlights the quotation coded at that point. Codes appearing in the margin can be filtered to families. (see Exercise 8.1)

2 Code listings per document: Filter the Code Manager list to those codes occurring in the current primary document through the Codes main menu using *Filter/Selected primary document*. Codes appearing in the Codes dropdown combo box and Code Manager and the margin view are filtered accordingly.

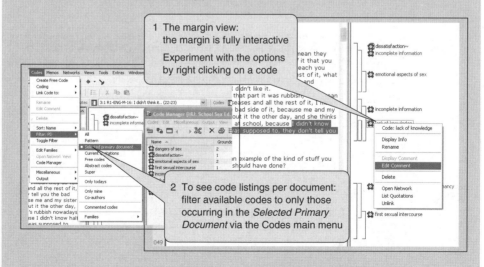

Figure 8.2 The margin view in ATLAS.ti5 (see Exercise 8.2)

(Continued)

(Continued)

3 Output all coded data for one document (not illustrated): either print the document with margin view through the Documents main menu using *Output/Print with Margin*; or, while filtered to codes for that document, from the Code Manager using *Output/All Codes with Quotations*.

The margin view is integrated with other aspects of the Hermeneutic Unit. Right clicking on a code in the margin provides various options, including unlinking the code from that quotation, listing all other quotations coded at that code across the dataset, opening the code's comment, or opening a network view on that code. Memos linked to quotations (Chapter 9) or hyperlinks between quotations (Chapter 4) will also appear in the margin, although objects appearing in the margin view can be restricted by type. Right click in the space of the margin to see options.

Exercise 8.3   ATLAS.ti5: recode data

In ATLAS.ti5 the procedures for recoding data are exactly the same as for coding for the first time. Whether in retrieval mode or looking through a document, you can always add new codes to existing quotations, or create new quotations and codes as relevant. See Exercise 8.1 step 3, and see Exercises 7.2 and 7.3.

Exercise 8.4   ATLAS.ti5: overview current coding status

The numbering of steps corresponds to Figure 8.3.

View coded references building up as you code:

1 The number of quotations referenced by a code is visible in the Code Manager listed in the Grounded column.
2 Clicking on the column header will list the codes in frequency order. Click the header again to switch between least frequent and most frequent at the top.

Generate output:

3 From Code Manager (or the Codes main menu) choose *Output/Codes Primary Documents Table*. Send either to an editor window to view immediately, or save as an Excel compatible .csv file to view in a spreadsheet application.

Note: Quotation frequencies listed in the Code Manager always relate to the whole dataset, whether they occur in text or multimedia documents, and whether filtered to particular subsets of data (see Chapter 12). Output files are external to ATLAS.ti5, and therefore the information they hold is not interactively linked to coded quotations.

(Continued)

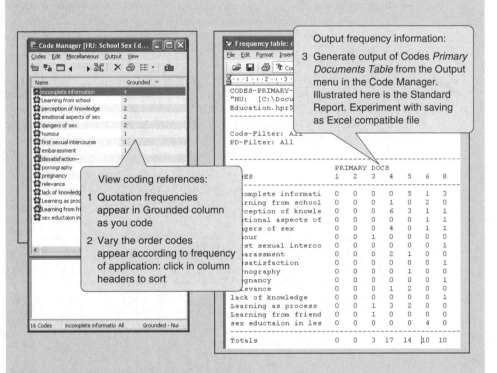

Figure 8.3 Overview current coding status in ATLAS.ti5 (see Exercise 8.4)

The View menu in the Code Manager provides various ways to change the format and content of information presented. Experiment with these different options to find a view which suits you best.

 Open a network on a (group of) codes to view them and their quotations visually (Chapter 10). Print documents with margin view as a way of checking coder consistency. Filter to groups of codes *and* documents to generate focused overview output (Chapter 12).

Exercises in MAXqda2

Retrieval of coded segments in MAXqda2 is based on the principle of *activation*, whereby you 'switch on' those codes and documents you are interested in. This simple process allows you to focus on parts of the dataset and coding scheme without navigating through dialogue boxes. Coded data are shown separately in the Retrieved Segments window, but they are interactively linked to source context in the main Text Browser. There are flexible ways to generate different forms of output, and sort the way results are displayed.

Exercise 8.5   MAXqda2: retrieve all data coded so far

The numbering of steps corresponds to Figure 8.4.

To retrieve data coded at one code

1 Right click on *Text Groups* in the Document System and click on *Activate All Texts*. This turns all the texts red (signifying they are activated). Or, if only interested in certain texts, activate one or a group. Remember to deactivate codes and texts before activating for a new purpose, to avoid 'hangovers' from previous exercises.

2 *Either* right click on a code (not a top-level hierarchical code: see below) and choose *Overview of Coded Segments*. This gives a table listing all segments coded at that code (across the whole dataset, unless you only activated certain text group(s)). Clicking on a row in the table provides interactive contact with source data in the Text Browser.

3 *Or* choose a top-level code, right click on it and *Activate*. This puts all the segments coded at that code and its subcodes in the Retrieved Segments window at the bottom right of the interface (across the whole dataset unless you only activated certain text group(s)).

To retrieve data coded at a group of codes

4 *Either* right click on a top-level code and click *Overview of Coded Segments*. This gives a table listing all segments coded at each code in that hierarchy and interactive contact with source data in the Text Browser.

5 *Or* activate a top-level code, which will automatically activate all the subcodes and put them into the Retrieved Segments window.

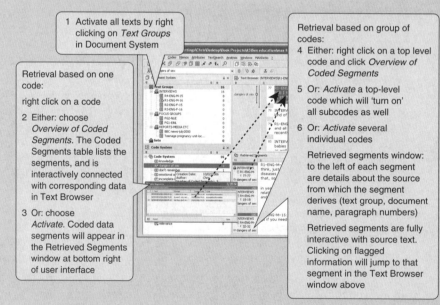

1 Activate all texts by right clicking on *Text Groups* in Document System

Retrieval based on one code:

right click on a code

2 Either: choose *Overview of Coded Segments*. The Coded Segments table lists the segments, and is interactively connected with corresponding data in Text Browser

3 Or: choose *Activate*. Coded data segments will appear in the Retrieved Segments window at bottom right of user interface

Retrieval based on group of codes:

4 Either: right click on a top level code and click *Overview of Coded Segments*

5 Or: *Activate* a top-level code which will 'turn on' all subcodes as well

6 Or: *Activate* several individual codes

Retrieved segments window: to the left of each segment are details about the source from which the segment derives (text group, document name, paragraph numbers)

Retrieved segments are fully interactive with source text. Clicking on flagged information will jump to that segment in the Text Browser window above

Figure 8.4   Retrieving coded data in MAXqda2 (see Exercise 8.5)

(Continued)

6   *Or* cherry pick codes from around the coding scheme and activate them. Coded segments
    will appear in the Retrieved Segments window. Full interactivity exists between retrieved
    segments and source data in the Text Browser window above.
7   *Or* use the Weight Filters to retrieve only segments which have been given a weight
    attribute between a specified range (not illustrated: see Analysis menu, and icons on the
    status bar). Note that weight filters affect all subsequent retrievals, including those using
    search tools, so you must check the states of activation regularly (see Chapter 12). If
    you do use the Weight Filter, cancel it by double clicking on the *Weight* icon on the
    status bar.

Generate output based on coded data (not illustrated)

8   Activate relevant documents and codes from the Codes main menu: choose either *Export
    Retrieved Segments* or *Print Retrieved Segments*. Save the file and open it in a word pro-
    cessing application.

Activate different text groups and sets to generate more focused retrieval. Activation is a very
simple yet effective and safe way to filter groups of codes and documents. Change the order
in which segments appear in the Retrieved Segments window by right clicking in the left-hand
grey margin and choosing *Ordered by Text Tree, Code Tree* or *Weight* (see Chapter 12).

Exercise 8.6   MAXqda2: view all codes appearing in one document

The numbering of steps corresponds to Figure 8.5.

The margin view

1   The MAXqda2 margin view is always on display and is resizable. Scrolling down through a text
    using the scroll arrows or the mouse wheel provides a clear overview of the current coding sta-
    tus of the text. Codes appearing in the margin will be green unless you have specified otherwise
    using code colour attributes, or by using the colour-coding bar (see Chapter 4). The margin is
    fully interactive; clicking on a code in the margin highlights the quotation coded at that point.
    Weight can be added to coded segments from the margin view by right clicking a code.

Index of coded segments

2   From the Codes main menu, choose *Index of Coded Segments*. This shows in tabular
    format all segments across the dataset coded so far.
3   Sort the Coded Segments table into text order by clicking on the Text column.
4   Interactive contact with source context: click on a row. This loads the corresponding text
    in the Text Browser, with that coded segment highlighted. There is a Comment column in
    this table: double click in a cell and type your comment before exporting.

(Continued)

(Continued)

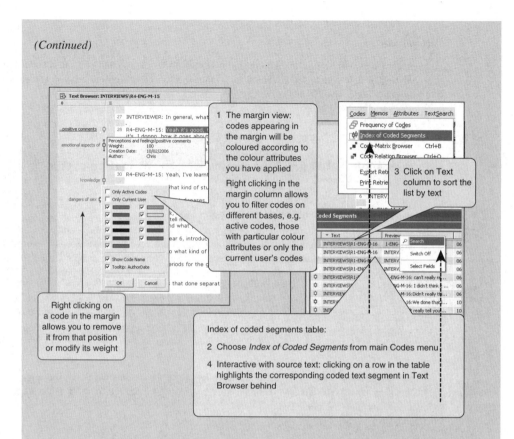

Figure 8.5   The Margin view and viewing all codes in one document in MAXqda2 (see Exercise 8.6)

5   Right click at the top of any header area of any column, select the fields you want included in the output file, click *OK* and choose *Export* in the Coded Segments window. Save the file and open in Excel or MS Word: it provides the summary information, but not the data.

Exercise 8.7   MAXqda2: recode data

Not illustrated here. See also Exercise 7.7 and Figure 7.8.

In MAXqda2 the procedures for recoding data are similar to those for coding for the first time. If in retrieval mode you have quick access to source context (once you have activated to get segments visible in retrieved segments window, click in cream margin information to left of

(Continued)

a segment, this will highlight segment in the Text Browser pane. Then you can recode segment to existing or new codes, see Exercise 7.7). Once the source is highlighted, you can recode by adding new codes to existing segments, or code new segments as relevant.

Exercise 8.8 MAXqda2: overview of current coding status

The numbering of steps corresponds to Figure 8.6.
View coded references building up as you code:

1 The Code System window always shows the number of segments coded at individual codes across the whole dataset. The hierarchical coding scheme can be sorted alphabetically (by right clicking on the top level and choosing *Sort Codes*) but not by frequency of coded segments. This table is fully interactive with coded segments.
2 From the Codes main menu choose *Frequency of Codes*.
3 The table shows all codes, indicating hierarchy where applicable. It can be sorted by any column header, and exported (as described in Exercise 8.6). Clicking on a row highlights the code in the Code System.

Import (groups of) codes into a map (Chapter 10). Print documents with margin view, as a way of checking coder consistency. Activate groups of codes and documents to generate focused overview output (Chapter 12).

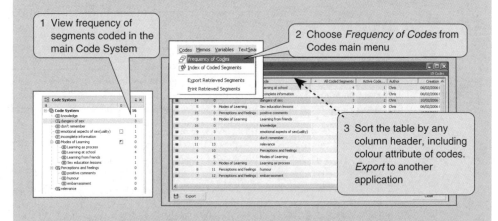

Figure 8.6 Overview current coding status in MAXqda2 (see Exercise 8.8)

Exercises in NVivo7

Retrieving coded data in NVivo7 works differently than described above in relation to ATLAS.ti5 and MAXqda2. While it is possible to return to the source context, in the first instance retrieval lifts coded passages *out* of context. You can recode either when looking at a source document, or when viewing coded data. Coded data can be easily exported and much frequency information is automatically provided within the software.

Exercise 8.9   NVivo7: retrieve all data coded so far

The numbering of steps corresponds to Figure 8.7.

To retrieve data coded at one code
1   Click on the *Nodes* option (bottom left of Navigation pane) to make this the active function.
2   Choose either the Free Nodes folder or the Tree Nodes folder. Find the relevant node and double click on it.
3   This lifts out all data coded so far at that node and brings them up in a *Detail* pane. Passages are listed by document. Above each coded passage the original source name is shown, together with the total number of passages from that document coded by this node and its *coverage* (the percentage of the whole source coded at the node).

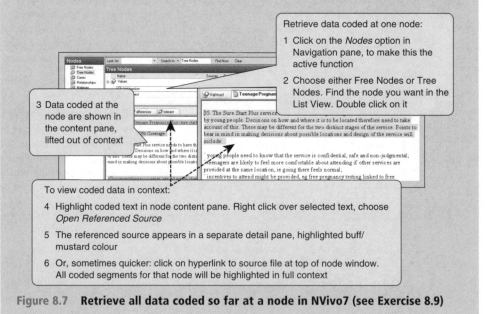

Figure 8.7   **Retrieve all data coded so far at a node in NVivo7 (see Exercise 8.9)**

(Continued)

To view coded data in context

4 Right click over a coded passage. Choose *Open Referenced Source.*

5 The original source document appears in a separate detail pane, with that passage high-lighted in a buff colour (colour varies slightly from computer to computer).

6 A quick way (sometimes) to see *all* the coded passages for that node in one document is to click on the hyperlink to the source file, underlined in blue, at the top of each document's coded segments. All coded passages for that node will be highlighted in a buff colour.

Further tasks

7 To retrieve data coded at a group of codes: several node content panes can be opened, but they appear separately. Iconized tabs appear above the detail view to move between.

| Val-trust | perc-SE change | differences | government announced |

8 Sets (see Chapter 7) allow nodes to be grouped, but again you must view the content of each node separately. It is only possible to view data coded at more than one node in the same place inside NVivo7 if you create a new node out of a collection of individual nodes. *Either* create a new node out of a node set by right clicking on a node set and choosing *Create as node.* Choose which folder to create the node in, click *OK* and name the new node. *Or* in node List View, select multiple nodes (from across the coding scheme if in *All Nodes* folder), right click, choose *Create As Node.* In order to see which data segments came from which individual constituent nodes, open coding stripes as described above.

Note: to remove additional information from the Content view, choose *Coding Source* in the View main menu, and choose to remove *names, references* or *coverage* as required. To view coding stripes in the margin, see Exercise 8.10 and Figure 8.8. To view all nodes together, choose the All Nodes folder. This lists all nodes at the same level, although it indicates their hierarchical positions. Experiment with undocking windows to see if this gives more flexibility in viewing the content of several windows.

Generate output based on coded data (not illustrated)

Choose the node you are interested in, right click on it and choose *Export Free/Tree Node.* Choose the additional information you would like in the report (e.g. name, description, paragraph numbers and links). Save the file. Open it in a word processing application. Export several nodes by highlighting those you are interested in while holding down the Ctrl key. Export multiple free and tree nodes by selecting them from *Search Folders/All Nodes.* They will be exported as separate files.

Exercise 8.10   NVivo7: view all codes appearing in one document

The numbering of steps corresponds to Figure 8.8.

1 To turn on coding stripes – to view all codes in margin view, go to *View/Coding Stripes/Show Nodes Coding Item* or *Nodes Coding Selection* (if you have text selected).

(Continued)

(Continued)

2 In the dialogue box, choose *Select All*.
3 All nodes showing: if you have asked for all nodes they will all appear listed at the top in the right-hand margin. As each coded segment appears, each node occupies its own *swim-lane* and appears in the same colour throughout the document.
4 The nodes appear in the margin. Each node occupies its own lane in the margin view. Right clicking on a node in the margin allows you to highlight the coded data, open that node or uncode from that position.
5 Alternatively, choose the basis upon which you want to view coding stripes, a limited selection of nodes, least/most coding item etc.
6 The grey coding density stripe gives an indication of the relative number of codes at each position, and when hovered over with the mouse it will tell you all codes at that point in the document.

Note: the Coding Stripes View must be turned on separately for each document or node opened.

When printing documents or nodes with the margin view, the data and the codes are printed on separate pages. Sticky tape will be needed!

Choose different bases upon which nodes appear in the margin. Choose from the nodes *most* coding item, nodes *least* coding item, nodes *recently* coding item or choose to only see *coding density*. View coding stripes when looking at coded data at a node. Experiment with the printing and exporting functions.

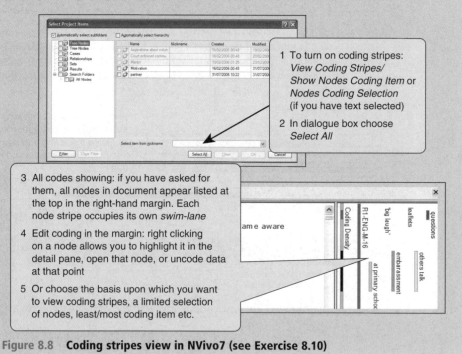

Figure 8.8   Coding stripes view in NVivo7 (see Exercise 8.10)

(Continued)

Viewing nodes coded at a document (not illustrated)

To view a list of all codes coding a source, an output report must be generated. From the Tools main menu, choose *Reports*. Several different types of report are available. Choose *Source Summary*. Specify the options you want to include in the report and click *OK*.

 ## Exercise 8.11   NVivo7: recode data

This is not illustrated here. See Exercise 7.12 and Figure 7.15.
In NVivo7 the procedures for recoding data are similar as for coding for the first time. However, you can also recode data when viewing the content of a node (i.e. when coded data are lifted out of the source context).

Exercise 8.12   NVivo7: overview current coding status

The numbering of steps corresponds to Figure 8.9.

View coded references building up as you code

1   As you code, the number of references build up in the Free Nodes and Tree Nodes views correspondingly. You can see the number of discrete passages (references) coded at a node across the whole dataset and the number of individual sources that code appears in across the whole dataset.

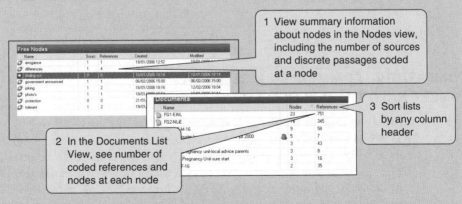

Figure 8.9   Overview of current coding status in NVivo7 (see Exercise 8.12)

(Continued)

(Continued)

2   In the Documents folders you can also see the number of nodes appearing in each document, and the number of discrete passages of text coded in each document.
3   Most lists can be sorted according to the column headers (not Tree Nodes).

Generate output (not illustrated)
From the Tools main menu, choose *Reports/Coding Summary*. You can specify different
options to include in the coding report. It initially presents the report on screen, but you can
print or save the file for viewing away from the computer software.
   Insert sets into a model (Chapter 10). Search for where groups of codes occur within certain sources to generate focused overview output (Chapter 12).

SUMMARY: BASIC WAYS TO RETRIEVE CODED DATA

Retrieval of coded data is central to all three software packages and central to the way most
researchers working with unwieldy amounts of qualitative data will expect to work.
Studying and annotating coded output, recoding, combining codes, are all aspects of
retrieval following on in turn from coding tasks. Focused retrieval is a major aspect of the
systematic management of data, enabling concentrated and iterative work on significant
data. You may eventually use more complex, filtered ways of interrogating the data using
query tools and it will be useful early on, in order to be aware of what they might further
achieve for your analysis, to have in mind a broader picture of what is possible (see
Chapter 12).

COMPARATIVE COMMENTS ON RETRIEVAL FUNCTIONALITY AND PROCESSES

Simple ways to begin interrogating the dataset
ATLAS.ti5 and MAXqda2 provide very simple ways to start focusing in on parts of the
dataset without having to use the search tools. The principle of activation in MAXqda2 is
intuitive and the ease with which you can see which groups of documents or codes are activated is useful and comforting. Unlike ATLAS.ti5 and NVivo7, in MAXqda2 the user must
specify from which texts to view coded data (i.e. it does not assume you are interested in
the whole dataset when retrieving data coded in basic ways). Filtering access to parts of

your work in ATLAS.ti5 according to (combinations of) codes and documents is also easy. In NVivo7 you have to build a more complex query to view passages coded from specific sources (see Chapter 12).

Closeness to data

Retrieving data in ATLAS.ti5 always locates coded quotations in context, keeping you very close to the source data at all times. If you need to lift coded quotations out of their source context you have to make an output report where there is no interactivity back to the source text. NVivo7 lifts coded data out of their source context in the first instance. It is possible from here to switch to a useful view of the respective source document for each coded passage and view all similarly coded data highlighted in context. Only one window opens at a time (undocking the windows to try to fix this does not always work satisfactorily, especially if other applications are open). MAXqda2 has the best of both worlds and puts coded segments in a separate window, each segment one click away from instant highlighting in source context: both windows are open at the same time, allowing coded segments to be viewed in isolation simultaneously with viewing coded segments in their source context.

The margin view

ATLAS.ti5 and MAXqda2 have very interactive and flexible margin views, both of which print out effectively. NVivo7 prints the data and the codes margin on separate pages which is less useful. The ability in MAXqda2 to assign colour attributes to codes is unique amongst the three packages, adding an additional way to filter the codes appearing in the margin. The ability in ATLAS.ti5 to view hyperlinks in the margin is unique, as is being able to choose between viewing only codes, memos or hyperlinks, or combinations of them. The NVivo7 margin view is less effective for viewing all codes, but the ability to filter the view by those 'least' or 'most' coding a document can be useful. The coding density stripe is unique to NVivo7, providing reminders of how data have been coded regardless of any filter set.

Viewing data coded at several codes

MAXqda2 provides the most flexibility in viewing data coded at several codes in one window within the software via the functional hierarchical system, or selective activation. The ability to alter the 'sort' order of how retrieved segments are presented within the software is also unique to MAXqda2. Code families in ATLAS.ti5 are flexible and allow easy navigation around quotations coded at a group of codes. Any selection of multiple codes and data can be outputted from the main codes list in ATLAS.ti5. It is not possible to view passages coded at multiple nodes in the same 'live' window within NVivo7 (unless a matrix query is run). Additionally, the lack of a way to see several clearly labelled codes and data output to the same file (enabled in the other programs) is a little frustrating. The ability in NVivo7 to easily make a new node or a set of nodes out of several selected codes via a couple of steps when right clicking is useful when thinking about generating broader brush or higher concept categories.

Interactivity between tables and data

MAXqda2 provides the most flexible interactivity in listing retrieved segments by (combinations) of texts and codes within the software. These tables provide full interactivity with coded segments; there is even a Comment column which can be edited in the table view in MAXqda2, prior to export. ATLAS.ti5 and NVivo7 provide tabular overview information but only as output, so there is no interactivity between the simple listings and the data (except by building matrix queries in NVivo7: see Chapter 12). An exclusive tool to MAXqda2 allows the instant conversion of any code to a numerical attribute which is applied to each document based on frequency of the code in each. This allows later interrogation and retrieval based e.g. on 'higher than' or 'lower than' frequencies.

Chapter 9
Managing Processes and Interpretations by Writing

Chapter 4 introduced annotation tools. Noting thoughts while exploring data, however, is only one way in which you can be writing as you progress. In addition to making annotations anchored to data you may need to write about a more general theme or aspect of your study in a centralized location. Part of making progress in the analytic process may be a movement away from text-level annotations to more abstract analytic memos. In addition to writing about documents, codes, themes, ideas etc. you will also need to keep an audit trail of the research process to track the development of the more practical aspects of the project and the analysis. This chapter builds on the issues discussed in previous chapters to consider strategies for effectively utilizing memo tools available in CAQDAS packages.

We first consider the importance of writing when conducting qualitative research. We then discuss memo functionality provided by the three featured software packages, illustrating ways in which memo systems can be efficiently and effectively managed. As with all other chapters you need to consider your own project needs and personal style in deciding which tools and strategies are most appropriate.

THE IMPORTANCE OF WRITING IN CONDUCTING QUALITATIVE DATA ANALYSIS

> Writing is thinking. It is natural to believe that you need to be clear in your mind what you are trying to express first before you can write it down. However, most of the time the opposite is true. You may think you have a clear idea, but it is only when you write it down that you can be certain that you do (or sadly, sometimes, that you do not). Having to communicate your ideas is an excellent test of how far you have a clear understanding and how coherent your ideas are. Writing is an ideal way of doing this. (Gibbs, 2005)

As mentioned in Chapter 4, the process of becoming aware of what is interesting and significant about the information and data you are collecting begins during the first moments of conceiving the research project and continues throughout. One of the key tasks we face as qualitative researchers is to ensure we note these thoughts, insights, questions and theories when they occur in order that they are useful when we return to them later. Doing so encourages a more consistent approach as it helps to ensure we follow up all potential avenues of enquiry, prompting us to revisit and rethink earlier ideas and build on them where appropriate. Whilst this is a necessary task in facilitating the analytic process and ensuring rigour in qualitative research, it is a messy one. As human beings our minds are able to continually have thoughts about different things, frequently simultaneously. It can often be very difficult to record them all, or to feel we can take the necessary 'time out' from the particular task we are currently performing to note them down. When working manually these issues are compounded because it is also difficult to subsequently search any written log we may have kept in order to retrieve those thoughts reliably.

Using a CAQDAS package can significantly help with the process of spontaneously noting observations and thoughts; managing them in a systematic and useful way; retrieving them in order to use at a later stage of the analysis; and outputting them in order to make use of them in the final written research product.

Thinking carefully about how to handle writing within your chosen software package is as important as organizing and managing the data and the coding scheme. As discussed in Chapter 1, it is when these three aspects of your work come together in a systematic and structured way that your use of software to manage your project as a whole can really start to be effective.

Writing as a continuous analytic process

In describing the process of conducting research it is common for the various aspects involved to be presented as discrete stages which happen sequentially and in isolation from one another. It is not unusual, for example, to hear students and researchers refer to their progress in a given research project in terms of whether they are engaged in 'data collection', 'analysis' or 'writing up'. Similarly, methodological texts often refer to such stages and discuss them separately. On one level, treating these aspects independently is both logical and necessary; it is common to distil a complex and multifaceted process into more easily manageable, digestible and understandable summaries. Indeed, this book by practical necessity is doing exactly that. However, viewing the nature and process of conducting qualitative research projects as sequential in this context is misleading, as one of its main characteristics (whatever the approach) is its iterative, reflexive and cyclical nature. This is usually the case during design and data collection as well as analysis (see Chapters 5 and 6 on coding and developing a coding scheme). Writing tools in software reflect and facilitate these processes.

Whilst some analytic tasks do occur sequentially, others are ongoing. For example, in Chapters 5 and 7 we discussed the sense in which various forms of coding may occur sequentially or in tandem and be revisited for various purposes. At some point, however, the task of coding comes to an end, since in itself it is not analysis. Interpretation through various forms of writing is, however, *the* one analytic task which starts at the beginning of the research process and continues throughout.

Writing about what is going on in the data, the patterns and relationships which you are identifying etc., will help in the process of analytic prioritization as you inevitably have to formalize those ideas through the act of writing.

FORMS AND PURPOSES OF WRITING

Field notes, the research diary and analytic memos are three well known elements of the writing process. The extent to which you use these and the function they play will depend on the nature of your research project.

Field notes

If you are conducting ethnographic or observational research, field notes are likely to be a primary source of data. Depending on the nature of the study and the technology available to you in the field, you may be able to write directly onto a computer. Even if you are not conducting an ethnographic study, keeping notes about thoughts and observations made whilst in 'the field' will be useful. If your field notes constitute data in themselves, think carefully about how you can best structure them for your chosen software (see later in this chapter, and Chapter 2 on data preparation and Chapter 11 on data organization).

Research journal(s)

A research diary or journal can perform several functions in your project. It is usually the main place where you record the various phases and day-to-day processes of your project, together with your thoughts about them. Qualitative researchers can add to transparency and rigour by systematically recording such information. This is invaluable if you need to justify your methodological approach and will act as a history or 'audit trail' of your project. In using a research journal within a CAQDAS package, consider the following:

- cross-referencing with literature
- including research proposal to assess progress
- tracking the various phases of the project (e.g. significant changes in direction, refinements in coding scheme etc.)
- recording the practical aspects of using the software (e.g. what was useful, how and why etc.)
- visualizing your progress in a map (see Chapter 11).

In team situations, research journals may be particularly useful for outlining responsibilities, tracking team discussions and recording action points. If you are coordinating a collaborative project it will be very helpful to have a record of decisions, responsibilities and progress.

Analytic or theoretical memos

You will also need to record the development of your interpretation. Writing analytic memos is a key aspect of grounded theory, seen as the place to theorize and comment about codes (concepts) and the coding process. For example, they will be used heavily during the phase of axial coding (see Chapter 5). Writing in relation to NVivo1.3, but equally relevant to other CAQDAS packages, Gibbs (2002) notes that software provides the ability to treat and work with memos as originally endorsed by Glaser (1978), i.e. as entirely separate from primary data. In so doing you can sort and search memos and use them to develop categories inductively (see also Chapter 5). Gibbs goes on to illustrate, however, that software provides an added flexibility in working with memos: the ability to link memos to other objects (codes, data segments) is a way of directly integrating your writing with the other elements of the project (see below). Similar processes are possible in most CAQDAS packages, including ATLAS.ti5 and MAXqda2.

Layder (1998) refers to *theoretical memos* in a similar manner. While he is discussing ways to analyse data with theory in mind, the following excerpt provides a useful illustration of the role of memos in qualitative analysis more generally and the practical processes involved in using them:

> From ... extended memos I developed discussions of many important concepts and ideas ... I did this by constructing a running discussion or commentary on the data contained in the interview transcripts and this involved two main elements. First, it required a continual reshuffling or rethinking of what the data meant (how, what and why questions) in order to produce new angles, ideas and explanations. Secondly, it involved a sustained teasing out (elaboration, extension, modification) of the concepts and ideas that were already playing a significant role in the analysis and interpretation of the data. (1998: 60–1)

You may have different memos relating to specific themes, concepts and ideas. In them you can flesh out your ideas and build upon them to develop a cohesive and coherent interpretation. Charmaz (2000) sees analytic memos as a pivotal intermediate step between coding and writing up the final report. This was also the experience in the Young People's Perceptions Project (see also Chapters 6 and 10). As illustrated by Figure 9.1, drawing models in tandem with developing ideas in memos assisted in furthering the interpretation. At the time, the model illustrated here as a network view in ATLAS.ti5, was drawn on paper, and is an early example of the processes involved in developing the eventual explanation. As discussed in Chapter 2, large amounts of data were collected from a variety of sources. The researcher was trying to untangle the complex factors inherent in the contrasting approaches to young people's sexual health within the Netherlands and England and Wales. In part, this involved writing about societal perceptions of young people as entities, and of sex and sexuality, as evidenced in different data sources. In doing so the tension between the state, religion and the individual became apparent, which in turn led to considering theories of structure and agency. Chapter 10 discusses the way this process developed in considering the roles of mapping in CAQDAS packages.

Whether your work is directed by or leading towards theory or not, writing memos will be an element of your process. As you progress, keep track of puzzling observations and lines of thought requiring further inquiry. You may choose to do so in a general research process journal (particularly if you want to keep hold of the sequence of their occurrence) or in annotations (if you want to quickly make notes and embed them at points in the text). Alternatively, you may decide to note these questions in an analytic memo about that general theme or topic. It usually makes sense to use methods consistently rather than switching between them sporadically, but noting observations and questions will act as reflective ponderings, to return to later once you have pursued a line of inquiry and built on an idea, or noticed something else of salience.

THE POTENTIAL VALUE OF SOFTWARE WRITING TOOLS

Software allows not only systematic management and retrieval of different forms of writing, but crucially the integration of writing with the rest of the project. First, the flexibility of software makes it very easy to record thoughts and ideas and link them to the data source which prompted them. Second, software allows the content of memos to be searched and retrieved with ease.

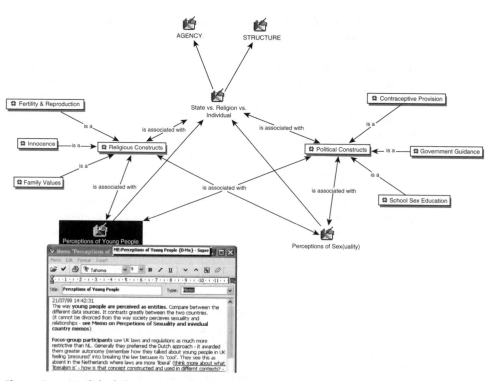

Figure 9.1 **Model of the process of writing memos to develop interpretation in the Young People's Perceptions (Silver, 2002) Project (illustrated as a network in ATLAS.ti5)**

Memos can also be 'linked' to codes in maps (see Chapter 11). Refer also to Chapter 6 concerning coding schemes and consider the role of writing in fleshing out how codes are related and grouped etc. This ability to integrate writing with the other aspects of the analysis in the CAQDAS package offers more analytic potential of writing itself than is conceivably possible when working manually.

Nevertheless, as with all the software tools we discuss throughout this book, this does not happen automatically simply because you happen to be working within a software package. All the packages have many different places in which to write and ways in which to manage that process. We argue that effective use of software writing tools, together with efficient management of the resultant material, can enhance the process of analysis and result in increased rigour, transparency and quality.

GENERIC TASKS FOR USING MEMOS

In previous chapters we have provided detailed step-by-step support for the exercises we have illustrated. Here, however, we differ in the way we present tasks. This is because the ways and reasons for creating and using memos, and the options provided by software, are more complex and varied than, for example, creating and using codes. In this section, therefore, we first list and discuss generic tasks which are possible in all three packages. In the software-specific sections which follow, we list the memo functionality provided by each package, in order to enable direct comparison. We focus on selected tools in providing screenshots to illustrate how they look within the software. The tools we show are those we think are particularly useful in each package. Given the variety of options available in each package, it is unlikely that you need to use all of them. Keep in mind the ways you like to write, and critically evaluate the tools we present in light of this and the needs of your project.

Managing your memo system

Because of the flexibility software provides in terms of writing, it is important to think carefully about how to manage and organize your writing. Some packages provide more sophisticated memo organization facilities than others. Whichever software package you are using, however, organizing your memo system is as important as organizing the data (Chapter 11) and the coding scheme (Chapter 6).

Creating memos

It can be tempting when using software to create a new memo every time you have a new idea, because you can create as many as you like and it is so easy to do so. This may be less problematic in some software packages than others but it is usually advisable to begin bringing together your writing about similar aspects early on. Study the devices provided which help you to retrieve memos, and think ahead about this issue. Your approach may necessitate the creation of many very specific memos, for example if you are interested in discourse or narrative. Consider carefully what a memo's function is before you create it. 'Less is often more' when it comes to the number of memos you have because proliferating writing in many different places can fragment your thinking. That said, you can both split broad thematic memos and pull many detailed notes together.

Free-standing centralized memo(s)

Some of your memos may be about a general aspect of your project and therefore usefully remain centralized and free from other aspects of your work. Logging the research process is a case in point. You may have one research log where you record all aspects of the research process, or you may prefer to keep different aspects of the process in separate logs (for example by creating one log to record the research process and another to act as a reflective diary).

Naming and dating memos

Naming your memos precisely and using consistent protocols for similar types of memo will help considerably in organizing your writing in a way which facilitates rather than hinders your analysis. If developing an accurate audit trail is important to you, always remember to date each entry you make in any memo (see Chapter 2 on naming protocols).

Grouping memos

Organizing your writing by grouping memos can be very helpful. Some software provides specific tools for grouping memos. Even where this is not the case, you can usually artificially group memos together by prefixing their titles. Groups may be based on research questions, emerging findings, theoretical ideas or perspectives, thesis chapters or report sections etc.

Structuring memos

However you use memos, there will inevitably be overlap in their content and the purpose of the writing within them. The way you handle this is something to consider carefully. You may decide to impose structure on your writing from the outset, or to do so when reviewing previous thoughts. Alternatively, you may decide that to structure your memos would disrupt the free flow of thoughts and ideas too much. The key thing is to think about these issues and decide on a general approach at the outset (whilst maintaining the possibility to change it).

If you are conducting a commissioned study then you may have predefined parameters for what is expected and therefore a mature reporting framework explicit from the outset. Undertaking a more explorative study, however, is inherently less formalized, and developing an idea of what the final written product will look like will therefore evolve more slowly. In both cases, however, stepping away from data and thinking more abstractly about how you will eventually pull your work together in a written format can be a welcome 'break' and also serve to refocus the mind and see the study in a different light. Stepping away from the data can often provide renewed direction and motivation.

There may be many different ways that you could usefully structure memos, and not necessarily one best way. Tools for structuring memos are generally very basic – headings, fonts, colour etc. – but can have great effect when used consistently.

INTEGRATING YOUR WRITING WITH THE REST OF YOUR PROJECT

The ability to integrate your writing with the rest of your work may be one of the main advantages of using software. At a practical level, linking objects to one another can simply serve to move around the different aspects of work in your software project more quickly. Importantly, when you are fleshing out an idea in a memo, linking relevant codes, documents and data will allow you to pull together those connected aspects later on. Writing analytic memos at relevant moments in tandem with the other analytic tasks stimulates progress. The links you make to other aspects of your work will only serve to improve the continuity of your thinking and cross-referencing. This is closely related to the ways you may work when mapping and coding.

Linking memos to documents

Linking memos to documents can be useful for writing contextual information concerning those documents. For example, in working with one-to-one interview data you may wish to compile descriptive information or build typologies concerning individual respondents at corresponding memos. This can be very useful in life history work when much contextual information is relevant. Another purpose of linking memos to documents may arise with focus-group data when you wish to link field notes about a particular discussion to the transcript.

Linking memos to codes

Linking memos to codes may help when thinking and writing at an abstract level about the relationships and connections within the data. Often this can serve the very practical function of reminding you about previous trains of thought, particularly when visualizing connections in a map or network (see Figure 9.1).

Coding your own writing

All three packages discussed here allow you to work with rich text format documents. This means you can create memos which can start as or become free-standing documents in their own right. This enables you to treat your own writing in the same way as primary and secondary qualitative data if you wish (i.e. to code, search etc.). The implications of doing so, however, differ between packages.

Search the content of a memo

It will be frustrating if you know you have written about an issue previously, but you can no longer find where. Searching the content to find a key word or phrase you know you have used in your own writing can be invaluable in such circumstances. This may also get you out of trouble if your memo system becomes unwieldy or overly fragmented.

 ## Outputting memos

Being able to get your written thoughts and ideas out of the software in flexible ways and in a format that you can easily convert, to form part of a final report, will probably be very important to you. This will especially be the case if you have taken the time to formulate your ideas clearly within a memo and want to use some of the content directly. Efficient

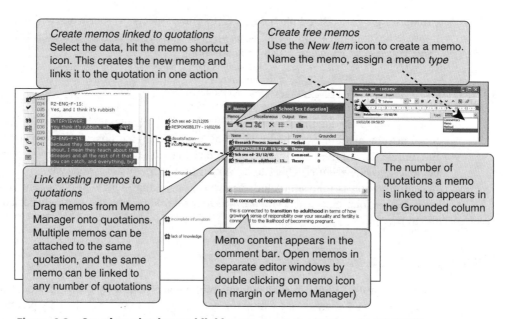

Figure 9.2 **Creating, viewing and linking memos to quotations in ATLAS.ti5**

output has much to do with efficient organization of memos in the software. Take a careful note early on to see the ways this is enabled in each package.

Outputting memos, just like outputting coded data, can be constructive at various moments throughout the analytic process. As previously suggested, there is often no substitute for printing information off and reflecting upon it away from the computer.

SOFTWARE-SPECIFIC MEMO FUNCTIONALITY

Memos in ATLAS.ti5

Memo capabilities in ATLAS.ti5 closely reflect the functionality of other aspects of the software (Figure 9.2). The central architectural characteristic of ATLAS.ti5 is that memos are independent objects, like quotations, codes and documents. This is quite different from the other packages considered here. One memo can therefore be linked to several different quotations, much like a code. This can be achieved for instance in a network (map), with the full text of each segment clearly on display, unlike any other package referred to in this book. Consequently, the relationship between memos in ATLAS.ti5 and other objects in the software is functional in quite distinctive ways. It is important, however, to be clear about the difference between memos and comments because this can be confusing.

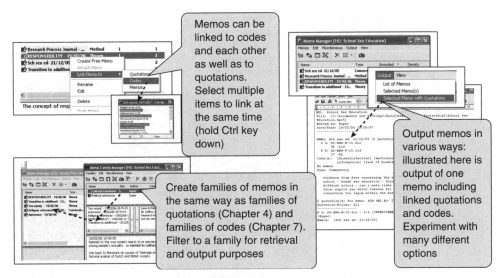

Figure 9.3   **Link, group, retrieve and output memos in ATLAS.ti5**

Memo functionality in ATLAS.ti5

See Figure 9.3.

- Any number of memos can be created.
- They can be entirely free standing in relation to any other aspect of your work.
- Create a memo at a selected quotation in a document.
- Link to combinations of documents, quotations or codes to organize and visualize (in networks) different theoretical /practical aspects of work.
- Assign *types* for sorting purposes.
- Group into *memo families*; a memo can belong to multiple families.
- View in a network with any other object.
- Use in a network to retrieve linked quotations.
- Convert into primary documents (in order to code etc.).
- Sort memos in the Memo Manager table by various column headings, including name, type, number of quotations linked, number of codes linked.
- Objects can be embedded into memos, e.g. Excel spreadsheets.
- All memos are listed in the Memo Manager.
- Any selection of memos can be exported to one file.
- Memos can be searched.
- Other ways to 'memo' include comments on *quotations* (see Chapter 4).

In relation to multimedia files in ATLAS.ti5, memos can be attached to quotations (parts of graphic files, clips of audiovisual files) in much the same way as to text. If you do link a memo to a video clip and other quotations, when opening the memo and all its linked quotes in a network, double clicking on the video clip reference will replay the clip. Hence in the network, the memo can act as a retrieval device.

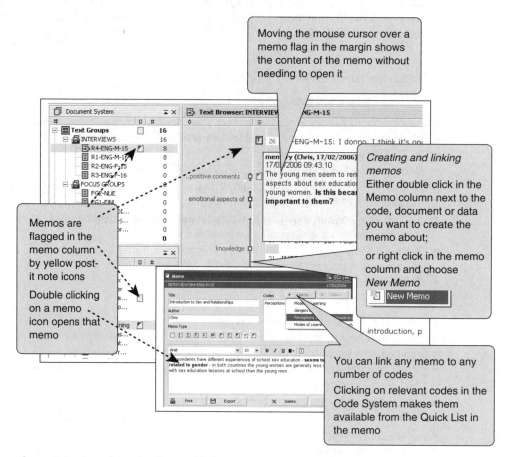

Figure 9.4   **Creating, viewing and linking memos in MAXqda2**

Memos in MAXqda2

The MAXqda2 memo functionality is simple, yet very powerful and flexible (Figure 9.4). In our opinion this is one of the key advantages to this software. Linking between memos and the other aspects of your work happens naturally, resulting in extremely flexible retrieval options. Earlier we stressed the importance of organizing memo systems, but this is less important in MAXqda2 as a direct result of this automatic and also purposeful linking. MAXqda2 provides the easiest way to output the content of all your memos. As with all aspects of working within MAXqda2, the interactivity between memos and the other aspects of the software are very good. The Document System, Code System and Text Browser panes all have a Memo column, where existing memos are shown by yellow post-it note icons. A more centralized location for writing could be a text itself – the content of which is codable like any other text (the content of memos cannot be coded, but codes can be linked to whole memos).

Memo functionality in MAXqda2
See Figure 9.5.

- Any number of memos can be created.
- Upon creation, memos are associated either with a position in individual texts, or codes, or text groups or sets of texts.
- Blank texts can also be created to act as free-standing memos.
- A *Link to* box in the Memo creation pane allows you to link e.g. text memos to any number of codes – allowing later retrieval at those topics.
- Text memos are automatically linked to the document, but importantly also to the text group or the set of documents in which the document sits.
- Memos can be given different icons to represent different types (appearing as different post-it note flags next to memos).
- They can be given a title.

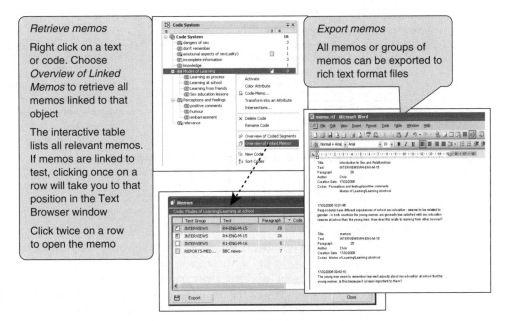

Figure 9.5   Retrieving and outputting memos MAXqda2

- The Memo System allows simultaneous searching, comparing and organizing of memos.
- Jump (single click) from a selected text memo in the list of memos to the corresponding text document at the position of the memo.
- Collect and view together, printed or exported to one file, all memos linked to one code, one document, one text group, or one set of files (unique to MAXqda2).
- Any selection of memos can be exported to a spreadsheet or word processing application.

Memos in NVivo7

There is no separate memo system in NVivo7 because memos are full-ranking documents (sources) in the same way as data files such as transcripts. This allows memos to be treated in exactly the same way as other forms of textual information (Figure 9.6). For example, you can annotate, code and search your own writing easily (see Chapter 4). NVivo7 does differentiate memos from other types of source, allowing them to be isolated, or excluded from other aspects of your project. There is no simple way, however, to output the content of selected memos together. With the above aspects in mind, we summarize the features of memos in NVivo7.

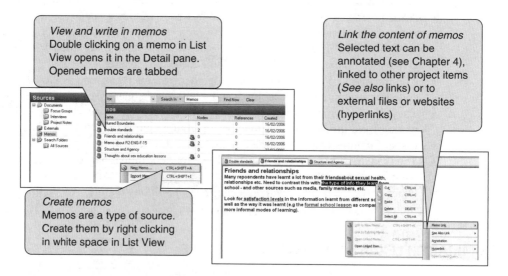

Figure 9.6   Creating, viewing and linking memos in NVivo7

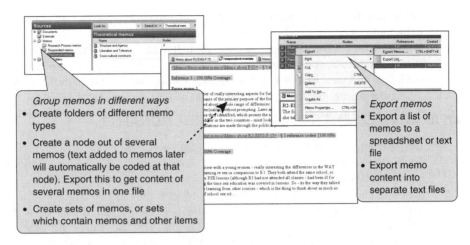

Group memos in different ways
- Create folders of different memo types
- Create a node out of several memos (text added to memos later will automatically be coded at that node). Export this to get content of several memos in one file
- Create sets of memos, or sets which contain memos and other items

Export memos
- Export a list of memos to a spreadsheet or text file
- Export memo content into separate text files

Figure 9.7   Group, retrieve and output memos in NVivo7

Memo functionality in NVivo7

See Figure 9.7.

- Memos (full-ranking documents) can be located in folder(s) of memos.
- Content can be coded, searched and retrieved on that basis.
- They can be included in models and linked to any other object via a relationship node (see Chapter 11).
- A memo can be linked to one other source and one other node (i.e. not several) via a memo link. Memos cannot be linked to each other.
- Content can be linked to (content of) other items via *See Also* links.
- Hyperlinks to external files can be embedded (see Chapter 4).
- Combinations of memos can be put together by a query, as long as they have been e.g. coded or structured in a way that can be built into a query (see Chapters 2 and 12).
- They can be combined into sets with other sources and nodes to gather related information from different places together (a feature unique to NVivo7).
- Lists of memos can be exported as spreadsheet or textual files.
- The content of memos can be printed or exported. Individual files are created for each memo on exportation.
- Other ways to 'memo' include using the *annotations* feature. Annotations operate as footnotes at end of each document (see Chapter 4).

SUMMARY: FLEXIBLE WRITING IN SOFTWARE

There are many differences in how memo systems work in ATLAS.ti5, MAXqda2 and NVivo7. That said, each software package will allow you to integrate your thoughts with the rest of your work and retrieve writing in various ways. If you are already using a software package you will be able to make effective use of memo tools to help you manage your interpretations about the data. If you are choosing between packages, the attractions of each system may rest as much on the way you work, and the way your mind works, as on the methodological needs of your project.

COMPARATIVE COMMENTS ON MEMO FUNCTIONALITY

Grouping, retrieving and exporting memos

Grouping memos to retrieve and export is central to their effectiveness. MAXqda2 has the most seamless and coherent approach, allowing uniform retrieval into one clearly labelled file of all memos based on or linked to any focal point within the project. Export functions work well in MAXqda2 and ATLAS.ti5, placing clearly labelled memos (with source data information where applicable) into the same file. ATLAS.ti5 uses the same tools to manage memos as it does for documents and codes, allowing full integration. NVivo7 places each requested memo in a separate file. Memos can be created as a node, which is unique to NVivo7 and allows exportation of multiple memos into one file, but this is an extra step. Sets in NVivo7 are also useful for grouping memos, especially with the ability to add sources and nodes to the same set.

Visualizing memos

The status of memos in ATLAS.ti5 is very evident at all times in one of the four combo boxes, and serves as a point of easy contact without moving away from the main text. The flexibility of ATLAS.ti5 is such that memos can be visualized in networks attached to codes, quotations and other memos. Memos themselves can be coat-hangers (in networks) using links to gather together different aspects of work. In MAXqda2 memos are also always evident against texts and codes via post-it note flags. NVivo7 treats memos as sources which can hide them away, even though they can be linked to other project items. Annotations are highlighted in documents and listed separately.

Chapter 10
Mapping Ideas and Linking Concepts

This chapter is short. It follows the chapter on memo tools since the relationship between writing and mapping can be strong. Different software applications can be used to create maps and diagrams which may help develop interpretations and add impact to an explanation or account. This chapter focuses on how integration with source data enhances mapping processes in CAQDAS packages. We suggest some starting points for creating graphic maps and illustrate how they help make and visualize connections. We also include guidance concerning routine tasks and ways to integrate mapping tools with other aspects of your work. The possibilities and creative uses of these graphic tools, however, far exceed the suggestions we can make here. There are many subjective variations in the ways to work with maps and diagrams in the software, so we list some particular functions in each software package. Maps are referred to in ATLAS.ti5 as *networks*, in MAXqda2 as *maps* and in NVivo7 as *models*.

THEORETICAL MODELS

Theoretical explanations are all about models, generally in terms of grand theory, and specifically in terms of particular authors' writings. As discussed in Chapter 6, many projects are informed from the outset by theoretical models (see Speller, 2000; Gulati, 2006). Theoretical mapping is also seen as a key aspect of analysis in many methodological approaches. Here we briefly introduce two of these.

Adaptive theory and the modelling process

Layder's (1998) description of 'adaptive theory' discusses the generation of theoretical models about the social reality under consideration. The logic of the analytic process is closely related to the early development of such theoretical models (which may be provisional or more concrete). Models act as 'templates' against which data are evaluated to see whether they fit into the 'conceptual scheme' of the model. Models therefore can contribute to the whole research process, imposing order upon it. However, they are also open to constant reformulation in light of empirical findings. (See Chapter 5 for discussion of Layder's adaptive theory and coding.)

Grounded theory and the mapping process

In Chapter 5, we discuss grounded theory and some of its principles at work in coding. In the Strauss and Corbin (1998) model of grounded theory, open coding leads to the next stage, axial coding. Drawing connections and defining relationships between codes is part of this process and can be facilitated by a diagrammatic mapping process. In the practical application of mapping techniques to grounded theory, Gibbs (2002) describes how, in going beyond what is illustrated in a hierarchical coding scheme, 'a richer and more complex set of linkages can be represented'. He creates a model in NVivo1.3 and uses alternative model styles offered in the package to illustrate explicit connections in the axial coding process to express different types of connections, e.g. intervening conditions, causal conditions for, strategies for etc.

MAPPING TOOLS: RELEVANT TRADITIONS

There is a broad literature on various mapping methodologies. In the context of the mapping tools provided by CAQDAS software, it is useful to draw attention to three approaches: mind mapping as conceived by Buzan (1995), concept mapping (Novak, 1993; Novak and Gowin, 1984) and cognitive mapping (Eden, 1988; Eden and Ackermann, 1998). Mind mapping generally focuses on a main idea and the aspects which radiate from it. Concept and cognitive mapping tend to produce more complex maps concerning multiple interconnections and more main focal points. The links between objects in these maps might be said to express more causal or directional connections. Cognitive mapping can be described as mental maps which model a theoretical approach, such as the mapping conventions created (Ackermann et al., 1992) on the model of personal construct theory (Eden, 1988).

MAPPING SOFTWARE PACKAGES

Mapping software packages have sometimes been created to emulate particular theoretical models. Decision Explorer, a mapping software tool widely used in academic and strategic management fields, was created with personal construct theory in mind, though its application and analytic functions are adaptable to other mapping traditions and modelling purposes. Other mapping tools like CMap have grown out of learning initiatives in higher education. Many others have been created to support strategic management decision making. We include a list of some of these in the resources section in Appendix D.

The general distinction between such mapping programs and the packages we focus on here is the integration between maps and the source data in CAQDAS packages. *Maps* and *mapping* are terms which are of course relevant to many methodologies, situations and sciences. Even within the software packages reviewed in Appendix C, maps may have different beginnings. In QDA Miner for instance (and other text-based manager packages), those using a constructionist, language-based approach to data would find the occurrence of words (and codes) mapped in a number of different representations. In QDA Miner, *dendrograms* and *cluster maps* chart proximity relationships between words and codes; interactive *heatmaps* map the position and concentrations of words within files and according to variables. Such tools are not, however, provided by most CAQDAS packages, including ATLAS.ti5, MAXqda2 and NVivo7.

MAPPING IN CAQDAS PACKAGES: GENERAL PURPOSES

Some users may not see graphic mapping tools as a necessary part of their analysis. It is true that mapping functions do not in themselves produce analysis. There are however many reasons for suggesting that because they help to work at a more abstract level they can facilitate the mental processes of analysis. In a general sense they encourage the visual depiction, and recall, of brainstorming sessions or the presentation of ideas to the reader or an audience. They can help to construct a visual structure of a complex account. In a more particular sense they help to integrate and connect abstract ideas with the data themselves. Used in tandem with other software tools, especially with writing tools and aspects of the coding scheme, they provide a visual way to cut across the dataset and rethink.

In the Young People's Perceptions Project, an existing theoretical model was drawn upon towards the latter stages of analysis to help rationalize and frame the empirical evidence. Analysis of the various forms of data (see Chapters 2 and 6) was indicating a complex interaction between individual and societal behaviour and perceptions. There are several different theoretical models to explain the relationship between 'structure' (e.g. political, social, religious and institutional systems) and 'agency' (the free will of individuals and their ability to act independently). Such models place more or less emphasis on the extent to which (societal, cultural etc.) structures determine individual behaviour. In simple terms, Giddens's (1984) 'theory of structuration' argues that neither structure nor agency should be given primacy in sociological explanations, viewing the relationship between them as a 'duality'. This model was used in the Young People's Perceptions Project as a theoretical lens through which to view the growing body of empirical data, and to help make sense of the interconnections seen within them. Data were not being 'tested' against Giddens's model, or being fitted to it, but the theoretical and empirical ideas behind it helped in highlighting aspects for further consideration. In particular, it helped in stepping back from the data to think and work at a more conceptual and theoretical level. As the analysis progressed, making graphic maps of the developing theory (continually adapted to reflect the growing interpretations) helped to further the analysis through the lens of the structuration model. CAQDAS software was not used at the time to create diagrams as the software being used (NUD*IST 4) did not incorporate this facility. Figure 9.1, however, illustrates in ATLAS.ti5 a map initially drawn on paper to help manage ideas about the role of religious and political structures in interpreting the differences between the Netherlands and England and Wales in school-based sex education provision.

In the software-specific sections to follow, we reproduce three additional aspects of modelling which facilitated the analytic process in the Young People's Perceptions Project, one in each of the featured packages. We illustrate that maps can be used for many purposes, and may not have any theoretical underpinning at all. The examples we use demonstrate three key roles of maps in the project: (1) retrieving and reviewing coded data to inform the rationalization of the coding scheme (illustrated in ATLAS.ti5); (2) deconstructing the learning processes of young people using layers in a map to compare modes of learning (illustrated in MAXqda2); and (3) planning the final written thesis structure to adequately reflect a complex argument within a linear format (illustrated in NVivo7). There were strong connections between analytic memoing and the creation of the models in this project, which is clearly illustrated in these maps.

Limits of CAQDAS mapping tools

As indicated above, the packages reviewed in Appendix C support rather different mapping functions. Table 10.1 describes particular functionality in the three software packages featured in this book. Keep the following in mind when using mapping tools in ATLAS.ti5, MAXqda2 and NVivo7:

- It is the user, not the software, that proactively creates links between objects such as codes, documents and memos.
- Maps can remind the user of connections which were made earlier or which occur having made use of other functions in the software – e.g. coding and subsequent links to coded data.

Possibilities with CAQDAS mapping tools

In the three software packages, you can perform the following tasks in the graphic diagram or map (network or model):

- View icons or objects representing codes, memos, documents.
- Make links between any of those objects.
- Define links in most situations (add a label to make the relationship explicit).
- Ask to see data or objects directly related or linked to the object (coded data, memo and document content) but not always in the map itself.
- Create new abstract objects, e.g. representing a process or a note or a new abstract idea. Link those to other objects if required.
- Change the format of the fonts, icons, backgrounds etc. to make a representation suitable for e.g. a presentation medium.
- Export a map to other applications or print it out.

Cautions

A map may be an oversimplification or at worst a fabrication of the full account. The map-maker has to be accountable for the connections being drawn. Mapping inside a CAQDAS package benefits from the integration with the source data. Continued contact with the evidence supporting the connections gives the map-maker a chance to develop or reflect on the visualization reliably.

Combine maps with memos and examples of data to improve transparency to counteract the glossing over of complex problems in the analysis (see Chapter 9).

GENERIC TASKS: MAPPING AND LINKING

The following list of tasks provides just suggestions. You do not have to make use of any of these options, although we do suggest using mapping tools early in your work with software in order to think about how they could be useful (see Chapter 3). In the software-specific exercise sections to follow, we focus on the distinctive aspects of respective mapping tools. Some of the best tools are only relevant to one or two packages and therefore do not appear in the following list of generic tasks:

1 Create a model of your project plan and timeline, by creating new abstract objects and linking them in a logical way. Experiment with layout and formatting options to familiarize yourself with the mapping tool.
2 If working from an *a priori* theoretical model, create objects (codes, memos and links) which represent abstract features of the theory.
3 Having examined and coded a document, create a map that models what you think are the prominent features of the particular respondent or case.
4 If you are working inductively, developing a theory or explanation as you progress, bring new codes into a map and begin to conjecture how things fit together and link

Table 10.1   *Mapping tasks and functionality*
(Networks in Atlas.ti5, Maps in MAXqda2, Models in NVivo7)

Tasks or function	Uses, ideas	Comparative comments
Start a map based on any existing object in the project or any new object, created in the map	A way of thinking in a different way: moving beyond a 'block', creating links around a focal point	All three offer slightly different ways of starting these tasks off. Atlas.ti5 has additional functions since quotations are independent 'objects' so can be brought into a network and remain interactively linked to source context. This is not possible in MAXqda2 or NVivo7
Connecting codes and labelling links	To create connections and reminders. Express relationships between different elements of thinking	All three packages enable this
Software remembers links?	Request that already linked codes are inserted into map to join a code already there	Only Atlas.ti5 automatically remembers the links made between two or more codes in subsequent maps where they appear. In other packages, maps are more like scribble pads. Both methods have advantages
Bring subcodes into the map, if you have a higher-level code already present	Useful for printing out graphical reminder of complex hierarchical substructures – stick on wall!	All three will import subcodes into a map. ATLAS.ti functionality is slightly different: subcodes based on families, or transitive links
	Up to user to express relationship between codes	Some relationships already in system in Atlas.ti5, others can be created. Relationships defining links have to be created in NVivo7 modeller or MAxqda2 maps
Connecting passages of text	A better way to track connections in the data (for narrative?)	Linking quotes/segments of data in network in ATLAS.ti5 enables effective hyperlinking (jumping) between multiple points in the text. Not enabled from maps in other software
Connecting code(s) to a memo	Another way to create (and remind you of) collections of codes, on different basis to main coding schema	Possible in all three. Again only Atlas.ti5 remembers such links in other/future networks
Creating models, based on existing or new 'objects'	Model your results or a process: may involve things other than existing codes, memos	Possible in all three
Code co-occurrence	Effective way of focusing on one concept and asking software what other codes overlap with it, in text	Atlas.ti5 and MAXqda fully enabled within network/map as well as by searching. Not possible in NVivo7
Layers	Allows user to assign objects in one map, to different layers, to enable display on selective basis, building up to the 'all' layer (another way to create abstract ideas)	Enabled in MAXqda. Groups device in NVivo7 creates layers. Not possible in Atlas.ti5

them – or create new abstract objects/concepts which help you to model the grounded codes into new higher concepts or axial codes.

5   Experiment with exporting maps to other software applications. Print off different maps to view and consider away from the computer.

Always give a map a meaningful name and date stamp it (see Chapter 2 for advice on consistent naming protocols). Define its use in the map description.

SOFTWARE-SPECIFIC MAPPING TOOLS

The following sections do not include full step-by-step support because the possibilities are so varied and their uses are often subjective and project specific. We describe the tools available in each software package, list possible ways to use them, and provide some starting point instructions for some tasks.

The Networking tool in ATLAS.ti5

It is important to note that the nature of *networks* in ATLAS.ti5 is rather different from that in the other two packages. In ATLAS.ti5 the links you make between two codes are functional and remembered. For example, if those two codes appear elsewhere in another network view, the same link will appear. This may work well. However, if it is likely that the relationship between the two codes changes with the next document you look at, this may indicate several things to you:

- The relationship is too varied to be a connection at all.
- The connection was made too early.
- Abstract or proxy codes (not yet linked to data) would be better used to express a *potential* link which is not yet generalizable or transferable (see also *super codes* in Chapter 12 for making propositions in ATLAS.ti5 to be tested later).

Main mapping functions and tasks in ATLAS.ti5
See Figures 9.1 and 10.1.

An empty network view can be created in ATLAS.ti5 from the Networks main menu into which any other project items can be dragged and dropped. Alternatively a network view can be opened *directly from* any selected objects, i.e. document(s), quotation, code(s) or memo(s), using *Open Network View*. Network views are displayed in the Network Editor, which has a menu bar showing Network, Nodes, Links, Layout, Display, Specials, Help. The Display menu is helpful for varying the way the network view appears.

General instructions
From any manager pane, or the PD margin area, you can right click on an object and open a network view which starts by inserting that object into the network view. In a network view, right clicking on any object, including links, offers a number of ways to view related

items, for example, to import other linked items, view related objects, change object properties and view quotations in source document context. Early tasks to practise include:

- *Create empty network views* and create new abstract objects – codes or memos – within the network views. You do not need data to start thinking abstractly in this way. Create an empty network view via *Networks New Network View.* In the network, choose *Nodes/New Node/Memo* or *Code.*
- *Open a network view on a code or any other object*: right click, *Open Network,* drag other codes in, make links between the codes (see earlier generic task list, item 4).
- ⌐ *Link items, e.g. codes*: in a network view, select a code, go to *Links/Link Nodes* (or use the shortcut icon shown). Click on the code to be linked *to,* and a list of relations appears. Either select one of the relations, or experiment and create your own via *Open Relation Editor.* Explore the nature and implication of the properties of relations in the online help. Semantic links have implications for retrieval in the Query Tool (see Chapter 12).
- *Stay integrated with data*: select one code in a network view, right click and *Import Neighbors,* i.e. the codes linked already or coded quotations (a more graphic method of *retrieval*). Vary the *Display/Quotation Verbosity* to get the whole quote included (see Figure 10.1).
- *See a graphic view* of a code family in the Code Family Manager: select family, *Open Network View.* Do the same for a memo family in Memo Manager.
- *Co-occurring codes* in the data: this allows you to focus on one code, newly opened in a network view (on its own). Right click and *Import Cooccurring.* This will show any overlapping codes (as they have been applied to data).
- *Create display for insertion/copying into a Word file*: in network view, *Network/Copy to Clipboard/Copy all nodes.* In Word, *Edit/Paste Special/Picture.* Experiment with other options to save graphic files.

Figure 10.1 shows how viewing codes in a network view in ATLAS.ti5 can help think more abstractly about relationships between codes, perhaps as part of reconceptualizing the coding scheme (see Chapter 6). You can work exclusively at the level of codes and concepts in a network or bring linked items into the view, for example coded quotations, co-occurring codes, primary documents and memos. In the Young People's Perceptions Project, codes have been linked using a combination of relationships such as 'is associated with', 'is a', 'is part of'. Note that objects in a network are interactively linked to their *neighbours*, enabling, for example, quotations to be viewed in their source context as well as within the network view itself.

Insert graphics into models. Save networks as snapshots to capture the layout if much work has gone into its format, or an analytic stage etc.

The mapping tool in MAXqda2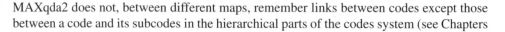

MAXqda2 does not, between different maps, remember links between codes except those between a code and its subcodes in the hierarchical parts of the codes system (see Chapters

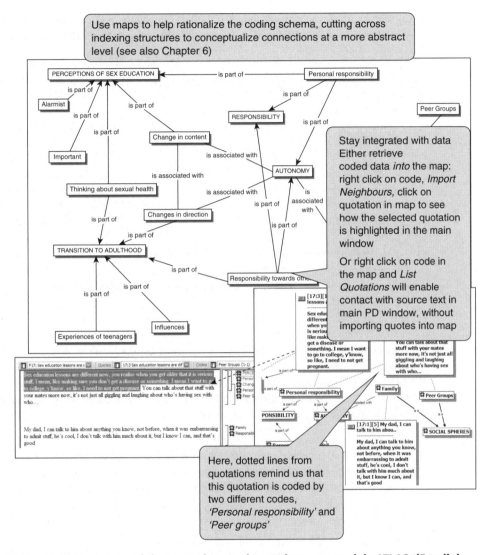

Figure 10.1   Young People's Perceptions Project: Using a network in ATLAS.ti5 to link codes and retrieve coded segments

6 and 7). Each map you save is listed to return to. MAXqda2 maps do remember linkages made from memos to codes, e.g. when creating or editing a memo (see Chapter 9). Maps are interactively linked with other project items: for example, you can see a listing of the data segments coded by a code appearing in a map. Data segments can be viewed in maps, and remain directly linked to the source text context from which they have been lifted. The implication of all this is that MAXqda2 maps remember links made outside the map, but

not within it. This enables the map to become a scribble pad, in which new visible links made in the map do not matter later; they only affect the development of the map in which they are created.

Main mapping functions in MAXqda2
See Figure 10.2.

General instructions
Open a map based on a code, a memo or a retrieved segment. There are three modes to work in (see icons along the top row of the map):

Selection mode allows the selection and creation of objects in the map. Alt + double click on a code, memo, data segment or document to bring it into the map. This also allows movement of individual objects around the map.

Link mode allows linking by holding the left mouse button down and dragging a line from one code to another.

Move mode allows you to move everything in the map together.

Features are as follows:

- *Stay integrated with data*: when the synchronized option (*Synchro Mode*) is checked, double clicking on any item takes you to that item in the main user interface.
- *Inserted icons to represent retrieved segments*: activate the codes and texts needed. In the Retrieved Segments window, select the margin area summary for the relevant segment, then Alt + double click etc. as above.
- *Create new objects*: e.g. in *selection mode*, click *New Free Object*.
- *Stay integrated with data*: maintain contact with supporting text and memos. Right click on code to see *Overview of Coded Segments* or *Overview of Linked Memos* associated with the code. Click once in the lists for instant contact with supporting data or memo.
- Create layers: in a map, click on the *Layers* icon and create *New*. Select one object or drag the cursor to select an area around several objects: right click over the selection and assign to the layer (see Figure 10.2).
- *Intersecting codes*: focus on one code, preferably on its own in a map. Select the code, right click, *Import intersecting Codes* to see how other codes overlap at segments in the data.
- *Create display for insertion/copying into Word file:* go to *Map/Save as File*. Insert the subsequent .jpeg file into a Word document.

Figure 10.2 illustrates layers in a MAXqda2 map using the Young People's Perceptions Project. Part of the analysis focused on different sources of information about sexual health and the learning processes experienced by the interview respondents (young people

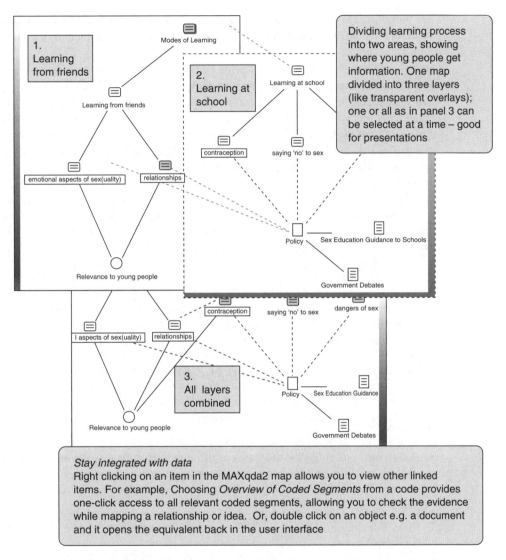

Figure 10.2   Young People's Perceptions Project: Using a map in MAXqda2 model to deconstruct young people's learning processes

living in the Netherlands and England and Wales). Here we illustrate the role of layers in deconstructing the learning processes of young people and comparing the modes of learning of those growing up in each country.

Insert thumbnail graphics into free objects within a map. Change the properties of free objects to enable the insertion of thumbnail photos/graphics and other inserts.

The modeller in NVivo7 ⊛

Models in NVivo7 are listed as an option in the Navigation view. Models can be treated in two principal ways: as static displays, or as dynamic models which retain connections to how things are changing in other views (e.g. changes of names of codes etc.). NVivo7 remembers links between project items which are created outside models (as relationship nodes), but not those created within models (using connectors). Links made between items in a model are visual connectors and have no implication beyond the model in which they were created. If project items have been linked via relationship nodes, however, these can be both visualized within a model, and used for retrieving coded data using the Query Tool (see Chapter 12). Shapes can be created easily in models to represent abstract ideas, or to help model processes or visualize connections. The model window provides a range of textual editing functions (such as colour, font, size etc.). Existing project items can also be added to models, together with associated project items (e.g. sources coded by a particular node or nodes directly linked to one another via relationship nodes etc.). Unlike ATLAS.ti5 and MAXqda2, coded passages cannot be visualized within an NVivo7 model, but project items such as nodes and sources can be opened from within a model into another window. Project items can be grouped in models and subsequently groups can be viewed in isolation or as layers over one another. The groups made in one model have no function within your project beyond the model in which they were created.

⊛ Main functions of modeller in NVivo7
See Figure 10.3.

General instructions
Once a model has been created, selecting an object and right clicking will reveal many optional extra tasks, e.g. to integrate with other project items. Most functionality in a model springs from this dropdown menu. Note that if the object is not selected, some options are greyed out.

- *Create model*: In Navigation View, select *Models*. Right click in List View to create a new model.
- *Add any NVivo item to a model*: a node, source, attribute, value or set.
- Connect any two objects by ctrl + select at both objects, right click to Create New Connector.
- ◇ *Choose style and shape of objects in the model*: drag shapes in to create new objects, ○ resize shapes by dragging in any dimension from one of the corner handles on the ▽ object, edit colours/fill/lines in Format menu and Editing button bar.
- Drag Note shape into the model and summarize the rationale of the model – or create a caption in the same way. Resize to fit text. Copy significant notes into relevant memos.
- *Create groups*: having added items to a model, to create new groups go to *Model/New Group/Name the Model*. Click on custom groups to right of model and, having checked on left-hand check box, double click on item to be added to group.

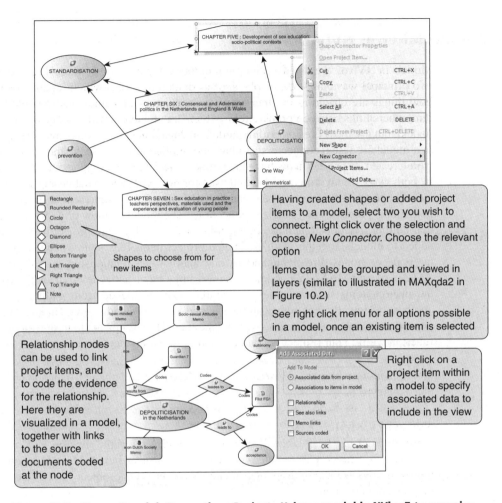

Figure 10.3 **Young People's Perceptions Project : Using a model in NVivo7 to organize the thesis structure**

- *Stay integrated with data*: select an object in the model and right click, then *Open Project Item*.
- *Make static or dynamic models*: click with right button in a model to preserve the model as a static snapshot of an aspect of the project at a point in time. Models are dynamic unless converted to static.
- *Show items connected* to e.g. a node: decide which items are required, e.g. documents so far coded to this node. Explore connections by right clicking on any item in model/Add associated data – make your choices and see links strike up in perhaps unexpected ways in the model.

- *Create display for insertion/copying into Word file*: choose the objects you want included, or go to Main menu, choose *Edit/Select All* then *Copy*.

Figure 10.3 illustrates in NVivo7 how the Young People's Perceptions Project used maps to help plan the final written thesis structure to adequately reflect a complex argument within a linear format. As in the examples above, memos were integrated in this model to help remind the researcher where relevant analytic notes were within the software project. In planning the thesis write-up, the order of arguments and chapters frequently changed, and modelling the structure in this way helped develop a logical presentation and keep in touch with cross-referencing with the literature and methodology chapters.

Experiment with static and dynamic versions of models to track processes or schedules of your project work. Undock the model window to have more space to work with.

SUMMARY: MAPPING FUNCTIONALITY

As discussed above, visualizing elements of your project in maps not only has close connections with the processes of memoing discussed in Chapter 9, but also can be used to bring together many elements of the project in a schematic way. Maps can therefore add to the sense of being in control or getting back in touch with the complex interrelatedness of different elements of analysis. If the creation of maps is based on an inaccurate premise however, the software will not tell you this on its own. Maps can have the effect of polishing a presentation or a piece of work but they can be flawed, they can oversimplify, and they can be used gratuitously and superfluously. Worse still they can be over-relied upon by their author, who might be allowing personal bias or an out-of-date idea to become entrenched in an early map. Once again, always try to be critical of the tools you are using and self-critical of the way you are using them. A map, if it is about something meaningful, must add something, and it must be founded on work that can be checked and backed up with solid evidence.

COMPARATIVE COMMENTS ON MAPPING FUNCTIONALITY

Integration with data, retrieval of data

All three packages offer good integration with all aspects of work. ATLAS.ti5 also offers the additional facility of retrieving coded segments in their entirety into a network, or using the network itself to create hyperlinks at text level (see Chapter 4) or to code data (see Chapter 7).

Layers, groups and 'remembered' links

MAXqda2 and NVivo7 provide layers or groups respectively within map views to collect similar items together and subsequently view limited aspects of a larger map in isolation. This can be very useful, for example, to incrementally view layers to demonstrate the development of an idea or a theory. Links that are created or changed between objects in ATLAS.ti5 are remembered across the project as a whole. The implications of proactively making links therefore in ATLAS.ti5 are more serious than in MAXqda2 or NVivo7.

The functionality of relationships at links

ATLAS.ti5 and NVivo7 allow the later retrieval of coded data based on certain relationships created between codes. ATLAS.ti5 allows you to create such relationships inside or outside a network, whereas relationships in NVivo7 can only be created in the corresponding List View, i.e. not within a model. Relationships in NVivo7 are another type of node, at which the evidence for the expressed statement can be coded data (coded by the relationship). Functional relationships (i.e. those enabling retrieval in the Query Tool) in ATLAS.ti5 are embodied in transitive (or hierarchical) links, such as 'is a', 'part of'; 'causes' etc. Data can be retrieved in the ATLAS.ti5 Query Tool based on transitivity. In MAXqda2, connections created by linking codes maps are not functional in this way.

Information gathering via maps

ATLAs.ti5 and MAXqda2 both have tools which allow the user to make easy investigations on one code at a time to find all its intersecting or co-occurring codes across the whole dataset. These are visualized in maps or networks and are based on other tools in the software, but they make sense of the ability to code multiply at any text segment, or overlapping segments. Though all three packages enable much information and associated items connected to an object to be retrieved into a map, NVivo7 and ATLAS.ti do this best in a graphic sense although connections to other interactive lists and tables elsewhere in the software is best in MAXqda2.

Chapter 11
Organizing Data to Known Characteristics

As discussed in Chapter 1, CAQDAS packages are powerful project management tools. One key element in this regard is the way in which data can be organized according to known characteristics. This enables you to narrow your focus onto (combinations of) subsets of data, thereby facilitating comparison. When conducting a large-scale project this aspect will be very important, but even when a project comprises only a small number of data files it will be useful to think about organizing them in a way which will facilitate the identification of patterns, relationships, contradictions etc. as well as enabling quick and easy access to parts of the dataset. When used in combination with other aspects of software capability such as conceptual coding, data organization can result in the dataset being interrogated according to complex combinations, helping to identify interesting relationships and facilitate the establishment of rigour (see Chapter 12).

This chapter considers the importance of data organization, looks at features which can be organized, and discusses different ways in which this can be achieved using CAQDAS packages. We then go on to provide step-by-step exercises in ATLAS.ti5, MAXqda2 and NVivo7.

THE IMPORTANCE OF ORGANIZING QUALITATIVE DATA

Whatever the purpose of your study, there will be inherent in its design an element of comparison. The larger the dataset, the more important it will be to organize the data efficiently, and the more reliance you will probably place on known characteristics when interrogating the dataset (see Chapter 12). If you are undertaking a small-scale study and have collected and transcribed all the primary data yourself, you will know and be able to remember more readily the characteristics which are important about the respondents. It remains important to organize the data accordingly even if your reliance on these features in terms of fragmenting and searching the data is less appropriate (due to the small number of respondents). Conversely, when conducting large-scale projects, for example service evaluations or public consultations, the amount of data collected will be greater and the types of respondents contributing more diverse. Indeed, you may be particularly interested in how certain types of people living in the area access and evaluate the service and therefore this information will be crucial to the analysis.

FEATURES IN DATA WHICH CAN BE ORGANIZED

When organizing qualitative data, most researchers think immediately about the social-demographic characteristics of respondents, such as gender, age, marital status etc. These are clearly very important to many projects, but from a software point of view any known characteristics among respondents or (repeated) features in the data can be organized. Identify 'factual' features about respondents and the data which you intend to compare, ask questions about or isolate. If your project comprises data collected from multiple sources it will be useful to organize the data according to their type or origin: interview, focus group, journal article, official guidance, email exchange, meeting minutes etc.

Secondary data and supplementary information (see Chapter 2) may also contain known characteristics which can be handled on this level. Examples might be: which journal an article was published in, and who the author is; which discussion group an email message was sent to, and how soon after the previous post; which government was in power when a policy was passed, and how long the topic was debated in parliament, and so on.

Your qualitative project may be part of a larger study, or have a more quantitative element. If, for example, you have quantitative data from a survey, you may wish to incorporate this information into the qualitative part of your work – particularly if interview or focus-group respondents have also filled in the questionnaires. Software enables integration of quantitative data for such purposes.

ORGANIZING QUALITATIVE DATA IN CAQDAS PACKAGES

CAQDAS packages organize known data characteristics differently, and use various terms to refer to them. ATLAS.ti5 refers to 'families', whereas MAXqda2 and NVivo7 refer to 'attributes'. Nevertheless, all three serve the same purpose: allowing you to bring the different elements of your project together in order to see new and interesting patterns and relationships.

Document 'families' and 'attributes'

There is no limit on the number of families or attributes you can create within a software project. The three packages we concentrate on here allow you to import spreadsheets which contain this information. This is particularly useful if you are integrating quantitative data which are already held in SPSS or MS Excel, although we do not illustrate this function. However, avoid creating or importing attributes unless you really intend to make use of them within the qualitative element of your project. It can be difficult to find the attributes you need if they are buried amongst large numbers of irrelevant characteristics. Avoiding unnecessary clutter will help maintain your focus. Always keep in mind how known characteristics will further your analysis. As illustrated further in Chapter 12, one way of interrogating your dataset may involve combining the organizational aspects (held in families or attributes) with the more conceptual aspects (held in codes). In deciding on which features to include as attributes, therefore, be thinking about the kinds of questions you want to ask, the ideas you want to test and the parts of your dataset you want to isolate. For example, you may want to look for how different kinds of respondents talk about an issue or theme differently. Or you may want to ask a question about a certain data type, just the interviews, or just the government reports. The general principle is that in order to ask a question about documents or respondents, you will need to have the (two or more) elements that comprise the question held at codes and/or attributes or their equivalent.

Differentiating between organizational features and 'conceptual' codes

We sometimes encounter confusion among researchers about when it is appropriate to use attributes as opposed to codes. It is useful to differentiate between their function by stating that organizing data using families or attributes allows you to capture 'known characteristics' or 'factual' information in the data. These aspects generally will not change: for example, whether respondents are male or female, where they live, which school they go to, what exam results they achieved, how satisfied they are with a service etc. That said, there may be situations when this information does change – particularly if you are conducting a longitudinal study, for example. Conceptual coding, conversely, is used to bring together segments of data which are similar in some way, as deemed by the researcher (see Chapter 5 on coding). As such, in relation to primary data, conceptual codes will generally be applied to parts of data files, where respondents are talking about a particular theme or where the researcher identifies data as representing a concept.

It can be particularly confusing when a known characteristic is the same as a concept you are interested in for more analytic purposes. To take a simple example, if conducting a study about perceptions of gender in newspaper articles about 'teenage pregnancy', you may need the organizational feature 'gender' to differentiate between whether the journalist is male or female, but you will also need conceptual codes to identify where the article discusses perceptions of gender differences generally, and men and women (or boys and girls) specifically. This will allow you to investigate, for example, both how the gender of journalists affects the way articles are written, and the way men and women are discussed within the articles, or in different publications etc.

Working incrementally

When you are using software, known characteristics can be assigned at any stage of the research process. They may not only be aspects about data or respondents which you are aware of at the sampling or data collection stages. As you progress through the analysis you will find out interesting things about some of your respondents or data sources. Where these findings can be deemed as 'factual' they can be added to the software project as families or attributes. For example, in the young people's project we identified clear differences in the ways young people evaluated the sex education lessons they attended at school. Although a relatively crude measurement, we could broadly group them into those who generally felt satisfied with sex education lessons, and those who were largely dissatisfied. This was useful in interrogating the data further according to these features: for example, whether those satisfied with school sex education behaved in different ways, or experienced relationships differently, or had more detailed knowledge about contraception etc.

Organizing whole data files

You may be working with data where each individual data file represents one respondent, instance or case. Examples of such data include one-to-one interview transcripts, journal articles, focus-group discussions (where you are interested in the group, not the individual opinion) etc. In this situation the organization of your data is straightforward because it is

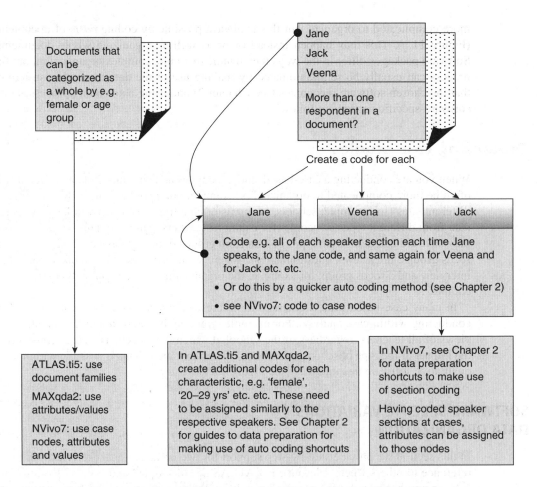

Figure 11.1   Subset organization of data, respondents, socio-demographic variables

usually possible to apply the relevant known characteristics to the whole data file – by creating and assigning families or attributes (Figure 11.1).

Organizing parts of data files

Attributes and families are usually assigned to whole data files within software and there-fore confusion can arise when you have documents in which multiple respondents, cases or contexts occur, for example focus groups, open-ended answers to survey data, field notes, minutes of meetings, email exchanges, web-based discussions etc. Such data are more complicated to organize, but this is always possible by coding *parts* of documents (Figure 11.1). This may happen instead of or as well as organizing whole documents. Software packages differ in the ways they handle this more complex organization, but the process can usually be semi-automated by making use of the data formatting structures that the chosen software recognizes (see Chapter 2) and using auto coding processes (see software-specific sections to follow).

Organizing case studies

When you are conducting a case-based study, the types and amounts of data collected will often be more complicated to organize. For example, you may be comparing a number of different sites (for example, schools, hospitals or countries), at which you have collected data from different types of people (for example, teachers, parents or pupils). Indeed, you may have collected different types of data from groups of those respondents (for example, focus groups, interviews, questionnaires). Where some respondents have taken part in an interview and a focus group, for example, the organization of their data will be even more complex.

In many case-based projects there is an interest in comparing across cases as well as conducting within-case analysis. For example, you may be interested in investigating the views of all teachers, regardless of the school at which they teach, as well as considering the impact of the type of school on the way lessons are taught. This is possible within most qualitative software in some way (see Figure 11.1).

SOFTWARE-SPECIFIC VARIATIONS: DATA ORGANIZATION

In this section we provide step-by-step support for two organizational exercises (but make reference to others where relevant). For ATLAS.ti5, MAXqda2 and NVivo7 we illustrate how to organize whole documents manually within the software, and how to use auto coding tools to quickly organize parts of documents, based on structure within the data (see also Chapter 2).

Exercises in ATLAS.ti5

Whole documents can be organized into subsets by creating document families. Families can be created easily within the software (see Figure 11.2). Tabular data in the correct format can be imported to automatically create families and quickly organize whole files into them (not illustrated). Information can be exported to work on in other applications (e.g. MS Excel or SPSS). Organizing parts of documents happens by coding (see Figure 11.3). Data organization by document family and coding can be combined in the Query Tool (see Chapter 12).

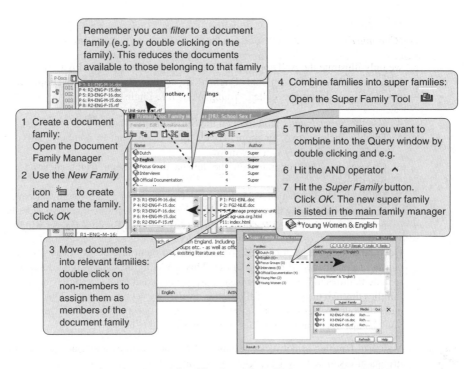

Remember you can *filter* to a document family (e.g. by double clicking on the family). This reduces the documents available to those belonging to that family

1 Create a document family:
Open the Document Family Manager

2 Use the *New Family* icon 📇 to create and name the family. Click *OK*

3 Move documents into relevant families: double click on non-members to assign them as members of the document family

4 Combine families into super families:
Open the Super Family Tool 📖

5 Throw the families you want to combine into the Query window by double clicking and e.g.

6 Hit the AND operator ∧

7 Hit the *Super Family* button. Click *OK*. The new super family is listed in the main family manager

👓*Young Women & English

Figure 11.2   Creating document families in ATLAS.ti5 (see Exercise 11.1)

Exercise 11.1   ATLAS.ti5: manually apply known characteristics to whole documents using document families

The numbering of steps corresponds to Figure 11.2

Families in ATLAS.ti5 are shortcuts to groups of documents (or codes and memos: see Chapters 8 and 9). Documents can belong to multiple families.

1   Open the Primary Document Family Manager from the Documents main menu via Edit Families/Open Family Manager. From here you can create, edit and delete families, add or remove family members, comment on the reasons for and uses of a family, set a family as a filter, and open the Super Family Tool.
2   Use the *New family* icon to create a new family. Give it a unique name and click OK.
3   Select the family in the top window. Move the relevant documents from the non-members list (in red on right) to the members list (in black on left) either by double clicking or by using the left-facing arrow.

Combine families into super families

Broad families can be combined into more specific and complex groups using the Super Family Tool. This process works by using Boolean operators including OR, AND, NOT (here

(Continued)

we only illustrate the AND operator). In the example illustrated in Figure 11.2, the individual families of 'Young Women' and 'English' are combined using the AND operator to create a new family of documents called 'Young Women & English'.

4 Use the *Super Family* icon to open the Super Family Tool.

5 Double click on two (or more) code families you want to combine. This throws those families into the grey Query window.

6 Choose the AND operator on the left-hand icon menu (right click on icons to see functions).

7 Hit the *Super Family* button. Accept the default name, or create your own (leave the * at the beginning if changing the name, as this indicates to the software that it is a super family). This new family is then listed in the main Primary Document Family Manager window.

Once families have been created you can filter to them in order to focus your attention on a subset of documents within the dataset. This works in the same way as described in relation to code families in Chapter 8 for basic retrieval of coded data. Combining document and code families through the process of filtering is a very easy yet useful way to look at and think about parts of your project without asking more complex questions using the Query Tool, although you can also make use of families in the Query Tool (Chapter 12).

Visualize families in networks (Chapter 10). Ask questions about how codes appear within groups of documents in the Query Tool (Chapter 12).

Exercise 11.2   Atlas.ti5: use auto coding tools to organize parts of documents

The numbering of steps corresponds to Figure 11.3.

Refer to the data preparation guidelines for ATLAS.ti5 in Chapter 2 if you intend to use this function.

1 Open the Auto Coding dialog box through the main Codes menu via *Coding/Auto Coding*.

2 Create a *New Code* at which to code the structure you are looking for. Name it accordingly (consider prefixing with xxx- to put it at the bottom of the codes list and away from the conceptual aspects of your coding scheme). Check this is the code that appears in the *Select Code* box (this is *important* to avoid coding at a conceptual code and thus messing up your coding).

3 Type the unique identifier (a speaker ID or other structuring device) into the *Enter or Select Search Expression* field.

4 Choose the relevant *Scope of Search*: the *Selected PD* (primary document, i.e. the one on display), *All current PDs* or a *PD Family*.

(Continued)

(Continued)

5 Choose the unit of context you wish to code in the *Create quotation from match extended to* area – either the *Single Hard Return* or *Multi Hard Returns* depending how you have structured your data (see Chapter 2).

6 If you want to see each paragraph as it is found and decide yourself whether to code it or skip it, click *Confirm always*. If you are confident your data have been prepared consistently you do not have to *Confirm always*.

7 Click *Start*.

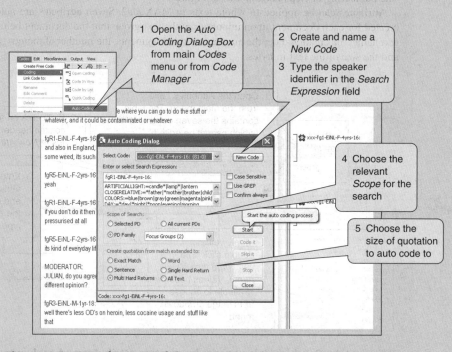

Figure 11.3   Organize parts of documents (e.g. focus-group speaker sections) using auto coding tools in ATLAS.ti5 (see Exercise 11.2)

Exercises in MAXqda2

Whole texts can be organized in MAXqda2, by creating either text groups or text sets. Text groups are discussed in Chapter 3 and must be created in order to import documents. You may therefore choose to create groups of different types of text when you import data files (e.g. interviews, focus groups etc.). Text sets are useful for code retrieval, frequency tables, retrieval of memos linked to documents etc. (see Chapter 7). In order to pose more complex questions about subsets of data (see Chapter 12), *attributes* can be applied to Texts (see Figure 11.4). Parts of documents are organized in MAXqda2 by coding. The text search tool allows quick coding of paragraphs.

Exercise 11.3   MAXqda2: manually apply known characteristics to whole documents using attributes

The numbering of steps corresponds to Figure 11.4.

Attributes can be applied to whole texts in MAXqda2. Seven attributes are automatically created for each document upon importation: the text group that the document belongs to; the text name; the creation date; the number of coded segments; the number of memos; the author; and the size of the text in bytes.

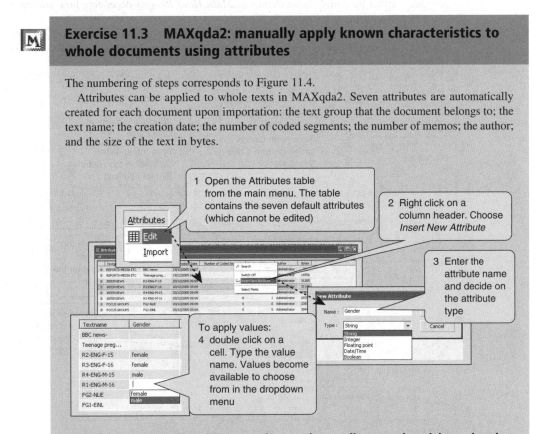

Figure 11.4   Organizing documents by creating attributes and applying values in MAXqda2 (see Exercise 11.3)

1   Open the Attributes table from the Attributes main menu *Edit,* or click the shortcut icon.
2   Right click on a column header in the table. Choose *Insert New Attribute.*
3   Enter the name and choose the appropriate attribute type (string, integer, floating point, date/time, Boolean).
4   Double click on a cell to create and apply the relevant value. As you create values, they become available in a dropdown menu from which to choose.

To only view attributes for a particular document, right click on the text in the Document System and choose *Overview of Attributes.* Attributes and values can be created for that document within the Attributes view. Columns can be hidden from view in any table, and clicking on the column header will sort texts according to the frequency of that column.

Exercise 11.4   MAXqda2: simple text search to organize parts of documents

The numbering of steps corresponds to Figure 11.5.

The instructions here relate to having prepared and formatted data for MAXqda2 as discussed in Chapter 2.

1 Create a new code in the Code System at which to save the results. Consider creating a hierarchy (e.g. focus-group respondents) under which to hang the individual codes for each respondent (see Chapter 7).
2 Open the Text Search window from the main menu.
3 Hit *New* and type the identifier you are searching for (e.g. the participant speaker identifier). Click *Run Search*.
4 The Search Results window appears, listing all finds in a table. (As with all tables in MAXqda2, there is interactive connectivity between the table rows and the data in the Text Browser window.)
5 Hit the *Options* button. In the Hits view, make sure the *Paragraph* radio button is ticked and that 0 is set as the number of paragraphs around each find to code. Close dialogue box.
6 Hit the *Code* button and choose the correct code (i.e. the code you created for the respondent). If the correct code is not listed in the 'quick list', choose it in the Code System. It will then appear in the quick list when you hit *Code* again. All the paragraphs in which the string you searched for will be coded.

Repeat steps 1–6 for other speaker sections.

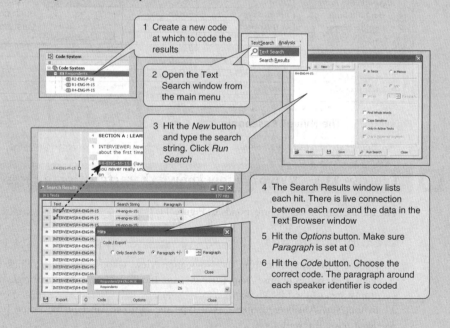

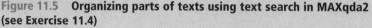

Figure 11.5   Organizing parts of texts using text search in MAXqda2 (see Exercise 11.4)

Exercises in NVivo7

In order to apply known characteristics to whole sources (documents) in NVivo7, sources first need to be coded as cases. Attribute values can be applied to cases but not other types of node. A case can comprise just one document (e.g. an individual respondent's interview transcript) or several documents (e.g. where several (parts of documents) refer to one respondent). When importing documents you can choose to automatically create them as cases (see Chapter 3) or this can be done later by a process of coding. The Casebook lists all project cases and their attribute values in a tabular format (see Figure 11.6). A Casebook can be created in a spreadsheet application and imported (not illustrated). Sets provide shortcuts to groups of documents or combinations of project items. Parts of documents can be coded at case nodes.

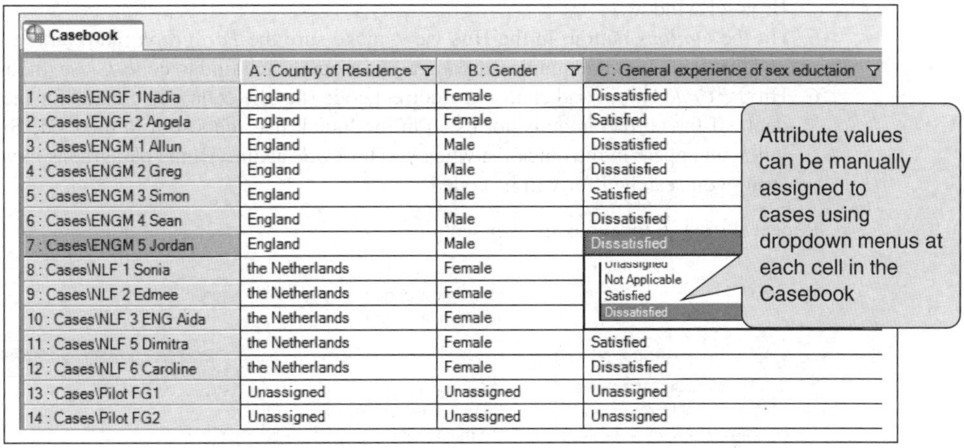

📖 Casebook			
	A : Country of Residence ▽	B : Gender ▽	C : General experience of sex eductaion ▽
1 : Cases\ENGF 1Nadia	England	Female	Dissatisfied
2 : Cases\ENGF 2 Angela	England	Female	Satisfied
3 : Cases\ENGM 1 Allun	England	Male	Dissatisfied
4 : Cases\ENGM 2 Greg	England	Male	Dissatisfied
5 : Cases\ENGM 3 Simon	England	Male	Satisfied
6 : Cases\ENGM 4 Sean	England	Male	Dissatisfied
7 : Cases\ENGM 5 Jordan	England	Male	Dissatisfied
8 : Cases\NLF 1 Sonia	the Netherlands	Female	Unassigned / Not Applicable / Satisfied / Dissatisfied
9 : Cases\NLF 2 Edmee	the Netherlands	Female	
10 : Cases\NLF 3 ENG Aida	the Netherlands	Female	
11 : Cases\NLF 5 Dimitra	the Netherlands	Female	Satisfied
12 : Cases\NLF 6 Caroline	the Netherlands	Female	Dissatisfied
13 : Cases\Pilot FG1	Unassigned	Unassigned	Unassigned
14 : Cases\Pilot FG2	Unassigned	Unassigned	Unassigned

Attribute values can be manually assigned to cases using dropdown menus at each cell in the Casebook

Figure 11.6   **The NVivo7 Casebook**

Exercise 11.5   NVivo7: apply known characteristics to cases

The numbering of steps corresponds to Figure 11.7.

Creating attributes

1 Choose *Classifications* from the Navigation View. Choose *Attributes*. Click in the List View area. Either choose *New Attribute* from the Project main menu, or right click in the empty area of the List View.
2 In the New Attribute dialogue box, type the attribute label in the Name field. Add a description if relevant.

(Continued)

(Continued)

3   Choose the attribute value type from the dropdown menu (string, number or date).
4   Click the *Values* tab. Click *Add* to create the value. Name it in the value cell. Describe the value if required. Check the *Default* box to set a value as the default for new cases if relevant.

Applying attribute values to cases

5   Navigate to the Nodes folder. Choose a case in the List View and right click on it. Choose *Case Properties*.
6   Hit the *Attribute Values* tab. Use the spinner arrows to choose the relevant value from the dropdown menus.

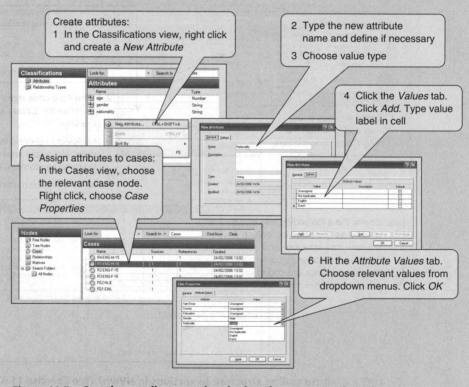

Figure 11.7   Creating attributes and assigning them to cases in NVivo7 (see Exercise 11.5)

Exercise 11.6   NVivo7: auto code parts of documents

The numbering of steps corresponds to Figure 11.8.

The instructions here relate to having prepared and formatted data for NVivo7 as discussed in Chapter 2.

NVivo7 provides the facility to auto code structured data to paragraphs or sections. Sections can be created using heading levels in MS Word, although this process can also be automated by search and replace tools inside NVivo7. In projects where, for example, the same respondent has taken part in a one-to-one interview and as a focus group, the ability to code parts of documents to case nodes is powerful. This is because this process unifies all data relating to one 'case' together, which is not enabled in ATLAS.ti5 or MAXqda2. In the following instructions we illustrate how to auto code questions in semi-structured interview transcripts.

First create a top-level tree node under which to auto code questions (not illustrated). To do so, click on *Trees*, and in the List View, right mouse to create a node. Name the new node. It's good practice to note in the description that these node trees are being made by auto coding.

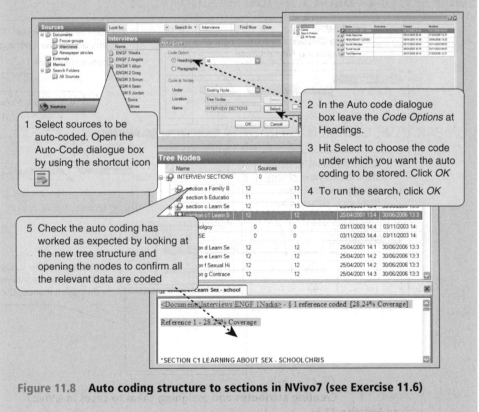

1 Select sources to be auto-coded. Open the Auto-Code dialogue box by using the shortcut icon

2 In the Auto code dialogue box leave the *Code Options* at Headings.

3 Hit Select to choose the code under which you want the auto coding to be stored. Click *OK*

4 To run the search, click *OK*

5 Check the auto coding has worked as expected by looking at the new tree structure and opening the nodes to confirm all the relevant data are coded

Figure 11.8   Auto coding structure to sections in NVivo7 (see Exercise 11.6)

(Continued)

(Continued)

1 Now go to the folder of sources you want to auto code. Select the items to be auto coded and click the *Auto Code* button on the Coding bar (or use the Project or context menu).
2 In the Auto Code dialogue box, leave options unchanged and click *Select* to find the relevant code under which to store the auto coded questions.
3 In the Select Project Items window, click on your new tree node, then click *OK*.
4 Confirm the *Auto Code* instruction by clicking *OK*.
5 Check the Tree Nodes to see that the process has worked as expected. The List View shows the nodes created and named and what coding was done automatically.
6 The three nodes created in this way can be moved, if appropriate, to case nodes where attributes and values can be assigned to them, e.g. for focus group speaker nodes.

SUMMARY: DATA ORGANIZATION FUNCTIONALITY

CAQDAS packages provide several means to organize data to known characteristics, and these tools are especially useful when a dataset is large or complex. As with many tasks, data organization can happen early in your use of software or at a later stage. The power of CAQDAS packages for your project may come when combining organizational features with the more conceptual aspects of your work held at codes (see Chapter 12).

COMPARATIVE COMMENTS ON DATA ORGANIZATION

Sophistication of tools

NVivo7 has more support for shortcut ways to organize types of data where more than one respondent appears in one data file, for instance, focus groups, open-ended questions to survey data etc. Paradoxically, because this tool is doing more complicated things, it is more difficult to work out the best way to organize your data in NVivo7. Similarly, more thought has to be given to formatting data for NVivo7.

Chapter 12
Interrogating the Dataset

In this chapter we discuss functions which allow you to interrogate, search or query the database, building on the tasks discussed in previous chapters. Despite the placing of this chapter, interrogating the dataset will probably be something you undertake at various moments in the analytic process: that is, it need not be left until, for example, coding has been completed. We list ideas and reasons for doing searches, illustrating how they can help you delve around the project for interesting relationships, patterns of occurrence and exceptions. We also raise some cautions and debates about searching tools, and discuss ways in which these tools provide additional methods of interrogation from those practically possible when working manually.

MOVING ON

If you have achieved a significant level of work using coding and organizing tools, you may be clear how you wish to proceed. Sometimes, having coded for some time, knowing where to go next can be mystifying. Search tools can be used to gain confidence in handling data and using the software at any stage of work. There may often be more than one way to achieve a similar result and early searching experiments will help you see what might be possible later. When the answer to a question is already known, a confirmatory search result will provide confidence in the way the search was built. This chapter provides support in commonly used searches, and some of the more sophisticated interrogatory functions. Though full step-by-step graphics are not given, we hope to provide enough support to help you begin searching with confidence. Remember, you cannot damage your software project by searching. The only dangers lie in being confused or uncertain about how to build a search or where the coding on which searches rely is unsound, patchy or inconsistent. The consequence may be dubious results, thereby leading to mistaken thinking. Interpreting the results of searches lies with you. Most tools focus on where items searched for exist in the data, but it is important to be aware that absence can be just as analytically significant as presence. Therefore view results in context and be reflexive about how searches are contributing to your understanding. Search tools will not in themselves produce good quality analysis.

DIFFERENT WAYS TO INTERROGATE THE DATABASE

There are many different ways to interrogate the dataset in ATLAS.ti5, MAXqda2 and NVivo7. Chapter 8 introduced some basic retrieval options; here we build on earlier work to interrogate the dataset in more powerful ways. Table 12.1 provides a summary of common searches and the terminology used in the three software packages.

Filtering and simple forms of retrieval

Filtering tools can be used at several levels, allowing you to focus on aspects of the project in isolation. They can be used in straightforward ways, for example to retrieve data coded at one issue or theme (see Chapter 8) or according to subsets of data (see

Chapter 11). Search tools combine both types of filter. Tables and matrices, for example, allow the comparison of how certain codes appear within certain types of data, providing frequency information as well as access to coded data.

Searching for content

Chapter 4 discussed the spontaneous exploration of text using 'find' and 'text searching' tools. This allows you to flick from serious coding or code creation mode to check the recurrence of a word or phrase in order, for example, to substantiate the relevance of a new code. This chapter builds on such tasks, illustrating the possibility of additionally coding or *auto coding* the results of text searches for content (see also Chapter 11 about auto coding structure in the data).

Code searches as iterative, incremental and repeatable

Code searches rely on the coding work you have already performed. The following are provided by *search* or *query* tools:

- combining codes to represent broader categories
- finding where codes occur together in the data
- finding where codes overlap or occur near to each other in the data
- finding where certain codes occur in a particular sequence
- finding data not coded by a particular code.

These searches can support the iterative analytic process, acting as ways to check out hunches as you progress. They can also facilitate incremental analysis in that further searches can be performed on the results of earlier ones. This either happens by building a previous search term into a new query or because the results of a previous search have been coded, enabling data coded at the new code to be used in a subsequent search. The variety of ways to combine work provides vast potential in interrogating the dataset.

Qualitative cross-tabulations in the form of tables and matrices

Software provides summary frequency information concerning the application of coding across the dataset, illustrating for example the number of times a code appears in a particular document. Although it is easier to achieve in some packages and each tabulates information differently, they all allow you to overview different aspects of your project in certain ways. Cross-tabulations are powerful ways to combine qualitative coding with the more descriptive organization of data. Where these tables are interactively connected with source data, they allow you to see summary (frequency) information and the corresponding qualitative data at the same time. Tables can be exported to other applications or printed.

Interrogating in maps

Although this chapter is mainly about interrogating the dataset by using search tools, it is important to remember that maps also offer ways to interrogate your work (see Chapter 10). For example, when based on what has already been accomplished through coding, maps help to visualize broad connections and linkages. This may often occur at a conceptual or abstract level, but it will be possible to flick back to the occurrence of a coded instance within its source context. Although mapping tools work in rather different ways, they all provide means to focus on one object, to see where it comes from and what other things it is connected or related to. In many ways, therefore, maps can act as starting points for other forms of interrogation. The connections illustrated in a map, for example, may prompt more detailed questions to be asked using the search or query tools. ATLAS.ti5 differs from most other software in that transitive (hierarchical) links between codes are functional as a means of retrieval. For example, where two or more codes have been linked using relationships such as 'is a cause of', 'is part of' or 'is a', quotations coded at related codes can be retrieved together in the query tool.

CHANGING TECHNIQUES OF QUALITATIVE DATA ANALYSIS

Ways to work with qualitative data have substantially changed with the improved access to data that software provides. Similarly, the sophistication of search tools and the variety of searches to choose from within software have increased. The potential of software to impact on the way qualitative analysis happens has been debated for many years (see for example Fielding and Lee, 1993). It is clear that many of the tools we discuss in this chapter allow interrogation to a level which is not possible without using a customized CAQDAS package. Analytic tasks can be integrated and methodological boundaries stretched by using tools in flexible and innovative ways. Conversely, if you are adhering to an established methodology then a more limited use of tools can also support specific analytic tasks effectively.

Cautions

Some tools have more potential to change the face of how qualitative data analysis is conducted than others. These include auto coding processes that search for and code verbatim content (see Chapters 4 and 11). John Seidel, himself one of the early pioneers of software development (The Ethnograph), was concerned that computer technology would lead to a sacrifice of 'resolution' in favour of 'scope'. His essays and thoughtful software manual recount how hours of in-depth examination of small sections of data revealed phenomena in midwifery care which would have been missed by faster methods of exploration and identification. He saw the value of analysis coming from careful immersion in relatively small qualitative datasets, and was concerned that this would be lost in the face of software developments which allow shallower exploration on larger and larger datasets (Seidel, 1991). These concerns were reflected in the absence of text searching tools in his own software. Conversely, Richards and Richards (1994), who were actively responsible for including such tools in early versions of NUD*IST, felt that text search functions were 'a necessary tool for gaining direct access to records rather than accessing them only through codes expressing the researcher's interpretation'. Weaver and Atkinson (1995) say something similar in describing the uses of text search tools 'as a useful means of checking the validity of analyses shaped by other strategies such as the coded segments strategy in interpretive research, or in the triangulation of methods'. Fisher (1997) stresses the slightly different efficiency dimension, suggesting that searching can counteract human failings by revealing possible 'aberrant cases', thereby ensuring that 'analysis is as comprehensive as possible'. These contrasting views are useful because they emphasize the value of two dimensions of work in qualitative data, while alerting us to the potential shortcomings of both.

Our own view is that the mechanistic text search tools with auto coding options available in CAQDAS packages can increase reflexivity and help to plough through a mass of data. To reverse the metaphor, however, when you are working in an interpretive way, the results only skim the surface of the data. It goes without saying that your data might refer richly to topics without ever using the key words you search for. If such tools are overused in an interpretive approach to the exclusion of other more careful work in the data, it is possible that the nature and purposes of some types of qualitative data analysis are being undervalued or misunderstood.

 Whatever type of search you conduct, it is important to be reflexive about its usefulness. Experimenting with searches early on will help you to practise building searches in different ways and think about how useful they will be later on.

GENERIC TASKS: SEARCHING

We now introduce the following generic tasks for interrogating the dataset: searching for content (text searching); code searching (for application of coding in the data); producing tabular data (for summary information); and creating 'signposts' for searches (to rerun later).

Searching for content

See Chapter 4, Task 4.3, for the various reasons to perform these searches. Amongst them are:

- searching for a powerful phrase or some jargon which demonstrates an attitude
- searching for a selection of words which encapsulate several occurrences of a similar topic
- searching for value-laden words.

Code searching

Table 12.1 summarizes detail about important searches in software. We cover some of these in the more practical software-specific areas to follow. They include:

- making one new larger code, e.g. a higher concept, out of many detailed codes, without losing the detailed codes
- comparing across cases or groups of respondents, to consider how they have each talked about an issue or several issues
- finding where one person or one case has talked about several separate or related issues
- finding where certain types of respondent have talked about an issue
- finding where respondents have talked about an issue near to talk about another issue
- finding where two or more topics have been coded at the same or overlapping places in the data.

Generating tabular data

Tasks here include:

- listing documents in which a topic is mentioned at all
- finding how many and which documents refer to a topic
- asking how many discrete passages have been coded to each code amongst certain document(s).

Creating signposts from searches

There are various ways to build 'signposts' into your work. Memos, special codes and particular maps can all be used to remind you of other pathways to be followed and investigations which deserve further attention. In a similar way, searches can be saved as pointers to future 'tests' on data. Saved search expressions can act as dynamic questions, repeatable on later accumulations of (coded) data. They can be built at a relatively early stage, when running them would return few results. All three software packages provide ways to save search expressions. For ATLAS.ti5, this is illustrated in Figures 12.1 and 12.2. The super code sits like a normal code in the main codes list but actually it represents a previous query and can be rerun. Similarly in NVivo7 a query can be added to the project and listed in the Queries pane (see Figures 12.5 and 12.6). MAXqda2 also allows search expressions to be rerun, though they are saved as files to be loaded later, outside the software (not illustrated).

SOFTWARE-SPECIFIC SEARCHING FUNCTIONS

The complexity and variety of the possible searches provided by software is impossible to include in detail and we must therefore be selective in those we illustrate. To provide an

Table 12.1   *Common search options in ATLAS.ti5, MAXqda2 and NVivo7*

(See software specific sections for *General Instructions* and other searches particular to individual packages). **NOTE**: Any of the searches listed here can be carried out on subsets of documents as well as across the whole dataset.

Purpose of search	Uses, options & variations	Easiest ways & terminology
Search for **one word, several words or phrase** in the content of textual data	Code a specified unit of context around each 'hit' (see Chapter 2) Processes similar to text searching for organizational purposes as illustrated in Chapter 11.	**A5** – *Codes/Autocoding* see Fig. 11.3 **MAX2** – Main menu/*TextSearch* use subsequent *Options* to autocode see Fig. 4.6 and Fig. 11.5 **NV7** – *Query/Text search* see Fig. 4.9
Collect together data segments coded at several codes, without losing the detail at the individual codes	Useful for generating higher level concepts when working inductively (see Chapter 5). View the results, then choose whether to create a new code to hold them.	**A5** – Select codes/Output/ *Selected Codes with full quotations see Fig. 8.1* **MAX2** – *Activate* by hierarchical top level, or individual codes and activate Texts reqd., by group or Set – see Fig. 12.3 **NV7** – *Select nodes/right click/Create new node see Fig. 8.7*
Find **codes which occur together** in the data	Useful to focus in on combinations of themes identified within the data, if for example working in a 'broad-brush', or deductive way (see Chapter 5)	*Where 2 or more codes occur exactly together* **A5** – Query/*AND* see Fig. 12.1 **MAX2** – *Intersection* or *Intersection (set)* See Fig. 12.3 **NV7** – Query/Advanced/AND see Fig. 12.5
	Software can find how codes occur together in different ways	*Where codes overlap in some way* **A5** – *Co-occurrence* or *Overlaps_by* or *Overlapping* – see Fig. 12.1 **MAX2** – *Overlapping* see Fig. 12.3 **NV7** – (see above) AND search then *Spread* see Fig. 12.5
Find **codes near to one another** in the data	Specify how near the codes occur and the sequence in which they occur (options vary).	**A5** – *Query/Follows* or *precedes* **MAX2** – TextRetrieval/*Near* OR *Followed by* see Fig. 12.3 **NV7** – Query/Advanced/NEAR OR PRECEDING See Fig. 12.5
Find **embedded** codes	Either where a code embeds another, or where a code is embedded by another	**A5** – *Within* or *Encloses* **MAX2** – *If Inside* or *If Outside* **NV7** – Query/SURROUNDING
To compare how groups of respondents (or data) contain certain code(s)		**A5** – see fuller descripe., in *Scope* in Fig. 12.1-fuller ATLAS.ti refs in Chap. 12 **MAXqda:** Code Relations matrix Fig. 12.4 **NV7** – *Query/Matrix* see Fig. 12.6 and fuller NVivo7 refs in Chap. 12

overview of functionality, we list multiple search options in each software package and refer you to Table 12.1. In providing fuller step-by-step support, we focus on the basic search building procedure in each software, and provide starting points for some others. The practical methods of conducting content-based searches have been covered either in Chapter 4 under text searching or in the auto coding procedures in Chapter 11, so we cross-refer to figures in those chapters.

Searching and interrogation tools in ATLAS.ti5

There are many ways to filter (see Chapter 8) and search the database in ATLAS.ti5 and distinctive ways for saving search expressions and integrating them into normal codes lists. Query tools and the auto coding of text (see Chapter 11) happen in two different windows. ATLAS.ti5 offers the additional ability to retrieve coded quotations based on the nature of the relationships created by linking codes.

General instructions
Right click mouse menus are very context specific in ATLAS.ti5. It is useful to experiment with interrogation via these menus by right clicking on objects. Look at the Tools main menu for additional interrogation/search options. The Query Tool allows the most complex means of interrogation. Refer also to generic tasks and Table 12.1 for ideas and reasons to search and interrogate.

HU-based interrogation/navigation in ATLAS.ti5

- The Object Crawler enables the entire 'HU' (project) to be searched for the existence of strings, words or phrases in the content of documents, memos, comments, quotations, families, links etc. Objects to search within can be specified and the results are interactively connected to source locations. Access the Object Crawler via the Tools main menu (not illustrated).
- The Object Explorer is a clickable expanding hierarchy that enables top-down navigation between linked objects. Each type of project object is listed hierarchically, under which all linked items are listed. This allows the visualization of the whole project, showing how each object is linked to other objects. Access the Object Explorer via the Tools main menu (not illustrated).
- The Cooccurrence Explorer is a clickable expanding hierarchy which enables either top-down exploration of the co-occurrence of codes with other codes (and then with quotations), or the co-occurrence of documents with codes (and then quotations). This is an easy way to check out some easily identifiable relationships, based on earlier work.

Searches for content and auto coding in ATLAS.ti5

- Use the Text Search tool to search for patterns or strings in a primary document (see Figure 4.3).

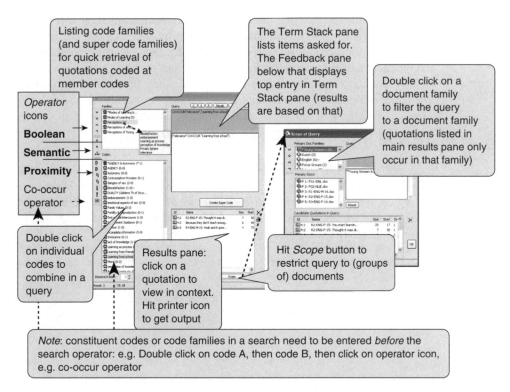

Figure 12.1   The ATLAS.ti Query Tool (not all functions described)

- From the Codes main menu, use *Coding/Auto Coding* (see Figure 11.3).
- The Word Cruncher will count the frequency of words across all or selected primary documents, producing an output report for viewing in a spreadsheet application. Hits are not interactively linked to source content (see Chapter 4).

Tabular interrogation in ATLAS.ti5

Access code by document frequency information via the Codes main menu using *Output/Codes Primary Documents Table*. Export directly to an MS Excel file or to a standard report for viewing immediately in an ATLAS.ti5 table (not illustrated). Tabular information in ATLAS.ti5 is not interactively linked to qualitative data.

Code searches in ATLAS.ti5

Open the Query Tool using the binoculars icon.

Query operators are listed as icons down the left side of the window. Right click on them to see the functions.

- Boolean operators: OR, EXCLUSIVE OR (XOR), AND, NOT.
- Semantic operators: DOWN (SUB), UP, SIB.
- Proximity operators: WITHIN, ENCLOSES, OVERLAPPED BY, OVERLAPS, FOLLOWS, PRECEDES, COOCCUR.

Note: in the above, constituent codes, code families etc. need to be entered into the search before the search operator. For example, double click on code A, again on code B, then click on the relevant operator icon.

Example code search tasks in ATLAS.ti5

- Compare across groups of data files: vary the query's scope to compare results by document families, or individual selections (see Figure 12.1).
- Simple retrieval by filtering to families of codes: see Chapter 8 and Table 12.1.
- Save query as a super code, i.e. as a dynamic code listed in the main codes list for constant reminders or signposts for tests or enquiries to make later on. To rerun the super code, double click on it in the codes list or the Query Tool.
- Snapshot super codes to capture the situation at a particular moment in time. This is particularly useful for longitudinal projects (see Figure 12.2).

Interrogating from networks in ATLAS.ti5

To see any co-occurring codes in a network, open a network view on a code, then right click over the selected code in the network view. Co-occurring codes can also be listed by right clicking on a code in the Query Tool. Quotations can also be retrieved within a network by right clicking on a code in a network view and Import Neighbors (see Chapter 10).

Retrieving quotations coded at codes linked by transitive relationships in ATLAS.ti5

Use the semantic operators to return quotations coded at a code above (UP), below (DOWN) or adjacent (SIB) to a code. Transitive links must exist between codes for these operators to function (see Chapter 10).

Summary of interrogation tools in ATLAS.ti5

As discussed in Chapter 8, ATLAS.ti5 provides simple ways (such as filtering) to begin interrogating the dataset. The Object Explorer and Object Crawler provide flexible ways to view the whole project and focus on parts of it without performing complicated searches. The search operators available in the Query Tool provide additional and more sophisticated ways to find patterns and relationships in the data. In particular, the super code ability and the semantic operators are distinctive to ATLAS.ti5 and both are useful additions to the standard collection of tools provided by CAQDAS packages.

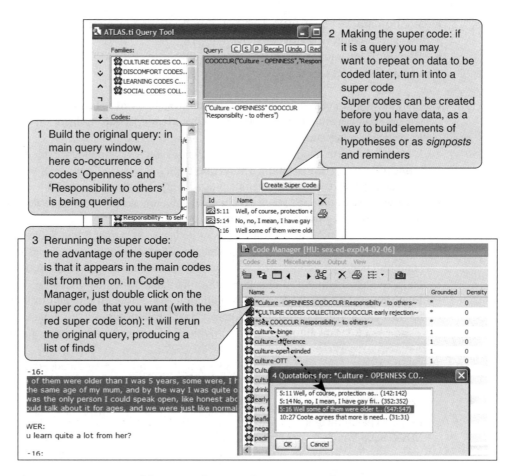

Figure 12.2   Query tool in ATLAS.ti5 – creating a super code

 ## Searching and interrogation tools in MAXqda2

MAXqda2 has a simple code searching tool called the Text Retriever which provides graphic and textual descriptors for each operator. Open it from the Analysis main menu via *Text Retrieval*. Tabular data can be generated and based on several project items – codes, memos, attributes and coded segments. Tables are interactively linked with text and are accessible without having to open the Text Retriever. The logic of activation underlies how searches enable interrogation of the dataset. Searching for content and coding the results (auto coding) happens in the Text Search function (see also Chapter 8, Figure 8.4). With the addition of MAXDictio (the add-on module to MAXqda2), word frequency with key word in context (KWIC) retrieval is enabled within the software. This is unique amongst the software packages discussed here. Outputs of coded data, memos and tabular information are easy to generate. Refer also to the earlier generic tasks for ideas and reasons to search and interrogate.

General instructions

- Find most options in main menus. Remember that selective activation of codes or texts has an easy, key role to play in the variation of summarized information in tables and in simple to more complex code retrieval using the Text Retriever.
- It is always worth choosing and right clicking on a text or code to explore options in terms of overview information. This provides easy access to, for example, an overview of coded segments or linked memos interactively linked to source text.
- Save any search that you think you may need to run again if it seems easier to do this than by rebuilding the search next time.

Content searching and auto coding in MAXqda2

- Auto coding of content can happen either via the Text Search option or via the Word Frequency tool if you also have MAXDictio. The surrounding paragraphs of hits can be auto coded (see Chapter 2 on automatically recognized units of context). Step-by-step instructions on auto coding are provided in Chapter 11 (see Figure 11.5).

- full step-by-step support for word frequency and text search tools with KWIC are provided in Chapter 4 (Figures 4.7 and 4.8). We introduced them as ways of exploring the occurrence of words as part of the early exploration of the data and they may also be useful at later stages of work. With the cautions discussed above in mind, the MAXDictio Word Frequency tool provides an additional way to explore data. Experiment with searching for words and phrases occurring in different combinations of activated texts and with creating your own dictionaries, which you can save to and run later.

Tabular interrogation in MAXqda2

There is much tabular information concerning aspects of the project automatically available from main menus or by right clicking on project items.

- Codes frequency table via Codes main menu to compare across different activated documents.
- Index of Coded Segments: across whole dataset via Codes main menu, or by (groups of) documents or code(s).
- Attributes table: via Attributes main menu, or ask for attributes relating to individual texts or text groups.
- Overviews of memos linked to particular codes, texts, groups of texts etc. (see Chapter 9).
- All tables can be exported and are interactively linked to source context.

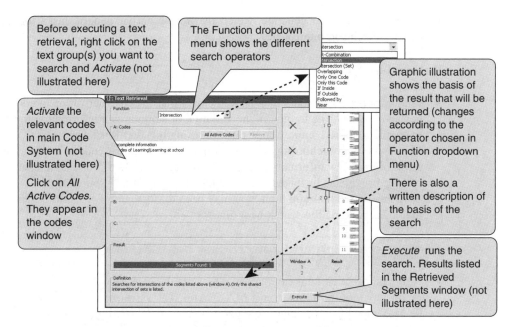

Figure 12.3   the MAXqda2 Text Retrieval (code searching) window

Code searching in MAXqda2

We discuss the functional hierarchical coding scheme provided by MAXqda2 in Chapters 6 and 8. Here we remind you of options and list main functions.

- Retrieve everything below a hierarchical level or several individual codes: see Figure 8.4.
- Hierarchies and subtrees can be treated as one code: use the *Subcodes* option in the Text Retrieval pane to find e.g. the intersection of one other code with the subsequent broad-brush code.
- Retrieval by groups of codes: see Table 12.1 and Figure 12.3.
- Text Retrieval tool (in Analysis menu) provides clear descriptors of ways to search, by Boolean or proximity bases (see Figure 12.3).
- Code Matrix Browser (under Visual Tools menu: see Figure 12.4) provides a code by document occurrence indicator, with different 'blobs' to indicate the strength of occurrence in each document. It is fully interactive.
- Code Relation Browser (under Visual Tools menu) enables you to find the co-occurrence of codes together in the data.
- Retrieve coded segments by weight: having assigned weight to coded segments to record an aspect of measure, activate the coded segments by weight via *Analysis/Use Weight Filter* (see also Chapter 8).

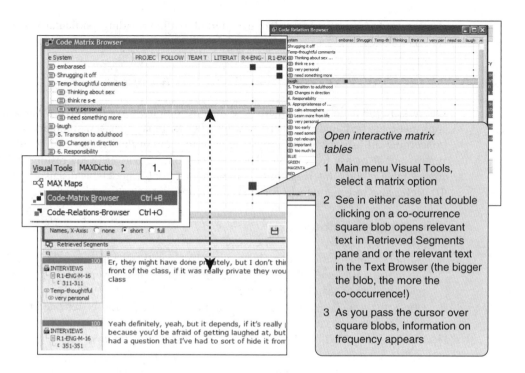

Figure 12.4   **MAXqda2 matrices – Code Matrix Browser (codes by document)**
Code Relations Browser (codes intersecting with other codes)

Interrogate by mapping in MAXqda2

In a map, find where codes co-occur in the data. See the main MAXqda2 functions in Chapter 10.

Summary of interrogation tools in MAXqda2

As discussed in Chapter 8, MAXqda2 provides simple ways such as activation to begin interrogating the dataset. In particular, the Code Matrix Browser and Code Relation Browser provide easy access to the co-occurrence of codes and texts in the data, and can be filtered according to current interest by activating particular texts and codes. Among the software discussed here, MAXqda2 is unique in this respect. While NVivo7 allows complex matrix searches (see later), it is a more step-by-step process to generate these presentations, and to vary the way information is provided. The visual and textual explanation of search operators is useful. The ability to add weight to coded segments and add a weight filter to searches and the Word Frequency tool provided by the addition of MAXDictio are distinctive in comparison to ATLAS.ti5 and NVivo7. Interrogating the dataset in MAXqda2 is easy to get started with, providing particularly easy-to-use dialogue boxes.

Searching and interrogation tools in NVivo7

Queries are the main way to interrogate data in complex ways in NVivo7. There is much information to be found elsewhere, however. For example, overview summary information concerning all aspects of the project is easy to view in the various List Views. Output reports are also easy to generate. There is good interactivity between results and data in matrix table reports. Interrogating via the mapping tools (models) is discussed in Chapter 10. Refer also to generic tasks for ideas and reasons to search and interrogate.

General instructions

- A *query* can be started when *Queries* is selected in the Navigation pane by right click-ing in the white space of the List pane. Or, use the *New* shortcut button and choose the relevant type of search (see below).
- Check the *Add To Project* box if you think this search could be repeated in the future on later data. You can specify how to view the results (see Figure 12.5).

Content searching and auto coding in NVivo7
See Figures 4.10, 12.5 and 12.6.

- Text searching: a type of query (see Figure 12.5; see also full step-by-step instructions in Chapter 4 and Figure 4.10).
- Find Tool (not illustrated): the main interface includes a Find bar, which is a simple way to locate project items. The tool searches the name and description of project items, but not their content (which can be searched for using a *text query*). Experiment with the advanced find options which allow groups of items to be retrieved, and con-sider grouping the results into sets if it seems relevant. The Find Tool is useful for locat-ing items, viewing items with similar names, and checking the characteristics of data.

Code searches in NVivo7
Queries provide starting points for many different variations in searches. Searches can be scoped to any project item.

- Simple code searches: find data coded at one node, perhaps filtered to certain sources. Or find data coded at cases which share an attribute (see Chapter 11).
- Advanced code searches: criteria for searching for the position of codes in the data are AND, OR, NEAR content, PRECEDING content, SURROUNDING content.
- Compound query: combine text and code queries to find words or phrases within data coded in particular ways (not illustrated).

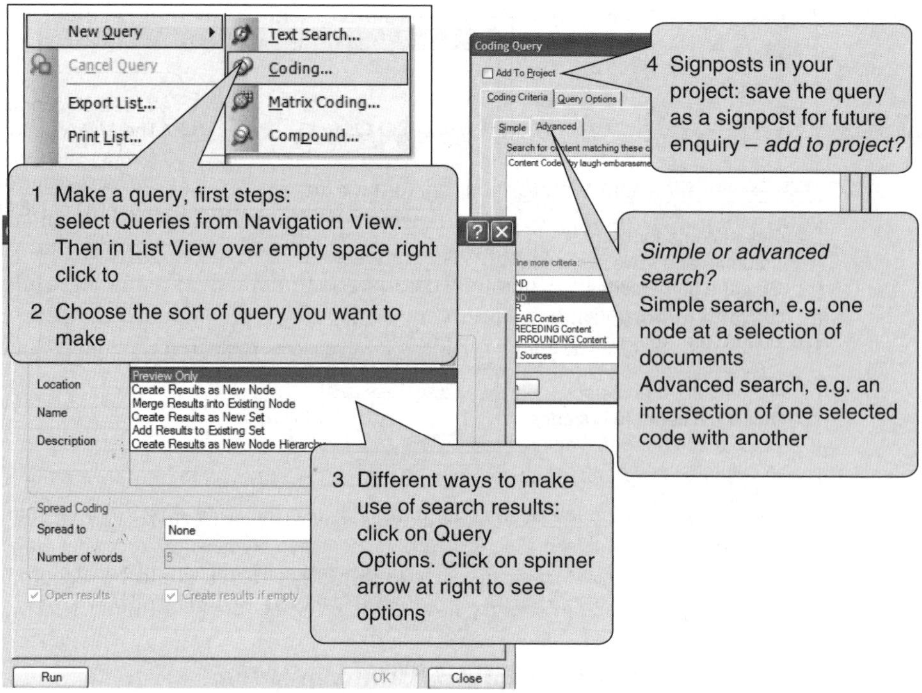

Figure 12.5   **NVivo7 – Starting points for creating various Queries**

Tabular queries in NVivo7

- Multiple tabular reports are accessible through *Tools/Reports,* providing summary information on various aspects of the project (nodes, sources, attributes, the whole project). Note that these reports are output and therefore not interactively linked with source context.
- Interactive matrix queries: the tables created by these searches provide frequency information according to, for example, the number of cases or passages coded. They allow retrieval of multiple attribute values in one table, facilitating the comparison of, for example, how various subsets of data talk about a range of issues (see Figures 12.5 and 12.6 for step-by-step instructions). The incorporation of multiple attribute values within one qualitative cross-tabulation is unique to QSR software (NUD*IST, NVivo2 and NVivo7).

Interrogate via models in NVivo7

Interrogate the project from the top down based on what you have done earlier. Find connections between different items by adding associated items in a model (see Figure 10.2).

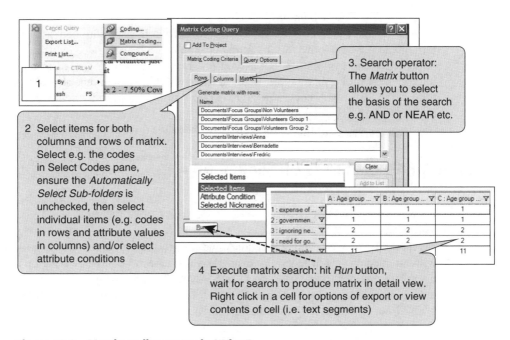

Figure 12.6   Matrix coding query in NVivo7

Summary of interrogation tools in NVivo7

As discussed in Chapter 8, NVivo7 provides simple ways, such as using sets, to begin interrogating the dataset. In addition to the standard search tools available in CAQDAS packages, NVivo7 provides a number of options which are distinctive among the packages we discuss here. In particular are the flexibility of matrix coding searches, the ability to vary options for how results are displayed, and the easy combination of coding and text searches using the compound query. However, NVivo7 lacks any word frequency tools such as those provided by ATLAS.ti5 and MAXqda2 (using MAXDictio). Although the sophistication and variety of queries in NVivo7 are one of its strengths, it is less straightforward to begin interrogating the dataset in comparison with ATLAS.ti5 and MAXqda2.

SUMMARY: REVIEWING SEARCHING AND INTERROGATION FUNCTIONALITY

While there are many similarities in the types of interrogation that can be facilitated by ATLAS.ti5, MAXqda2 and NVivo7, there are also many differences. Some of these are quite subtle, while others are more significant in terms of both the sophistication of options and the ease with which results can be generated. It is not within the scope of this book to describe and discuss all the variations, but we have focused in this chapter on those which we consider are important to your understanding of the way each software package functions and those which are particularly useful or distinctive. We have not included a separate chapter on reporting and outputting, but have mentioned at various points throughout the book how various forms of output can be generated. Much searching will be tentative and exploratory, but as you progress there will be a need to formalize your interpretations for a final report. Refer to Chapter 9 for a discussion of memo writing, and think reflexively about how retrieval of earlier writing can usefully be integrated with output of the evidence supporting your interpretation. Here we list some key aspects of getting to grips with searching which differ between the three software packages.

COMPARATIVE COMMENTS ON SEARCHING AND INTERROGATING THE DATASET

Basic ways of searching and the ease of specifying searches

In ATLAS.ti5 and MAXqda2 it is quick and easy to focus attention on parts of the dataset without opening search tools. For example, in ATLAS.ti5 double clicking on code and/or document families filters your work. In MAXqda2 this is achieved by activating individual codes and texts or a code hierarchy or text group. This type of filtering is possible in NVivo7 but it requires the building of queries.

Interface of search tools

The MAXqda2 search tool is neat and easy to understand, with clear visual representations and textual descriptions showing the results which will be returned for each operator. ATLAS.ti5 and NVivo7 query functions are more difficult to feel comfortable with immediately.

Saving search expressions

Although it is possible to save search expressions in MAXqda2 and NVivo7, the super codes option in ATLAS.ti5 provides the most obvious signposts to later tasks involving the rerun of searches, since they are listed and executable in the main codes list. NVivo7 lists saved queries in a separate area, and MAXqda2 saves them outside the software.

Qualitative cross-tabulations

NVivo7 can produce complex qualitative cross-tabulations of multiple codes by e.g. multiple subsets of data in one search, providing varied interactive frequency information. MAXqda2 has an even more impressive set of matrix options, and if coding is done in ways to support it, these can also be used to compare subsets with even less effort, though tabulation of frequency is not quite so varied. In ATLAS.ti5 this information is provided in separate places, i.e. you need to run a separate search for each individual subset of data. The interactivity of matrices in NVivo7 and MAXqda2 is exceptionally good. ATLAS.ti5 lacks interactivity between tables and the qualitative data. All three packages allow you to export tabular information.

Chapter 13
Convergence, Closeness, Choice

PLANNING FOR THE USE OF SOFTWARE

We hope to have provided some pointers to the differences in available software packages, some considerations in planning for software use and some ideas about working with the packages. The issues raised in the example projects are common to many situations. They were referred to at strategic moments in the task-based chapters in order to illustrate some of the successes and predicaments we encounter in our day-to-day work. They demonstrate how researchers in different contexts manipulate software to suit their needs. These researchers selectively and critically used tools to develop their own strategies.

Working as an individual or working in a team raise different issues in terms of using software. Team projects are more complicated and rely heavily on the organizational aspects of the software as well as the dynamics of the team. They also require more planning. The three collaborative projects we feature (CDHPP, NFER and VIA) developed distinctive ways of managing the practical aspects of teamworking using software (see Appendix A). We have not provided a comprehensive guide to working collaboratively here, but have drawn attention to elements of the process which are particularly relevant to teams.

Researchers working individually with software have many more choices and can allow the ways they work with software tools to evolve more organically. However, they may feel more isolated and in need of local support which is not always available. Interviews collected as part of the 'Online support for QDA and CAQDAS' project[1] strongly confirmed gaps in local support. Though the CAQDAS Networking Project is often called upon to help, these interviews illustrate that researchers want to be self-reliant and do not like to 'keep asking for help'.

The rationale of this book, and the philosophy behind the CAQDAS Networking Project (see Appendix D), has always been to supplement the gap in support which was the natural consequence of new technologies emerging during a period when qualitative projects, and qualitative elements in broader research studies, were increasing in number. The CAQDAS Networking Project itself has contributed to a significant growth in the numbers of expert users, but it remains difficult to convert this into institutional support on a local basis. Graham Gibbs's University of Huddersfield initiative in combination with the CAQDAS team at the University of Surrey to provide 'just in time' support seeks to address this issue. The online resource providing information about doing qualitative data analysis (QDA) and using CAQDAS provides easily accessible support (see Appendix D).

CONVERGENCE OF TASKS AND TOOLS: SOFTWARE AS A CONTAINER FOR YOUR WORK

In writing this book we encountered a number of challenges. At the outset our aim was twofold: first, to demystify the field of qualitative software by illustrating the range of packages and tools currently on the market; and second, to illustrate ways in which using software can reflect and enhance the cyclical and iterative process of doing qualitative analysis. What we found, as we wrote the task-based chapters, was that separating tasks creates artificial differentiations. What we actually do when handling qualitative data in software is to shuffle between panes, multitasking with different tools. In a typical five-minute period we might slip from carefully reading and coding the data to using fast exploration tools in order to find similar occurrences of a particular word or phrase, to reviewing what has been coded so far, and to annotating what we see. We jot down insights, references to other work and reminders for follow-up action. It is rare, as in life, that reasoning processes happen in a linear and orderly way, and CAQDAS packages certainly free us from having to be linear. The three main aspects of work – organizing the data, organizing ideas about the data, and developing interpretations about the data and their convergence within the software container – represent the key benefit of using a customized CAQDAS package. This does not happen by chance, however, and it can be difficult to work out how to effectively combine these aspects. We have cross-referenced frequently between tasks to enable and encourage the meshing of different aspects of work.

CLOSENESS TO DATA: INSIDE SOFTWARE AND OUTSIDE IT

In Chapter 5 we alluded to scepticism concerning the use of CAQDAS packages in supporting qualitative data analysis. These are discussed in more detail by Gibbs et al. (2002).

We understand such concerns, but it is also important to challenge the idea that CAQDAS packages 'take the researcher away from the data'. This was raised when these packages first became commercially available and, despite subsequent developments, such concerns persist, especially amongst some experienced qualitative researchers. Fielding and Lee (1998), in their study of CAQDAS users, found some researchers felt closer to their data when working more 'manually'. The feeling is that using a computer will put an artificial barrier between the researcher and the data. Reluctance to change from carefully developed routines and systems is understandable.

Since the Fielding and Lee study, software programs have improved beyond the expectations of early users. In terms of data themselves, the increased range of formats directly handled by software and the improvements in types and presentations of output make conceptual work easier. Key advances in memoing and mapping tools, basic retrieval options and searching possibilities provide the researcher with options that might never have been considered before. In methodological terms, some users would need to place different emphases on certain tools. A narrative analysis of a relatively small amount of data might only make use of annotation and memoing tools. An interpretive approach to a larger dataset might make heavy use of coding devices. The relative role of theory in each project would vary the way codes are created and the directions of travel in the software. One way or another, as we discussed in Chapter 4, software keeps us within touching distance, throughout the analysis, with the fundamentals of information and data.

A CAQDAS package can bring the researcher closer to the data in a variety of ways. This can be true when you are *inside* the software. For example, hyperlinking and annotation tools provide ways of staying close to data without abstracting from them. Software will obviate the need to use highlighter pens and piles of paper whilst coding. However, the variety of output options available allows you to be very close to different combinations of data *outside* the software and *away* from the computer. Paper still has its place in qualitative data analysis, but the computer can help to provide you with the right bits of paper! Tactile contact with printouts is a dimension of work which enables you to see, think about and annotate data in different ways. Often the most insightful thoughts occur at unexpected times, away from the computer, and away from the data.

WORKING WITHIN YOUR COMFORT ZONE: FOCUSED EFFECTIVE USE OF SOFTWARE

We often see researchers using software in very innovative and sophisticated ways. However, we also frequently see projects in which relatively few tools are used, but to great effect. Researchers sometimes worry that they are not using software to its 'full potential', and that this somehow means their analysis is falling short of what is expected. We made the point in Chapter 4 that the use of software can conventionalize data and assumptions about how they should be analysed. We challenge the idea that there is one ideal way of using any CAQDAS package. Such ideas undervalue the usefulness of the software and the ability of the user to make discerning choices. Our central message is that *you* should determine what is useful. There will be ways to do things differently, and tools which you have yet to use. Almost every time we use and teach a package we see an alternative way of using a tool, or learn something new.

NOTE

1 Joint ESRC funded 'Online support for QDA and CAQDAS', G. Gibbs and C. Taylor, University of Huddersfield and A. Lewins and N. Fielding, University of Surrey (http://onlineqda.hud.ac/).

Appendix A
Background and Summary of Example Projects

EXAMPLE 1

Young People's Perceptions Project
Christina Silver (2002)
'The development of school-based sex education in England and Wales and the Netherlands: culture, politics and practice'
Using NUD*IST 4, but worked up in ATLAS.ti5, MAXqda2 and NVivo7 for this book

This project concerns the development and exploration of the cultural politics and practice in school-based sex education in England and Wales and the Netherlands. These countries have experienced significantly different rates of conceptions by 'teenage' women over the last four decades and this provided the policy background to the project. Previous (comparative) research largely considered the effectiveness of school-based sex education in terms of specific aspects, including content, timing and teaching environment, knowledge attained and the inclusion of young men's needs. Here the focus was on the role of wider social, cultural and political influences in understanding historical approaches towards school-based sex education. This interest was largely informed by the researcher's dual English-Dutch nationality. Having lived most of her life in England, she wanted to explore what it was about the Netherlands and about being a young Dutch person which has contributed to the low incidence of unintended pregnancies amongst young women in comparison to England and Wales. School-based sex education was used as the sociological lens through which to do so.

The project was broad in scope and exploratory in nature and did not adhere to any formal set of empirical or analytic guidelines. It did not take place in a theoretical vacuum, however. For example, the areas of interest and the nature of the initial research questions reflect a social or cultural constructionist perspective in that an underlying assumption was that the analysis of a country's social, cultural and political history can add to the understanding of one particular area of policy development, implementation and effectiveness. The research design evolved as the project proceeded. Large amounts of various forms of primary and secondary data were used including primary data collected through questionnaires, focus groups and interviews, and secondary data derived from various forms of documentary evidence (see Chapter 2).

The variety and nature of the data necessitated a flexible and open approach to the analysis. As described more fully in Chapters 5 and 6, the different forms of data were handled and analysed differently according to both their inherent nature and their function within the project as a whole. Towards the latter stages, theoretical writings were revisited in order to further contextualize the growing interpretation (see Chapter 9). The most influential of these was Giddens's (1984) 'theory of structuration' (see Chapter 10). Whilst the interpretation presented in the final written thesis had been developed by the close analysis of the data and was very much grounded in a young person's perspective, it was informed by external theoretical ideas and understandings.

EXAMPLE 2

'The relocation of Arkwright'
Gerda Speller (2000)
Using NUD*IST 4

Arkwright was a north Derbyshire coal mining village which narrowly avoided a major explosion in 1988 when methane gas was seeping into the houses from the local disused coal mine. The 100-year-old village of 177 households was blighted. In 1990 British Coal Opencast put forward a plan to opencast mine the area. Together with the North East Derbyshire District Council a plan was agreed to build a new village nearby at a cost of £15 million in exchange for planning permission to opencast, thereby also providing a solution to the ongoing methane problem.

The main purposes of the study were to identify the psychosocial processes involved in detaching oneself from a place and forming new attachments to a future place, and to explore the relationship to individual and community identity. *Place attachment* (emotional bond with place) is a concept within environmental psychology that has a clear link with identity theories within social psychology. Thus the theoretical framework for this study was provided by Breakwell's (1986; 1992) *identity process theory* (IPT) as it integrates change and dynamic temporal processes (see Chapter 6).

The unusually high compensation offered (terraced houses replaced with semi-detached houses) resulted in an imposed transition from a working class environment to a middle class environment. An additional aim of this work was to observe whether this transition was a positive or a negative experience for residents and whether it was seen as a facilitator or an inhibitor to forming place attachment. As there was little empirical work on place attachment, it was hoped that this study would ultimately serve to refine the current theories.

The study was longitudinal over a six-year period (1992–8). The in-depth data were collected at five points in time: three data waves before the relocation and two after the relocation of the residents. A total of 259 interviews were transcribed and loaded into the NUD*IST 4 database, resulting in 181,147 text units (lines) that formed the basis for coding, comparing, creating categories and memo writing across all five time phases (T1–T5).

Since there is little empirical work on place attachment, the major variations in participants' behaviours and perceptions were grounded in the data and had not been envisaged before the completion of the analysis. This, to begin with, resulted in many free nodes that through the process of comparison were later categorized. The next stage in the analysis involved printing out participants' responses in this concentrated form. This highlighted complexities within a category, including nuances or differences which frequently resulted in splitting the category or merging it with others. This process of searching for relationships between themes and emerging patterns also brought to the fore what Opie (1992) calls 'multiple realities' or inconsistencies in participants' accounts. These often represented or were an indication of the process of adaptation to a new environment and were therefore considered an important element for inclusion in the analysis. The final main categories for place attachment emerged as 'sense of security'; 'sense of autonomy'; 'desire and ability to engage in appropriation'; 'optimal levels of internal and external stimulation'; and 'place congruence'.

In terms of individual and collective identity and its relationship to place (Speller et al., 2002), the analysis was informed by the intention to investigate the presence of the IPT principles – 'distinctiveness for the person', 'continuity across time and situation', 'self-esteem' (feeling of personal worth or social value), and 'self-efficacy' (a person's perceived ability to function in an environment) – and how the spatial change was associated with a change in the salience of these principles. Hence this part of the analysis was theoretical and confirmatory. Seeing the appropriate quotations in this concentrated format made it clear that the previous collective identity had changed to a much greater individual identity by T5, with a concomitant change in the residents' sense of community.

EXAMPLE 3

'Video intervention/prevention assessment-Transitions (VIA)'
Centre on Media and Child Health, Children's Hospital Boston (VIA 1994 onwards)
Rich, Chalfen, Szymczak and Patashnick (in progress)
www.viaproject.org viaproject@childrens.harvard.edu
Using NVivo

Video intervention/prevention assessment (VIA) developed from the observation of a considerable gap in communication between dieticians and young patients with chronic health conditions. Michael Rich MD MPH drew on his previous experience as a film maker to devise an innovative and powerful way of bridging these gaps. VIA utilizes audiovisual media to reveal and communicate aspects of living with a chronic-illness as a young person which cannot be achieved through traditional clinician–patient interactions. The techniques employed comprise an innovative methodology applicable to a range of socially mediated situations or conditions. VIA provides very useful examples of how software can support complex cross-disciplinary, team-based and longitudinal projects. It also provides a proven method for analysing vast amounts of audiovisual material.

VIA lends camcorders to children and adolescents with a range of chronic medical conditions (including asthma, obesity, spina bifida, sickle cell disease, cystic fibrosis and perinatally acquired HIV). Participants are given a very wide brief, simply being asked to 'teach your doctor about your life and your condition'. They document their day-to-day experiences of living with their illness in the form of 'video diaries'. This allows them the freedom to express personal experiences, feelings and responses in their own terms. The resultant video is both detailed and powerful, with participants creating up to 150 hours of video each.

Such vast amounts of video require a systematic analytic approach. The quantity of video generated as well as VIA's emphasis on life in context means it is not feasible to analyse the video frame by frame. In addition, when VIA began there were no suitable software packages available to support direct analysis of video. The team has therefore developed a unique analytic method which until 1999, when they began using QSR NVivo, was carried out manually. Informed by ethnography, participant observation and visual anthropology, VIA's analysis process draws on principles of grounded theory to generate themes which unify participants' illness experiences. Prior to coding, master copies of each participant's videos are generated and each frame of tape is assigned a unique numerical identifier. This allows precise location of specific audiovisual data for analysis.

Logging is the first analytic stage which involves documenting what is observable on the videotape, but does not constitute a full verbatim transcription. Rather, it results in a detailed but simplified description of the video's content to allow scenes, situations or concepts to be located easily and quickly. Each log is structured using different styles of text to depict certain key aspects of the audiovisual narrative. Completed logs are exported from MS Word to NVivo, where the ability to recognize textual styles in up to nine levels of heading is used very effectively to structure the complex logs and enable linking to particularly pertinent video clips. The logs are then analysed through theoretical frameworks of medicine, public health, psychology, clinical social work and anthropology. The coding approach combines deductive and inductive strategies (see Chapter 5), and the team has developed an unusual but highly effective way to make use of coding scheme structures to manage the process (see Chapter 6).

EXAMPLE 4

'Health and social care needs of people over 50'
East Surrey Health Authority: ESHA (2000)
Using ATLAS.ti4

The research aimed to find out the present and future health and social care needs of people aged over 50 living in an affluent area where many older people have unmet needs. The research was based on postal questionnaires, one-to-one interviews and three focus groups, one with health and social care professionals and two with representatives of the community and community organizations.

A researcher was commissioned (post data collection) to pull the dominant themes from transcripts of focus groups, each composed of end users or relatives/carers and professionals or providers of services. The client had requested that ATLAS.ti (version 4) be used to assist in the process, and delivery of the results in the form of an awareness raising presentation of both the software and the output. At this stage the client had no theoretical concerns and simply needed to be given a list of the themes and the segments of data supporting them. Word frequency information was also requested. Further analysis and writing up would be based on the delivered material. Each focus group covered their main concerns which had been flagged up at the beginning of each focus group's discussion (e.g. day care, health care, transport, personal safety).

Conclusions and recommendations are grouped under the following headings:

- information about local services
- housing for independent living
- expanding the role of Cobham Centre
- the role of health and medical centres
- care-related needs and carers' needs
- hospice care
- personal safety
- transport
- consultation on service development.

EXAMPLE 5

'Curriculum progression in the arts'
National Foundation for Educational Research (NFER): Taggart, Whitby and Sharp (2004)
Using MAXqda

The National Foundation for Educational Research (NFER) is the largest independent educational research institution in Europe. It is a not-for-profit organization and a registered charity.

Since 1946 the NFER has been working to equip decision makers, managers and practitioners with the most innovative thinking, practical research and responsive assessment programmes to underpin the drive towards excellence in education and lifelong learning. The aim of the Foundation is to improve education and training, nationally and internationally, by undertaking research, development and dissemination activities and by providing information services.

Teams of researchers undertake around 200 research projects every year and their work spans all sectors of education, from preschool to lifelong learning. The majority of the Foundation's work (about 69 per cent of income) is funded through securing research, evaluation, test development and information service contracts from government departments, charitable organizations and public agencies in the UK and abroad.

These factors – the size of the NFER, the number of projects undertaken, and the funding mechanisms – led to the choice of MAXqda as the most appropriate qualitative data analysis software package for the Foundation. MAXqda is a very accessible package, and as such has a low lead-in time and is user-friendly for the wide range of staff working at the NFER as well as their sponsors, as is demonstrated in the project described here.

'Curriculum progression in the arts' is a thematic probe commissioned by the Qualifications and Curriculum Authority (QCA) as part of the International Review of Curriculum and Assessment Frameworks Archive (INCA). Thematic probes are comparative education reports providing snapshot cross-national data on specific subject areas and themes of interest across the INCA countries. The project aimed to define the content, progression and assessment of the arts curriculum in the compulsory phase of education from an international perspective. In order to gather data, a questionnaire was emailed to 41 educational specialists in 23 countries/states. Twenty-one countries/states replied electronically and the data were exported directly into MAXqda. Electronic versions of curriculum documentation were also entered into the software.

In this format, the research team (one researcher, one senior researcher and one principal researcher) were all able to access the project data and contribute to the coding. After top-level coding was completed, the research team met with the sponsors. At this meeting the research team explained the basics of MAXqda, presented the interim findings using the software and discussed the coding and analysis. By the end of the meeting, the sponsors themselves were able to contribute to labelling and coding the data. The ability of 'lay people' to understand and use the software was one of the key features that made the use of MAXqda on this project so successful (Taggart et al., 2004).

EXAMPLE 6

'Understanding knowledge construction in online courses'
Shalni Gulati (2006)
Using Atlas.ti5

ATLAS.ti (version 5.0) was used in the doctorate research that investigated how postgraduate learners constructed meaning in online and blended courses. The research questions and methodology were situated in the constructivist paradigm. The method used George Kelly's (1970) repertory grid technique to elicit 29 learners' construction processes during online and blended courses. Data collected included audiotaped interviews, repertory (numerical) grids saved in Excel, factor analysis correlation data output (quantitative analysis results), graphical representation of learning dimensions saved in PowerPoint, and metaphorical pictorial representation of individual learning spaces.

The aim was to explore individual differences in learning constructions and to identify emerging themes using the grounded theory principles (Strauss and Corbin, 1998). The textual, numerical and visual (graphical representations and learning metaphoric representations) data were imported into ATLAS.ti (version 5.0) and assigned as primary documents. The textual and visual data were coded, and deconstructed using memos, quotations, comments, links, families, co-occurrences, query tool, output and network views in ATLAS.ti. As the coding proceeded, prefixes were used to classify closely related codes. This classification helped to ask different questions through co-occurrence outputs for families, prefixed codes and individual codes (see Chapter 6).

There were limitations in using ATLAS.ti to code numerical data. The numerical data could be imported to ATLAS but it was not possible to code and develop networks of individual rows and columns. In the repertory grid method, such coding would be useful to connect the quantified data with the emerging qualitative meaning.

The query tool and outputs were particularly useful in drawing out the similarities and differences in knowledge construction for online and blended learners. They helped to identify main themes which surfaced as an emerging theory of online learning.

EXAMPLE 7

'Evaluation of flexible thinking workshops'
Centre for the Development of Healthcare Policy and Practice (CDHPP), University of Leeds: Haynes, O'Neill, McNichol and Silver (2005)
Using ATLAS.ti version 5

The Centre for the Development of Healthcare Policy and Practice (CDHPP) supports individuals, teams and healthcare organizations in delivering high quality services. It offers a range of evidence-based programmes designed to meet the challenges of health-related services by promoting different ways of working. Programmes are offered in the areas of empowerment, leadership, practice development, and enterprise and innovation. Included in the last category are 'flexible thinking' workshops which introduce strategies to tackle old tasks in new ways. These include mind mapping and speed reading techniques as well as developing ways of being more creative and innovative at work. CDHPP constantly evaluates and revises its programmes to ensure they represent research in the field and that they are relevant to those who take part. This project was part of the evaluation process, focusing specifically on the flexible thinking set of workshops.

Data were collected from workshop participants immediately after a workshop in the form of 'reaction sheets' and again three months later in the form of an open-ended questionnaire. The data collection tools and analysis framework were jointly developed by the CDHPP evaluation team and the independent researcher. The need to generate focused information which would feed back into further programme and workshop developments informed the project design. As discussed in Chapter 5, this necessitated analysis on two levels. First, conceptual and thematic analysis across the question-based structure was undertaken. This involved a grounded approach to code generation, highlighting organizational barriers and enablers to creativity and innovation in the workplace. Second, a relatively deductive and quantitatively oriented analysis was undertaken according to the questions asked. This allowed for workshop objectives, such as whether participants felt the intended outcomes had been achieved, to be interrogated. The analysis was undertaken using ATLAS.ti5 by the researcher, in close collaboration with the CDHPP evaluation team. While the researcher was undertaking the analysis and was responsible for writing the final report, the CDHPP team have experience of ATLAS.ti5 and therefore were involved in the process.

Appendix B
Keyboard Shortcuts for ATLAS.ti5, MAXqda2 and NVivo7

MAIN MENUS AND SUBCOMMANDS COMMON TO ALL THREE PACKAGES

- To open any main menu: press Alt + the first (or underlined) initial of the menu name.
- Within each main menu: on the keyboard, select the first (or underlined) initial for each command.
- In MAXqda2 and NVivo7, the relevant initial is underlined.

SOFTWARE-SPECIFIC SHORTCUTS

Not all are listed. You will find more in individual software manuals in the relevant software function sections.

ATLAS.ti5

There is no specific section referring to shortcuts in the ATLAS.ti5 manual since there are very many uses of e.g. the Ctrl key at different moments to vary the way commands are executed. In the manual, shortcuts are provided in context with descriptions of separate functions. See the help menu or the manual at http://www.atlasti.com/manual.html

Ctrl + S	Saves work
Ctrl + O	Opens an HU file
Ctrl + left mouse click	Deselects any item selected in a list/manager pane or network
Alt + C + O	Allows open coding on selected text
Alt + C + F	Creates free node (see other main menu combinations)
Alt +	See above for all other main menu combinations
P	Plays a video/sound file (if open in PD window)

Spacebar	Pauses play (as above)
Ctrl + RB	Shows links to select data
Ctrl + double left mouse click	Clears a filter: e.g. in Filter field on a manager window to clear a filter
Ctrl + F	Activates text search
Ctrl + N	In a network: selects linked neighbours to an already selected node
Ctrl + A	In a network: selects all nodes in the network
Ctrl + I	In a network: deselects all (if all nodes selected) or inverts selection if some nodes are selected
Ctrl + Shift + Z	In a network: undo import neighbours
Ctrl + Z	In a network: undo last positioning/layout
Ctrl + 3	In a network: switches on or cancels shadow appearance on selected node
Ctrl	Holding Ctrl key down when selecting a code, quotation, memo or document and choosing *Open network* will list all networks in which the relevant object is included

MAXqda2

See the '?' menu: from the appendix of the online manual.

Ctrl + W	When text is selected, this will open up a window for entering a new code
Alt + N	When in the Code System menu, this creates a new code
Ctrl + L	When data are selected, this creates a link point in the text, in order to link up to another text selection using hyperlinks
Ctrl + I	Creates an *in vivo* code from a text selection in Text Browser
Ctrl + Q	Codes selected text in Text Browser to code which appears in codes toolbar
Ctrl + T	Creates and opens a new text in edit mode in the Text Browser, ready to be edited
Ctrl + V	Creates a new attribute when in the Attributes table pane
Ctrl + B	Open the Code Matrix Browser
Ctrl + O	Opens the Code Relation Browser

NVivo7

Shortcuts are listed in the online help.

Ctrl + A	Select all items in a list or text in a source, depending on the context
Ctrl + C	Copy selected text

Ctrl + F	Find text in a source or a node
Ctrl + G	Go to specified heading level, paragraph, *See Also* link or annotation, in a source or a node
Ctrl + H	Replace text in a source
Ctrl + N	Create a new project
Ctrl + O	Open an existing project
Ctrl + P	Print selected item
Ctrl + S	Save the project
Ctrl + V	Paste selected text
Ctrl + X	Cut selected text
Ctrl + Z	Undo previous action (up to five levels)
Ctrl + Shift + A	Add a new item (folder, source, node etc.) depending on the context
Ctrl + Shift + C	Open the Casebook for the project
Ctrl + Shift + I	Import documents or Casebook depending on the context
Ctrl + 1	Open Sources group in Navigation View
Ctrl + 2	Open Nodes group in Navigation View
Ctrl + 3	Open Sets group in Navigation View
Ctrl + 4	Open Queries group in Navigation View
Ctrl + 5	Open Models group in Navigation View
Ctrl + 6	Open Links group in Navigation View
Ctrl + 7	Open Classifications folder in Navigation View
Ctrl + 8	Show all folders in Navigation View
Ctrl + Enter	Enter a carriage return (make a new line) in text fields such as *Descriptions* and annotations in the *Annotations* tab
F1	Open online help
F5	Refresh
Alt + F1	Hide Navigation View

We recommend these sections are read in conjunction with Chapter 1.

ATLAS.ti5

ATLAS.ti was initially developed at the Technical University of Berlin as an interdisciplinary collaborative project between the psychology department, computer scientists, linguists and future users (1989–92). The prototype was then further developed by Thomas Muhr, and the company ATLAS.ti Scientific Software Development GmbH, formed in 2004, continues to develop and support the software.

Here we review version 5 of ATLAS.ti. Refer to chapters in the main body of the book for illustrations and step-by-step instructions about various aspects of ATLAS.ti5. ATLAS.ti5 is a large and flexible software program: we do not attempt to make this a comprehensive catalogue of all its tools and very many ways of working.

Minimum system specifications (recommended by developer)

MS Windows 98 or later (Windows 2000 or XP recommended); RAM 64 MB (minimum), 256 MB (recommended); 25 MB free disk space (minimum), 45 MB (recommended).

Structure of work in ATLAS.ti5

ATLAS.ti5 functions using what we call an 'external' database system. The Hermeneutic Unit (HU) is the file containing project information. Data files (documents) are held externally, assigned and then referred to from within ATLAS.ti5. Functions operate from main menus and four dropdown menus: Documents, Quotations, Codes and Memos. These can be accessed through floating manager views (see Figure 3.2).

Data types and formats in ATLAS.ti5

- *Textual formats*: text only (.txt), rich text format (.rtf) or MS Word (.doc). Rich text format (RTF) documents can be marked and edited. Other objects (such as graphics, tables etc.) can be embedded into RTF files. MS Word documents cannot be edited after being assigned to the HU.
- *Multimedia formats*: digital video, sound and graphic files can be directly assigned to the project and handled in similar ways as textual formats. Formats include: .jpg, .jpeg, .gif, .bmp, .wav, .avi, .mpg, .mpeg, .mp3. See developer information for complete list (see also Chapter 2).

Closeness to data and interactivity in ATLAS.ti5

- *Quotations*: segments of data can be selected and listed separately as quotations which may subsequently be coded, but they can also be treated independently. The independence of quotations is a central functionality of the software and enables flexible text-level work, including hyperlinks (see below and Chapter 4). Whether coded or not, navigating around quotations always locates them in the source context. Quotations can be created in multimedia data, enabling individual clips of sound or video to be played in isolation, annotated, coded, hyperlinked etc.
- *The margin view* provides an overview of embedded quotations, codes, hyperlinks and memos and is fully interactive. For example, highlighting an object (code/hyperlink/memo) in the margin displays the linked quotation. The content of objects can be accessed and edited from the margin view. Interactivity is excellent between all project objects (documents, quotations, codes, memos and networks) (see Chapters 7, 8 and 10). Objects appearing in the margin can be filtered according to groupings (families) and textual documents with margin view can be printed effectively.

Coding scheme in ATLAS.ti5

- *Non-hierarchical code listing*: in its main listing and structure, the coding scheme is non-hierarchical.
- *Families of codes* enable several codes to be grouped together. Any code can belong to any number of families. Filter work to a code family to view or generate output on an aspect of the coding scheme. Create *super families* from combinations of families.
- *Hierarchical or semantic links* between codes can be used to impose structure on the coding scheme and express relationships between concepts, themes etc. Links can be viewed in a network or the Object Explorer but not in the main codes list. Coded quotations can be searched for based on the properties of links (see Chapters 6, 7 and 12).

Coding processes in ATLAS.ti5

- *Drag and drop* codes onto clips in multimedia documents in the same way as onto highlighted text.
- *Shortcut icons*: there are a range of coding shortcut icons, and multiple codes can be applied to a data segment simultaneously.
- *Functional margin display*: codes and memos can be edited and accessed from the margin (see Chapter 7).

Basic retrieval of coded data in ATLAS.ti5

- *Navigate around coded date* to view quotations in source context. Textual and graphic quotations are highlighted, audio/video quotations are played back. Filtering to families of codes and/or documents focuses retrieval. Coded segments which can be output to one file lifts segments out of the context (see Chapter 8).
- *Margin display* provides overview of how documents are coded in their entirety. Hyperlinks and memos linked to quotations also appear in the margin. Vary the objects display in the margin (see Chapter 8).

Data organization in ATLAS.ti5

Document families allow whole documents to be organized into subsets. Tabular information can be imported to quickly organize documents into families. Whole or parts of files can also be categorized by coding. Family functionality replicates that for organizing codes and memos (see Chapter 11).

Writing tools in ATLAS.ti5

ATLAS.ti5 allows the user to write in many different places.

- *Memos* are a main object at the same level as documents, quotations and codes. The content of several memos can easily be outputted into one file. Links created between memos and other objects are functional in that opening a network on a memo will include any other linked items (see Chapters 4 and 9).
- *Comments* can be attached to documents, codes, quotations, networks etc.

Searching and interrogating the database in ATLAS.ti5

- *Filtering* to combinations of families is an easy way to begin interrogating the dataset (see 'basic retrieval of coded data' above).
- *The Query Tool* enables coded segments to be searched for based on a number of standard Boolean, semantic and proximity operators.

- *Super codes* are saved queries listed as codes. They can be rerun on data that are coded subsequently to constituent codes in the query, thereby enabling up-to-date navigation around complex combinations of codes. Snapshot super codes to capture a search at a specific point in time. Super codes can be combined with other codes in the formulation of a more complex 'query'.
- *Cooccurrence Explorer* is a hierarchically expanding list based on primary documents and codes and the direct associations of each. Documents co-occur with codes, and codes expand to show where they sit in quotations. Similarly, codes co-occurring with other codes in the data are listed, and those codes when expanded co-occur with quotations. Provides two different ways to approach an exploration of what has been done so far at data level – a good way to see potentially close connections.
- *View co-occurring codes* in a network springs from the above tool and provides a graphic view of the code Cooccurrence Explorer. Any code which overlaps or coincides with the original selected code is imported into the network.
- *The Object Crawler* allows searching for strings (e.g. words or phrases) in the entire HU (documents, codes, memos, networks and comments). Finds are interactively linked to source context.
- *Certain relational links* created between codes function as semantic search operators in the Query Tool, retrieving e.g. everything connected to a code via a series of unidirectional transitive links (see Chapters 8, 11 and 12).
- *The Word Cruncher* counts the occurrence of words across the whole dataset, or a single document. Results can be saved into an exported spreadsheet file or pasted into a memo (see Chapter 4).
- *Auto coding* processes provide immediate contact to the searched-for word or phrase in its surrounding context. Several different units of context can be coded around each find, including word, sentence, paragraphs separated by single hard carriage returns, and paragraphs separated by multiple hard carriage returns (see Chapter 11).

Linking devices in ATLAS.ti5

Linking is very flexible in that almost any project object can be linked to any other. Linking is usually functional in that, when opening a network on one of those linked objects, other objects it is linked to are automatically imported. Effective hyperlinking between points in the data is enabled due to the centrality of the quotation. This allows the tracking of sequence or process within or between data files. Relationships between hyperlinked quotations can also be created (see Chapters 4 and 10).

Mapping using the networking tool in ATLAS.ti5

Functional links between objects can be created in the networking tool. Hyperlinks between quotations can be created and visualized in networks. Links between any codes are functional, in that wherever two or more of the same linked codes appear in any network view they will be linked in the same way (see Chapter 10 and Figure 10.1).

Output in ATLAS.ti5

- *Coded output* is distinguished by labelling of each segment with code, source document and paragraph numbers. Output can be varied to produce summaries – lists of codes and how they are connected to other codes. Multiple codes and their quotations/segments can be exported into one file in a clearly labelled format. Vary output to produce summaries including lists of codes and how they are connected to other codes.
- *Tabular output* displaying frequency of codes by documents can be filtered to show comparisons between document subsets and code families. Both varieties can be exported e.g. into Word or Excel, or printed. Word frequency tables can be exported to Excel or run in the software (although they are not interactively connected to source context) (see Chapter 7).
- *Network output* is enabled via the clipboard or by saving as a graphic file.
- *Project export*: the whole HU can be exported into an SPSS, XML or HTML file. XML representation can be converted into a wide variety of other representations. Outputting the HU allows team members or interested non-software users to navigate around XML generated reports from a webpage.

Teamworking in ATLAS.ti5

Separate team members can share data files due to the external database system. The Merge Tool allows many different models and choices in merging HUs.

Comments on ATLAS.ti5

- *ATLAS.ti5 offers good flexibility* and provides many different ways of working to suit different purposes. Functionality goes far beyond code and retrieve, yet if that is all the user needs it is very easy to get to that point. The flexibility provided by the quotation structure and the ability to hyperlink between places in the data is useful. If used extensively the user must devise ways of managing these linkages.
- *The external database* makes the process of saving and moving the HU and data more difficult to manage than other packages, although the Copy Bundle function in the Tools menu makes this process easier (see Chapter 3). If editing data files within the HU, care needs to be taken in the management and diligent saving of changes. Difficulties may relate to the synchronization of changes between data files and the HU. Working with MS Word files would offer more protection since these are not able to be edited inside the software (and, of course, must not be edited outside ATLAS.ti5). New users especially need to be aware of the implications of the external database.
- *The quotation structure* is rather different to other software and has implications for the way some searches might work later. For instance a search for all data *not* coded by a code would produce quotations not coded, not all the text where the code does not appear. This may not matter except to a researcher wanting a proportionate idea of volume of data coded or not coded in a certain way.

- *The main working code list*: the Code Manager does not have a functioning hierarchical structure to choose from, though it is possible to create code connections and collections of a hierarchical nature. To some users this is an attraction because they feel restricted by hierarchies. To others it lacks choice since hierarchical structures can provide a way to systematically 'tidy up' a codes list. It can be argued that a cosmetically prefixed alphabetic list of codes can keep the user in better contact with all codes in such a quasi-hierarchy than a hierearchical system which hides subcodes away. It would certainly be a disciplining factor against the creation of too many 'levels' where loss of contact with codes can be a problem.
- *The super codes function* is an excellent way to pose and store questions or hypotheses in order to test ideas and connections. In comparison to similar functions in other software, super codes provide the easiest way to be reminded of earlier 'hunches' and to rerun simple or complex queries. Every query has the potential to be saved as a super code. The presence of super codes in the codes list is a constant reminder of potential questions to be asked, or previously posed queries which might need to be rerun – facilitating continuity and rigour.
- *Filtering* provides easy ways to begin interrogating the dataset. The Query Tool is easy to use for simple searches. Some search operators have very precise parameters and the user must be aware of these to interpret results and their implications reliably. However, the Query Tool lacks the ability to integrate searches for text with searches for coded data.
- *The co-occurring codes function* is very useful, particularly for identifying other more complex questions or trends in the data. ATLAS.ti5 led the way with this major enhancement in interrogating tools.
- *The network tool is very flexible* in that any object can be linked to anything else. The software remembers the links between any two objects, so the user needs to be sure the connection remains relevant, or use proxy objects (codes or memos) to illustrate an abstract model.
- *The Object Crawler* provides a way to search the whole project and helps particularly in the recovery of notes in comments which are dispersed in many places around the software.
- *The ability to export the software project* to SPSS, HTML or XML is useful and the HTML export is the simplest way to allow the non-user in a team to navigate around a project and see its major 'workings'. This facility is extremely useful in team situations and the presentation is user-friendly.

HyperRESEARCH 2.6

HyperRESEARCH was first developed in 1990 by Sharlene Hesse-Biber, T. Scott Kinder and Paul Dupuis in Boston, Massachusetts, USA. From 1991 HyperResearch has been developed by ResearchWare Inc. who continue to develop and support the software. In 2005 ResearchWare Inc. launched HyperTRANSCRIBE, a tool for transcribing audio and video files. Both HyperRESEARCH and HyperTRANSCRIBE are available for Mac and Windows platforms. This chapter reviews version 2.6 of HyperRESEARCH.

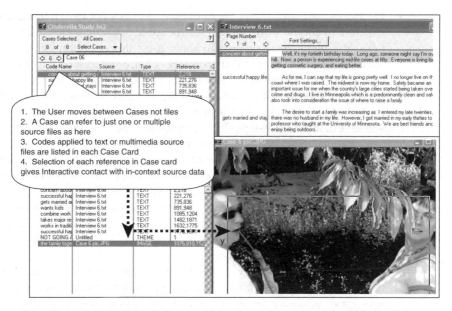

Figure C.1   HyperRESEARCH 2.6: the user interface, the case card and hyperlinks to text and multimedia data

Minimum system specifications (recommended by developer)

Cross-platform Mac and Windows, MS Windows 95 or later, Mac OS8 or later; RAM 64 MB; 5 MB disk space.

Structure of work in HyperRESEARCH 2.6

The project as a whole is called a *study*. The database is 'external' in that source files are accessed by the study, but not contained within it. There is a *case structure*: a study comprises *cases* which can refer to one source data file or many. A file may belong to several different cases. The case structure functionality is quite different from other packages reviewed here. For example, the *case card* lists coded references for each case separately. Functions operate from main menu options. Panes open as free-standing windows which can be resized and moved around the workspace as required (Figure C.1).

Data types and formats in HyperRESEARCH 2.6

- *Textual formats*: text only.
- *Multimedia formats*: digital video, sound and graphic files can be directly assigned to the study and treated in similar ways as textual formats accepted multimedia file

formats include .jpeg, .wav, .avi, .mov, .mpeg, .mp3. See developer information for complete list.

Closeness to data and interactivity in HyperRESEARCH 2.6

Font settings (typeface and size) can be customized in the text source file window. Contact between the study and source data is created by coded references in a case card. Hyperlinks connect annotations, case card coded references etc. to source file position (one click) whether the file is textual or multimedia (e.g. the coded video clip will replay as the reference is selected). The coded margin display is interactive, and reports containing references to coded passages are hyperlinked back to source while viewed in the software.

Coding scheme in HyperRESEARCH 2.6

The coding scheme is not hierarchical and codes are listed alphabetically. Codes cannot be grouped except by cosmetic labelling.

Coding processes in HyperRESEARCH 2.6

- *Coding data at a case card*: whilst the correct case card plus source file is selected (on view), codes are assigned to selected text by menu selection. The coding reference appears in the case card of the case that is selected (Figure C.1).
- *Double clicking on the code* from the codes list assigns code to selected data. The code appears in the margin of the file. One click on the code in the margin highlights codes text, and the relevant reference in the case card, but this is the extent of interactivity of the margin view.
- *Coding multimedia data*: codes can be applied to parts of graphic files, or to clips of audio/video files. Coded multimedia segments are listed in the corresponding case card in the same way as textual quotations. Double clicking on a coded reference in the case card replays the coded clip. Hyperlinked coded references to multimedia files will appear in generated reports, but not the actual clip of e.g. the audiovisual file. While in the software, however, clicking on any hyperlinked coded reference in the report will replay the clip.

Basic retrieval of coded data in HyperRESEARCH 2.6

- *Select cases* based on various simple to more complex criteria, e.g. on the basis of the case name or the presence, absence on co-occurrence of codes appearing in a case. View coded segments in context by selecting individual coded references in the case card.

- *Select codes*: filter to view only codes that have been selected by name of code, or by criteria, e.g. a code's presence or absence in a case, or its inclusion with other codes in a case.

Data organization in HyperRESEARCH 2.6

Basic organization happens at the level of the case. Whole or parts of files can also be categorized by coding which will enable selections and filtering on the basis of 'organizational' codes appearing e.g. in case together with other codes.

Writing tools in HyperRESEARCH 2.6

Comments can be attached to coded references on each case card, and these annotations are flagged in a column next to the coded reference. Annotations are hyperlinked (one click) to both the text of the annotation and the source file position. In reverse, clicking on a code in the margin opens up any annotation at that coded reference in the case card. They can be included in output reports on coded data etc.

Searching and interrogating the dataset in HyperRESEARCH 2.6

- *Selection of cases or codes*: 'searching' happens in the software by a process of filtering or selecting combinations of codes and/or cases. Codes can be selected by name, by criteria (inclusion, overlaps etc), by code map or by specifying and running a hypothesis (see below). Coded references listed in case cards reflect the selection. Similarly, cases can be selected on the basis of name, code or criteria; cases which do not satisfy the specified criteria are filtered out of view within the software. However, in a subsequent report based on the selection, each page of the report, if sorted by case, announces the presence or absence of the selections in each case. Typically a complex search might be incrementally based on several selections, a selection of codes applied to an already filtered case list or vice versa.
- *Hypothesis Testing Tool* works similarly to the selection of codes or cases but allows the user to formalize and save searches. Test the existence or coexistence of codes in cases to do two things: (1) to add a higher concept (*theme*) to whole cases; and (2) to build rules in order to progressively test elements of a whole hypothesis. Hypotheses can be saved and rerun on newly coded data. Themes applied to cases at each rule state do not act like new codes in terms of hyperlinkages to source text, but act as filters to allow navigation through cases in which they do appear (or do not appear) and can act as criteria for building retrieval, reports or further hypotheses.
- *Searching by applying code map*: the code map view allows the creation of connections between codes. Individual or linked codes can be selected from the code map to

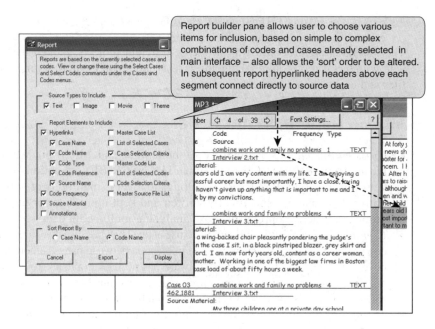

Figure C.2   HyperRESEARCH 2.6: retrieval and reporting in reports, hyperlinked to source text

retrieve coded data segments. For example, select all codes within one, two or more levels of connectivity (i.e.1 = immediately connected to selected code, 2 = connected at one remove etc.). This then shows which cases, if any, have any of the codes defined by the *Apply* operation.

- *Auto coding* allows searching for words or phrases and for resulting 'hits' to be coded. Context around hits can be coded to include specified numbers of words or characters before and after hits, or the whole file. Sentences are not recognized. Search settings can be saved and reloaded (and amended) for future searches.

Output in HyperRESEARCH 2.6

- *Reports of coded retrieval* are initially viewed within the software and any included data segments are hyperlinked back to source files (Figure C.2). The report builder includes a large range of options for inclusion and is always based on the current status of selection in software on codes/cases. Output can be ordered by case or code. Reports can be exported as text only files.
- *Report parameters*: the way a report is specified can be saved and loaded again. The information saved includes the original code and case selections, as well as the information you wish to be included in the report.
- *Code matrix*: code frequency across cases can be exported to e.g. Excel.
- *Code map* (only one editable map currently possible) can be exported into MS Word.

Teamworking in HyperRESEARCH 2.6

There is no straightforward way to merge different projects, though the developers can help with this if it is required. Hypothesis tests and report (search) settings can be saved as files and easily shared between studies.

Comments on HyperRESEARCH 2.6

- *Cross platform*: the availability of both Mac and Microsoft Windows versions means HyperRESEARCH (and HyperTRANSCRIBE) are options for a wide number of users. HyperRESEARCH belongs to a very small body of software for qualitative data analysis specifically written and kept up to date for the Mac user. It is often an attractive option for those analyzing multimedia data.
- *User interface*: the software is simple to use at one level because there are few possible windows to have on display. There is good interaction between panes, although some dialogue boxes are quite step by step. The software has no backdrop/background so the interface does not obscure other non-minimized applications: this can be a nuisance. Unlike other software packages there are a very limited number of ways to do the same thing.
- *The unit of the analysis* is the case, not the file: this may appeal to some users. Any number of files (or just one) can be referenced to a case (or to any number of cases). This means files are not 'hard wired' to cases, so that when in coding mode the user must always be aware what case is open so that the coding for a file goes to the correct case card. This can be tricky. The restriction to text only format files for textual data is a bit dated, but then not many software packages allow the direct analysis of both text and multimedia.
- *Multimedia data and text*: one of very few packages (ATLAS.ti5 is another) which integrates direct analysis of multimedia and textual data, and as such it has a special value.
- *The hypothesis tester and the 'themes'*, which can then be assigned to cases as a result of testing, provide an understandable and clearly visible way of categorizing cases by higher concepts. The fact that further hypothesis tests can include these 'themes' as criteria for selection underlines the importance of understanding how, at this stage, the case increasingly becomes the unit of analysis (though of course you may only have one file in each case). Applying themes to coded segments can be a useful way of grouping codes and can be used effectively; in combination with the code map. This way of handling incremental analysis is rather different than in the other software reviewed here.
- *The report builder* is easy and useful. The user has complete control about how information is included in a report. Reports clearly label coded segments which are hyperlinked to source text (one click). This is the same whether the coded segment is included in the report or only the reference to the segment is listed as in multimedia. This is useful as it provides a broad overview of coded data whilst maintaining easy access to source context. It is important to be aware that the contents of the windows and the report builder, and therefore the contents of reports, reflect the current code and/or case selection. Inclusion of this detail in a report is important; and, because the incremental process of selection is sometimes complex, being able to save the settings of reports is beneficial.

- *Moving the study*: there is no simple way to 'pack up' all the elements of the study (i.e. the study file and also all the source files) if, for instance, you wish to move the files to another computer. If this is required it is important to practise early on and develop a workable protocol for safely moving work.

MAXqda2

This description includes MAXDictio (add-on content analysis feature) and MAX Maps (add-on visual mapping tool).

MAXqda2 is the latest in a software stream originally developed by Udo Kuckartz in order to manage political discourse data on the environment. Its application has widened to multiple academic disciplines and applied research areas. Optional add-on software MAXDictio (extra cost) expands the functionality to provide basic content analysis style indexing and counting or all words in the dataset. MAX Maps (extra cost) adds the ability to draw graphic maps which are interactively linked to other project items. Here we review version 2 of MAXqda and where appropriate (and when we have permission from the developers) we refer to selected features planned for the next version of the software, MAXqda3. Refer to chapters in main body of the book for illustrations of aspects of MAXqda2 and step-by-step information.

Minimum system specifications (recommended by developer)

Pentium III or better (minimum 700 MHz); available RAM 128 MB (minimum); Microsoft Windows 98, Windows ME, Windows 2000; monitor 1024 × 768 resolution or better.

Structure of work in MAXqda2

MAXqda2 functions using an 'internal' database system. Files are imported into and then contained within one *project* file. This makes backing up and moving work straightforward. The user interface comprises four windows: the Document System list project data files which are called 'texts'; the Code System houses the coding scheme; the Text Browser displays individual texts; and the Retrieved Segments window displays coded data. Windows can be resized, opened and closed as required. Data line wraps to fit the available window. The interface in MAXqda3 will be enhanced by the addition of more easily accessible functions, including new toolbars (see Figure 3.6).

Data types and format in MAXqda2

- *Textual formats*: rich text format only Objects, including files (e.g. Excel spreadsheets, PowerPoint files) and graphics, can be embedded into RTF files and activated from within the software (see Chapter 2).

- *Text pre-processor tool*, unique to MAXqda, organizes texts according to how they have been prestructured. At transcription stage codes, using specific syntax can also be attached to segments before importing into MAXqda2 for quick auto coding upon importation. This is especially useful for large and/or structured datasets.
- *MAXqda3, the next version, will work with Unicode*, enabling a wide range of character sets and languages (including Chinese and Arabic) to be fully recognized, i.e. as code labels, and incorporated with searches as well as within source texts and memos. Importing texts will also be easier and more flexible in MAXqda3; for example, texts will no longer have to be imported directly into text groups (see Chapter 3).

Closeness to data and interactivity in MAXqda2

Maxqda2 provides full interactivity between the different aspects of work (usually just one click between functions and views). Windows displaying different elements of work can be viewed and worked with simultaneously. The compact structure of the user interface enhances contact with the whole project. MAXDictio provides interactive frequency tables and fully interactive key word in context (KWIC). Coded data can be viewed in the source context at the same time as in isolation. The margin display is fully interactive, resizable and always on display. Codes on view in the margin can be easily filtered in various respects and print well (see Chapters 3 and 8). Text links allow pairs of text segments to be linked. (see Chapter 4) and hyperlinks to URLs can be placed in the text.

Coding scheme in MAXqda2

The coding scheme can be as hierarchical or as non-hierarchical as required. If hierarchies are created, they can be functional for retrieval purposes (see Chapters 6 and 8). Drag and drop allows easy reorganization of codes. Assign colour attributes to codes to add an additional layer of organization. Coloured codes appear in the margin (see Figure 8.5 and Chapter 6). In MAXqda3, subcodes will inherit the colour attribute of higher-level codes.

Coding processes in MAXqda2

Drag and drop selected text onto a code. Assign recently used codes from dropdown menu. Undo recent coding actions. Apply weight to coded segments within a range of 1 to 100. A unique tool in MAXqda is the ability to convert code frequencies into numeric attributes for each document – a key way to integrate more quantitative analysis and manipulation of data should this be required. For instance, activation of all documents coded at a certain frequency level by a code could be very useful for close examination of certain trends in data (see Chapter 7).

Basic retrieval of coded data in MAXqda2

Activation is the central retrieval principle, allowing combinations of codes and text to be 'turned on' (activated) to display relevant data in the Retrieved Segments window. Codes can be activated by weight and texts by attributes. Functional hierarchies allow quick retrieval of data coded at the top level and all subcodes together (see Chapter 8).

Data organization in MAXqda2

Descriptive organization happens by applying attributes to whole texts or parts of them. Sets of documents provide shortcuts to groups of texts (see Chapter 11). MAXqda3 will include the ability to apply colour attributes to texts in the document system in the same way as is provided for codes in MAXqda2. The range of colours to choose from will also be extended. Attribute views in MAXqda3 will be similar to standard statistical packages, such as the 'data view' and 'variable view' in SPSS.

Writing tools in MAXqda2

Memos can be attached to text segments, codes and texts. They are displayed as post-it note icons adjacent to the linked object. Individual memos can be linked to any number of codes and organized by coloured flags. There is flexible retrieval of memos into collections based on several different criteria, e.g. all memos linked to a particular code, all memos within one text, all memos for a set of texts, all memos for a text group. Output memos based on these criteria (see Chapter 9).

Searching and interrogating the dataset in MAXqda2

Interrogate aspects of the dataset by simple or complex states of activation or by utilizing automatically generated overview tables, for example the index of Coded Segments and the matrix browser options discussed below. Activation by weight adds an extra dimension to searching. Results of searches can be exported to word processor and spreadsheet applications, or saved as HTML files. MAXqda3 will include an overview of retrieved segments alongside the current retrieval view, similar to the MAXqda2 index of Coded Segments.

- *Interactive matrix browsers* provide interactive chart-like visualization of code co-occurrences. The Code Relation Browser (easy one-click menu option) shows codes co-occurring with each other, reflecting relative frequency of co-occurrence, and co-occurrence of codes in subsets of data if codes on that bases have been applied. Clicking on the knots of co-occurrences runs an instant search, and segments appear in the Retrieved Segments pane.

- *The Code Matrix Browser* tabulates codes and their relative frequency in documents, and the frequency of codes occurring in individual documents. Charts are interactively connected to source data and can be filtered according to activated codes and/or texts. Double clicking on a knot in a matrix runs that search, and coded segments appear in Retrieved Segments. MAXqda3 will have additional visual interrogation tools, including a 'text comparison chart' for comparing text segments and a 'personal document picture' which will show colours associated with codes in sequential order.
- *The Text Retrieval* tool allows searching for the occurrence of codes using standard Boolean operators. The basis on which search operators retrieve data is visually represented and described in the Text Retrieval dialogue box. The results of searches can be coded.
- *Codes frequency tables* show the frequency of codes across the whole dataset or amongst combinations of activated texts and codes.
- *Text searching* provides key word in context (KWIC) retrieval. Text searching can be combined with the search for coded data (see Chapter 12). Results of text searches can be auto coded to the search string or a number of paragraphs around each hit; paragraphs are identified by one hard return (see Chapter 2).

Linking devices in MAXqda2

MAXqda2 provides a number of linking devices. Pairs of text segments can be linked through internal links. In MAXqda3 there will be a Text Link Browser window for managing these links. External links to websites can be inserted into texts. Link memos to one another in maps (visual link only) or link memos to codes to enable functional retrieval of memos (see Chapters 4, 9 and 10).

Mapping in MAXqda2

MAX Maps allows the creation of visual maps based on objects already created within the project (codes, memos, texts etc.) or by creating free objects representing a new idea, theory etc. Text and graphics can be added to a map. Any number of maps can be created, and objects' properties can be changed within the map view. Individual maps are not automatically linked to one another; therefore relationships created do not affect the main structure of the coding scheme, for example. Objects within a map are, however, interactively linked to the relevant source context within the project. Objects within maps can be added to layers for incremental viewing (see Figure 10.2).

Output in MAXqda2

Selected memos can be outputted into one file (all memos, all memos linked to one data file or a set of files, or all memos linked to one code). Any interactive table produced inside the software can be exported to view in a spreadsheet application. Exporting in HTML format is possible: export memos, attributes and coded text segments in HTML format to display in a web browser. Print texts including margin view.

Content analysis features in MAXqda2

MAXDictio (add-on module) provides word frequency counts across (groups of) texts, providing a tabular index with interactive KWIC retrieval. A dictionary can be created to build lists of words to include in frequency counts, which can be used in combination with other tools (see Chapter 4).

Teamworking in MAXqda2

Aspects of work can be merged, including individual documents, or a whole project's database can be imported into another. Colour-coding devices are useful to indicate different researchers' work, and HTML output for sharing information.

Comments on MAXqda2

- *The MAXqda2 user interface* is compact, appealing and tidy. It enhances interactive contact with different aspects of work, keeping the user close to the source data at all times. Auto arranging but resizable windows allow easy customization and isolation of element(s). It is difficult to find anything wrong with the user interface and the speed with which the user can move around its intuitive functionality.
- *Maxqda2 is intuitive and simple*: it is easy to learn and to begin working effectively. It includes some simple yet appealing features which users often request and are not available in many leading software packages, including the ability to colour codes and print off the margin display easily and satisfactorily. Even at its most sophisticated levels, it retains a simplicity which recommends it.
- *MAXqda2 has excellent memo tools*: easy, varied and systematic memo retrieval options are particularly useful for team situations. MAXqda2 has one of the best memo retrieval systems available since memos are automatically linked to other project objects. They can be sorted and therefore retrieved in many different ways, including according to the icons you have assigned to certain types of memo. The varied nature of retrieving memos means it is less important to be consciously systematic in organizing writing than in other software packages.
- *Sets of documents*, in MAXqda2 are very useful. The lack of code sets is limiting in comparison to other software. However, freedom to activate codes to produce retrieval on different bases is very easy.
- *In the team situation*, users can be selective about which items they merge together, thereby allowing progressive accumulation and comparison of work.
- *The principle of activation* allows quick and uncomplicated retrieval. Interrogation of the dataset is easy to grasp and manipulate. The Code Relation Browser and Code Matrix browser provide quick access without the need to construct complicated search expressions.
- *Auto coding tools* are less flexible than in other software packages because the only units of context to which you can automatically code are the search string itself of the paragraph.

- *With the addition of MAXDictio* the software has a small but useful range of content analysis tools not currently available in most other code-based packages (apart from QDA Miner). They provide interactive (KWIC) connection to the source context.

QDA Miner 2.0

This description includes
WordStat, an add-on content analysis and text mining module.

Normand Peladeau, a former program evaluator, believed that software should be created to facilitate the analysis of numerical and textual data within one program. He mixes graphical and statistical tools with the features characteristic of qualitative software. QDA Miner is the CAQDAS qualitative tool. With the add-on WordStat, the range of exploration and analytic techniques is extended to the more mathematical *content analysis* of data. Potentially handling thousands of cases, the combined software spans the CAQDAS, text retriever and text-based manager categories of software (see Chapter 1). QDA Miner is therefore part of a new generation of qualitative software, crossing methodological boundaries. Here we review version 2.0 of QDA Miner. It is recommended that this review is read in combination with Chapter 1 which enumerates in more detail the basic functionality which most of these software packages have in common.

Minimum System Specifications (recommended by developer)

Windows 95, 98, 2000 or XP (or Mac with virtual PC); RAM 128 MB; 9 MB of hard disk space (36 MB when used with the WordStat content analysis module).

Structure of work in QDA Miner 2.0

QDA Miner functions using an 'internal' database structure, so documents are imported into the database and work is held in one project file. The ability to archive and compress the project file facilitates backing up and movement of projects. The compression reduces the file size to between 15 and 20 per cent of the original. The interface is tidy, divided up into resizeable areas with lists of variables (and documents), and the codes list and main document window (with coded margin) are viewable simultaneously throughout. Other windows providing output come on top (see Figure C.3).

- *Variables structure*: QDA Miner operates using a variables structure, which is unusual amongst CAQDAS packages. A new tool on creating a new project makes this process easy, offering a number of different ways and starting points to start a project, such as from a list of documents, from a database using quantitative variables, using a document converter etc. Different document type 'variables' act like holders for different types of qualitative information, and new documents can be added at any time to handle additional types of data, e.g. notes files for each document.

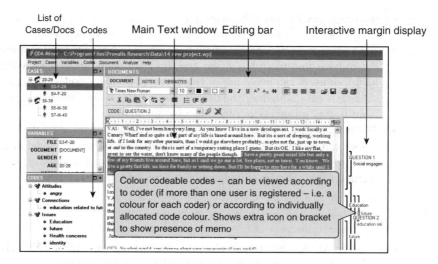

List of
Cases/Docs Codes   Main Text window Editing bar   Interactive margin display

Figure C.3   The QDA Miner user interface – in coding mode

- *Quantitative variables* hold respondent/case information which are used for case filtering and comparison. This information can be imported from a spreadsheet.

Data types and formats in QDA Miner 2.0

- *Textual formats*: QDA Miner only directly stores text saved as rich text format (.rtf) (see Chapter 2). However, the Document Conversion Wizard can convert various file formats such as MS Word, WordPerfect, rich text, HTML and Adobe Acrobat to work with inside the software. Textual data are fully editable using standard Windows formatting toolbars.
- *Other formats*: several database and spreadsheet file formats (including MS Access Excel, dBASE, Paradox) and any data file with an ODBC driver (Oracle, MS SQL etc.) can also be imported. Objects such as tables and graphic elements can be embedded into RTF documents.

Closeness to data and interactivity in QDA Miner 2.0

Documents open with one click from the listing in the main window (see Figure C.3). The codes margin area provides interactive contact with coded text. Interactivity between windows is very good: for example, one click on a text segment in the coded retrieval window connects with source data and highlights a segment within its source context.

Coding scheme in QDA Miner 2.0

- *Hierarchy*: the QDA Miner coding scheme can be completely non-hierarchical (with the proviso that there has to be one top-level code, underneath which all the others hang), or users can make use of five levels to organize codes. Reorganizing the coding scheme is easy with drag and drop to move codes within and between categories. There is no way to group codes other than by hierarchies.
- *The margin display* shows colour-codable codes as defined by the user; any Windows colour can be applied to any code. Viewing coloured codes in the margin allows comparison of codes assigned, for example, by different coders or according to broad themes. Codes can be edited, annotated, resized, removed etc. from the margin view.

Coding processes in QDA Miner 2.0

Coding can be assigned to any chunk of text, to one or several table cells, or to a whole graphic or other embedded object. Drag and drop codes onto text, or double click on a code to assign it to selection. Codes can be applied to whole paragraphs without manual text selection by drag and drop.

Basic retrieval of coded data in QDA Miner 2.0

- Basic retrieval of coded text is enabled at single and/or multiple codes. This happens in a dialogue box where boxes adjacent to required codes are ticked. Other/new codes can be assigned to any group of retrieved codes.
- Code list/output: a tabular codes listing provides description and frequency across documents *and* cases.

Data organization in QDA Miner 2.0

Documents are organized by cases for filtering. Cases are presented as a simple list with documents associated. In addition, any numerical, categorical, logical and date data may be used to categorize cases. QDA Miner can handle up to 2030 variables and several million cases.

Writing tools in QDA Miner 2.0

Annotations can be attached to codes in the code list or at the code mark in the margin area. Coded segments can also be annotated. A notes file is automatically created and linked to each case. Editable memo files can be created as documents, and then coded, annotated and searched etc. like any other file by creating a new document type variable.

Searching and interrogating the database in QDA Miner 2.0

- *The thesaurus facility* allows the program to return a hit every time any one of the words or phrases associated with the thesaurus item is found.
- *Integrated text searching on coded data*: search different units of text, i.e. the whole document, a paragraph, a sentence, or previously coded text segments associated with a specific or several codes.
- *The code sequences retrieval tool* allows exploration of common code sequences to gauge some idea of what codes are following each other in the text. A limited number of codes can be requested, or all codes: you define whether overlapping codes count or not. A tabular list of sequences is produced between pairs of codes (in both orders: code A followed by code B, and vice versa) together with frequency of the recurring sequences. This then allows the user to select a pair of codes in a particular sequence, producing a result window listing the full text of each coded segment or both codes, interactively connected to full context in source file. New coding can be applied to one result or all results in the results pane (see Figure C.4).
- *Auto coding and section retrieval feature*: uses text delimiters to auto code structured documents or fixed structure reports or text files (e.g. PsycINFO or Medline database searches).
- *Auto coding and text searching*: interactive tabular list of hits highlights the original text segment. Coding may be done on selected hits or on the entire list of hits.

Output in QDA Miner 2.0

- *Tabular outputs* to be printed or exported to Excel, HTML, Comma or tab delimited files. Coding retrieval results may also be exported as a new QDA Miner project.
- *Text outputs*: text documents and reports may be saved to disk in rich text, MS Word, ASCII or HTML format.
- *Graphical displays*: cluster plots, heatmaps etc. can be copied to the clipboard, pasted into a word processor, and exported to .bmp, .wmf, .png and .jpg formats.
- *Whole project export* can be to spreadsheet and database file formats, e.g. Quattro Pro, Lotus, Excel, Paradox, dBASE.

Teamworking in QDA Miner 2.0

- *Multi-user logon*: allows several coders to work on the same project (not concurrently) either with full access or with access to limited features and no access to other coders' work. Alternatively, several users may work on different copies of a project or different subsets of cases.

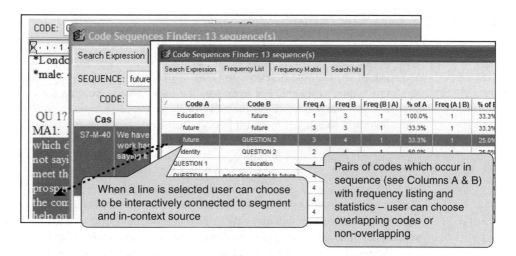

Figure C.4   **QDA Miner: sample automatic retrieval – Code Sequences tool**

- *Merge feature* consolidates several project files into a master project.
- *Intercoder reliability tool* computes agreement measures and the identification of common disagreements.

Content analysis features in QDA Miner 2.0

- *Add-on module WordStat*: comprehensive quantitative content analysis and text mining module. It has lemmatization, stemming, stop lists, hierarchical categorization of words, word patterns and phrases, KWIC lists, links to lexical databases, vocabulary and phrase extractors.
- *Exploratory tools and graphical charting* for hierarchical clustering, multidimensional scaling, proximity plots, interactive heatmaps, correspondence analysis etc. Compare by numerical or nominal variable.
- *Analysis of case or document similarities*: clusters cases based on their similarity of coding.

Comments on QDA Miner 2.0

These comments are based mainly on the interpretive (QDA Miner) part of the software. Please enquire further for other fuller, recent reviews of the content analysis features of WordStat.

Comments on QDA Miner

- *The coding scheme in QDA Miner* has a restricted number of hierarchy levels enabled. This can be a good disciplining factor, as too many levels fragment ideas and hide codes out of site. Simple functions in QDA Miner are handled really well – often those missing in other software. For example, the user can use colours for codes as they appear in the margin, based on meaning or based on differential colour coding for a team member. In single or multiple code retrieval, just tick the codes wanted, for clearly labelled retrieval.
- *User interface and structure*: the central 'variable-based' structure of the software is different to other software and potentially more difficult if your focus and experience are very qualitative to the exclusion of quantitative. However, everything is done to make getting started as easy as possible. The crossover between quantitative text mining and qualitative functionality make this a potentially useful tool for mixed-methods approaches. The text mining terminology in the program can be a bit demanding, however. Potentially a researcher working interpretively could make good use of the software, but the package is perhaps more ideal for those who also need to have one foot in the text mining approach to data analysis. The developer is responsively working very hard to make the software accessible to the interpretive researcher.
- *Extra functions.* (1) The thesaurus facility and the search category tool extend the potential of the text search tool in catching meaningfully related words. (2) The in-house conversion of Adobe Acrobat. (pdf). files using the Document Conversion Wizard is a first amongst the featured software. (3) The Code Sequences Analyser is a very useful and unique tool, replacing what would be complicated searches in other software. It is impossible to overestimate the value of this tool. It offers the user the ability to list not only co-occuring or overlapping codes in the data, but separated sequential paired occurrences of all codes with each other across the whole dataset. Results tables are interactively connected to source data.
- *The export features* are well organized and easy to create. When viewing the results table of a coded retrieval, the report is created at one click of an icon. The option to export coded segments, and in the process create a new project with them, is unusual and makes good data reduction sense when dealing with hundreds or thousands of documents or records. The exported code labels become case names, and the segments are contained within a document type variable for each case.

QSR NVivo7

Tom Richards and Lyn Richards originally developed NUD*IST as a scroll mode Mac package at La Trobe University, Melbourne, to support Lyn Richards in her work as a family sociologist. Subsequently QSR International was formed which now develops and supports all QSR software products. QSR software stopped being developed for the Mac platform after NUD*IST 4 (N4). This chapter reviews version 7 of NVivo updated with Service Pack 2. The software combines the functionality of the previous NVivo2 and N6 (the last of the QSR NUD*IST strand of software). Refer to chapters in the main body of the book for illustrations of aspects of NVivo7.

Minimum system specifications (recommended by developer)

Pentium 4 at 2 GHz or faster; 512 MB RAM or more; 1024 × 768 screen resolution or higher; Windows XP Service Pack 2 or later; approximately 1 GB of available hard disk space; internet connection; MS SQL Server (comes with software).

Structure of work in NVivo7

NVivo7 functions using an 'internal' database system and one *project* file holds all project information. The NVivo7 interface looks like MS Outlook in which the 'workspace' provides access to the different elements of your work. The interface can be customized in certain respects (e.g. where different panes appear etc.). The main views in the workspace are the Navigation View (providing access to project folders, e.g. sources, nodes, models, links etc.); the List View (listing items within each folder); and the Detail View (where the content of an item is displayed) (see Figure 3.9).

Data types and formats in NVivo7

- *Textual formats*: text only (.txt) rich text format (.rtf) or MS Word (.doc).
- *Graphics* can be embedded into RTF files. Documents can be given read-only properties. Files are imported into or created within the project as sources. There are three types of source: documents the source materials (e.g. transcripts); memos, to record thoughts; and externals, proxy files to represent files outside the NVivo7 database.

Closeness to data and interactivity in NVivo7

- *The content of sources and nodes are viewed* in the Detail View, and once opened, are tabbed, providing access without having to use the navigation buttons. Text does not line wrap, and viewing coded data initially lifts text passages out of source context.
- *The interface* is familiar, but functionality is separated. Detail View windows can be undocked, however, to view detailed content in separate windows at the same time. Linking devices (see below) and sets can increase integration between project items.
- *Sets* are shortcuts to project items, allowing items to be gathered together (e.g. a combination of sources and nodes can belong to the same set) (see Chapter 8).

Coding scheme in NVivo7

- *The coding scheme* can be as hierarchical or non-hierarchical as required. There are five types of node: Free nodes and tree nodes (for housing non-organized and hierarchical thematic codes), cases (for organizing documents and subset information), *relationships* (for creating and coding links between items) and *matrices* (to save results of qualitative cross-tabulations).

• *Nodes are visible in separate folders* in the Nodes Folder View. The contents of each folder are viewed in the corresponding List View. An All Nodes folder allows access to all current nodes, regardless of the type. Sets of nodes enable alternative grouping of nodes without affecting the coding scheme.

Coding processes in NVivo7

Free and tree nodes can be created up-front or developed from data level. Drag and drop selected text onto existing nodes. Shortcut coding icons and a coding toolbar speed up the coding process (see Chapter 7).

Basic retrieval of coded data in NVivo7

• *Basic retrieval of data* coded at one code is viewed by double clicking on the node and viewing in the Detail View. This lifts coded passages out of source context, but the Detail View allows recoding while in this view (see Chapter 8).
• *Coding stripes* allow up to 200 nodes to be viewed in a right-hand margin. Choose according to, for example, all codes, codes most coding item, codes least coding item, codes recently coding item, or manually choose codes. Coding Stripes View shows relative coding density at any one point. The Coding Stripes View has some interactivity: selecting a code highlights the relevant text; coded data can be accessed and segments uncoded.

Data organization in NVivo7

The organization of data happens by creating cases and applying attributes. A case can comprise one or several sources and/or parts of sources. Case and attribute information can be imported from or exported to a spreadsheet application. Cases are a type of node. Case nodes can be assigned attributes (e.g. socio-demographic variables) but other types of node cannot have attributes (see Chapter 11).

Sources can be auto coded according to prestructured formatting of files (see Chapter 11). Headings (identified by MS Word styles) or paragraphs (identified by one hard return) are automatically recognized for auto coding processes (see Chapter 2). Sets of documents can be created at any time to group sources in different ways.

Writing tools in NVivo7

• *Memos* are blank documents which can be created at any time, and linked to an existing document or node. These are full ranking documents and therefore can also be coded and searched etc. (see Chapter 9).

- *Annotations*: comments can be embedded at any point in any document and reopened when required. Each annotation is hyperlinked back to its anchoring text, an excellent tool, although further cramping the available space when on view. Annotations appear like footnotes at the end of the source or node and a list of annotations can be exported to a spreadsheet application (see Chapter 4 and Figure 4.9).

Searching and interrogating the dataset in NVivo7

The database can be interrogated by creating and running queries (see Chapter 12). There are four types of query:

- *Text search*: for content in sources, nodes, sets or annotations.
- *Coding query*: simple queries find e.g. where cases with a particular attribute are coded at a particular node; advanced queries allow searching for position of nodes in the data (e.g. Boolean or proximity operators).
- *Matrix coding*: compares pairs of project items and displays in a table.
- *Compound query*: search for specified text in or near coded data.

Queries can be saved to rerun later. Results of queries can be previewed, saved and outputted.

The Find Tool retrieves project items by searching item names for specified text strings.

Linking devices in NVivo7

There are five types of linking device:

- *Memo links*: a memo can be linked to either a node, a document or an external (but not to several).
- *See Also links*: text segments linked to other project items (including passages of text in other documents).
- *Annotations*: write comments about text segments.
- *Hyperlinks*: link text segments to files or websites held outside NVivo.
- *Relationships*: a type of node which defines a connection between two project items. Different relationship types can be created, and the data which support that relationship coded accordingly.

Modelling in NVivo7

Models can be either static or dynamic. Items in *static* models are not connected to any other project item. *Dynamic* models provide *live* connection between projects existing within the model, and the project items they represent. Relationships (see above) can be visualized in a model. Items can be grouped in a model (acting as layers) (see Chapter 10).

Output in NVivo7

There are several forms of output in NVivo7. The content of project items (sources, nodes, matrices and the casebook) can be exported, but it is not possible to export multiple items into the same file. It is possible to print a document or node with the coding stripes on view, but text and codes are printed on separate pages.

- *Tabular output* provides summaries on individual aspects of the project: source summary, node summary, relationship summary, attribute summary and coding summary.
- *Coding comparison report* shows similarities and differences in how two sources have been coded.

Teamworking in NVivo7

One or more projects can be imported into the 'master' project. All items or selected items can be imported.

Comments on NVivo7

- *QSR's goal of normalization* is achieved to some extent with the use of an interface which looks like MS Outlook. Many people do find it easy to move around the software. It has been achieved at a cost however, since the system specifications are higher in almost every respect than the other packages.
- *The user interface,* while familiar, means that you can only view one type of function at a time, i.e. either sources, or codes, or sets, or queries etc. Compared to other software packages reviewed here, this impacts on the sense of contact you have across different aspects of your work. The movement between different aspects of work is not as fluid as in earlier versions of NVivo or in other software. Visual assurance that a task has been executed is sometimes missing, which is often unnerving for new users. The software is slow compared to other software and has a cramped feel. The latter is exacerbated by missing basic requirements like line wrapping which restricts the ability to resize the text window or the margin view. The familiarity of the folder structure, especially for documents, is appealing. Beginners tend to like the software; those used to using earlier versions have too many comparative criticisms.
- *The case structure* for organizing data is the best attempt amongst the software packages discussed here in unifying and simplifying the process. Thought needs to be given to this aspect of work early, however, to make the best use of available tools. The systematic support NVivo7 provides is excellent and the structures provided for organizing the data throughout the software provide the best flexibility of all the software packages with respect to later interrogation of data.
- *The codes stripes view* is partially interactive and has to be closed and re-opened to bring it up to date when a new code is applied in the document. The coding density stripe is unique to NVivo7, though it has less relevance now that the number of codes potentially visible in the margin area is effectively all – providing you can scroll to see them all – rather

than the limit on seven as in the pre Service Pack 2 software. Text with its margin view can be printed but appears on separate sheets of paper, making precise consideration of how data are coded and comparing across and between printouts cumbersome.

- *Sets are flexible* in NVivo7. The ability to add sources and codes to the same set is unique amongst the software packages reviewed here. This provides useful ways to isolate parts of a project, or to group aspects together for many different reasons. However, simple to achieve and clearly labelled output in one file of multiple codes and data segments is missing.
- *The Query Tool is easy to get started with* and the range of outcomes from queries is good. Matrix searches in particular offer flexible ways of conducting multiple searches at one time and accessing results. The ability to save the way queries are built in a list is useful. The query dialogue boxes, however, are step by step and it can be easy to miss important options, and it is quite difficult to see what the process should be in the more complex searches.
- *Linking tools* are not as versatile as in other packages. This applies to the links between memos and data files also. While it is possible to link between pairs of points in the text using *See Also* links, subsequently navigating around the dataset according to the links is really cumbersome via menus and submenus and cannot be regarded as hyperlinking. *See Also* links are cumbersome to make and navigate, but the usefulness of them might be the fact that they are listed in a systematic way enabling the researcher to see at a glance the number and nature of links in each document. They are poor compensation for the former, flexible linking tools in NVivo2. The best linking device is the Annotation tool which is in effect a footnote hyperlinked back to the text to which it is anchored. This could provide an effective way of clicking fast through different parts of one document.

QUALRUS

Qualrus is developed by Idea Works, Inc. with initial support from qualitative researchers including Howard Becker. It differs significantly from other CAQDAS packages because it uses 'intelligent computational strategies' to assist the researcher with certain tasks. It may therefore be seen as the first in a new generation of qualitative data analysis software packages. It is recommended that this review is read in conjunction with Chapter 1, which more fully describes commonality and the usual functionality of CAQDAS programs.

Minimum system specification (recommended by developer)

MS Windows 95 or higher; RAM 48 MB (required), 128 MB (recommended).

Structure of work in Qualrus

Qualrus functions using an 'external' database structure whereby the software refers to source files located outside it. It has an efficient and easy to grasp pack and go system for condensing the project file and all data files for backing up or moving to another computer.

The user interface comprises three main parts: the project overview, which contains links to project items (sources, codes, links, views, scripts, reports and lists); the sources window, where data files are viewed; and the margin view, where codes appear as they are assigned to data (see Figure C.5). Other functions are accessed through main menu options and a small number of shortcut icons.

The *segment* is the basic unit of analysis and is created upon coding. This affects the way certain search tools function, and it is important to be aware of this structure early on.

Data types and formats in Qualrus

- *Textual formats*: Text only and rich text format.
- *Graphic formats*: .bmp, .jpg.
- *Video formats*: .avi, .mpeg, .mpg etc.
- *Audio formats*: .wav, mp3 etc.
- *HTML formats*: .htm, .html etc.

It is also possible to navigate the internet from within Qualrus and save pages as sources. See the developer website for a complete list of acceptable source file formats.

Closeness to data and interactivity in Qualrus

- *Sources are viewed* in the sources window and loaded sources are tabbed for quick access. There is usually good interaction between different windows, although limited drag and drop functionality.
- *The margin view* is interactive, providing quick access to memos, the coding scheme and other project items.

Coding scheme in Qualrus

The coding scheme can be hierarchical or non-hierarchical as required. Hierarchy is imposed by linking codes in a semantic network rather than creating subcodes. Code labels can be given synonyms, and attribute–value pairs (e.g. gender–female) can be applied to codes where relevant. Summary information concerning each code is held in the code editor window, which also provides quick access to coded segments and visualization of links between codes.

Project overview   Sources window   Margin: showing codes

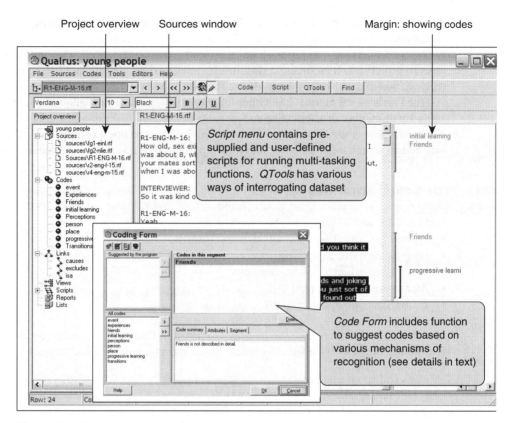

Figure C.5   The Qualrus user interface

The approach to coding and the structure of the coding scheme can depend on whether and how suggestive coding functions (see below) are made use of.

Coding processes in Qualrus

Suggestive coding, if utilized, provides an active role in coding processes. Codes are suggested for application to text segments based on the combination of natural language patterns, user-defined code synonyms and links between codes. For example, the software compares strings in a selected segment with how similar text passages and previous passages were coded in order to decide which codes to suggest. The software 'learns' as coding proceeds, based on the acceptance or rejection of previous suggestions.

Suggestive coding features work incrementally: codes are initially suggested upon text selection because (1) the code label itself or a synonym (or its root) appears in the selected text, or (2) a code has been applied earlier in the document (constant comparison). Upon applying a code X to a text segment (whether suggested by the program or not), further codes may be suggested because (1) code Y has previously also been applied to text segments coded by X; or (2) a one-directional link exists between code X and code Y.

The coding form allows application of suggested codes or any other codes. Codes can only be applied to segments, but a segment is defined by the user and can be any size.

Basic retrieval of coded data in Qualrus

Retrieval of coded data happens via the code editor or by using the search tools (QTools). In the first instance, segments are 'lifted out' of context, but there is good interactivity between the results pane and the source text.

Data organization in Qualrus

Organization of data to known characteristics such as socio-demographic variables can be achieved by coding or by assigning attribute–value pairs to codes.

Writing tools in Qualrus

Memos can be attached to sources, codes and segments, although there is no central memo system where all memos are listed. Empty sources can be created as memos and worked with like any other source. QTools allow searching for coded segments with memo attached.

Searching and interrogating the dataset in Qularus

A number of ways to interrogate coding in addition to standard Bolean operators are accessed through QTools. Much information is automatically generated without having to construct complicated search expressions. Together with good interactivity between QTools results and source context, this facilitates comparison and cross-checking.

- *The statistics tool* assists with theoretical sampling, providing basic summary statistics (e.g. frequency of code application per source and frequency of code co-occurrence at a particular coded text segment).
- *The coincidental codes tool* examines the co-occurrence of each possible pair of codes in segments, ordering pairs by how frequently they co-occur.
- *The categorizing tool* allows coded text segments to be sorted into stacks which themselves can be assigned codes. This is particularly useful for generating higher order categories outside the main coding scheme, and reflects manual methods of working.

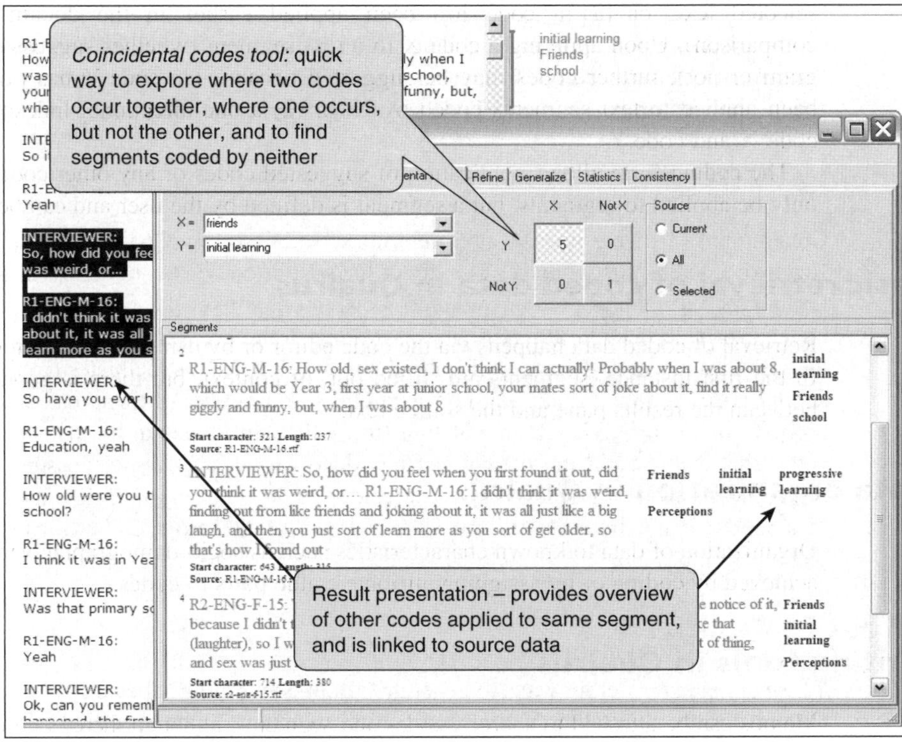

Figure C.6   The coincidental codes tool in Qualrus

- *The hypothesis testing tool* examines all segments to test specific user-defined hypotheses. For example, search for where two or more codes are applied to segments and specify for another code to be assigned to all finds, using standard IF, THEN protocols. All possible combinations of the codes asked for are presented in a matrix result which facilitates the 'finding' of where co-occurrences are not present in the data, as well as where they are.
- *The refine tool* examines codes or relationships among codes and can be used effectively to build on work done in the hypothesis testing tool.
- *Auto coding tools* are based on the use of a script that first assigns a dummy code to a segment. The software then checks to see if it should be coded with the auto code specifications, then uncodes it if it is still coded with the dummy code.
- *Lists* save results upon which to build further questions.

Linking devices in Qualrus

Codes can be linked to one another using default or user-defined links. Default links are 'causes', 'excludes' and 'is a'. Suggestive coding is partly reliant on links specified between codes, although this feature can be disabled if required. Links between codes can be created at any time and are centrally visualized in the code editor. Specific parts of the semantic network can be further interrogated and visualized in maps by working in different view editors (see below). Data segments cannot be linked independently.

Mapping in Qualrus

Creating links between codes can be central aspect of work in Qualrus when making use of suggestive coding functionality. The direct links from one code are shown in the code editor, but the view editor provides ways to focus in on parts of the coding scheme to visualize and manage links in different ways. Working in the network view, for example, allows the visualization of any number of links chained together. This facilitates the comparison of similar codes and the visualization of hierarchy. Certain types of links (e.g. 'causes' or 'is a property of') can be viewed in isolation from other link types in the network view. Only codes that exist within the project can be added to views; it is not possible to add non-project items such as graphics, or to use colour or layers to group different aspects. Codes in a view are not interactively linked to the rest of the project. Views can be saved as pictures (.bmp files).

Output in Qualrus

These are many different ways to generate output concerning aspects of works in Qualrus. Output options allow the content and format of output to be specified in various ways. Reports save output for viewing in other applications; reports can be saved in basic or dynamic HTML format.

Extensibility in Qualrus

Qualrus is extensible in that the program can be modified to fit particular needs. Write scripts using an object-oriented scripting language (similar to C++ or Java) to extend and tailor the software.

Teamworking in Qualrus

- *The merge facility* allows all or selected aspects of one project to be imported into another.
- *The coder consistency tool* facilitates teamworking by providing statistical data showing how consistent each coder is with the recommendations of the program.
- *Logging*: the software automatically logs all aspects of work, thereby providing information concerning, for example, the details of a code (its name, the list of segments applied to the code, when the code was created, by whom and how it was chosen, i.e. whether selected manually by the user or as the result of a program suggestion).

Comments on Qualrus

- *Sophisticated software* in some unique respects, although it can be used effectively without making extensive use of sophisticated tools. It is easy to get started with, although it takes time to become familiar with the range of options available. Several functions are more quantitative than is usual amongst CAQDAS packages, providing alternative ways to compare, for example, the application of codes statistically.
- *Use of artificial intelligence*, in particular, takes qualitative software to a new level while also being a controversial aspect amongst some users. The expert user may make good use of the A1 features, although the functioning of this aspect of the software needs to be well understood early on in order to make effective and appropriate use of available tools.
- *Suggestive coding* may be seen as a way to speed up coding processes, but, more importantly, it can serve to increase the rigour and consistency of coding. Making full use of suggestive coding is facilitated by developing a fairly mature coding scheme at the outset, and may therefore be particularly useful to those working in deductive ways. That said, Qualrus is equally appropriate for more inductive approaches to analysis, and the nature of its A1 constant comparison with segments coded earlier has some considerable resonance with grounded theory (Glaser and Strauss, 1967).
- *The segment structure is a little restrictive* in comparison to other CAQDAS packages, specifically the current inability to search for where codes merely overlap in the data and are not applied to exactly the same segment. There is not yet a straightforward way to compare codes across subsets of data.
- *Interactivity* in most windows is good with other aspects of work, although some dialogue boxes, including the coding editor, are somewhat 'clunky'.
- *Extensibility* means that some of the program's limitations can be overcome by the confident computer user willing to learn the scripting language. Where this is the case, its potential is almost unlimited.
- *The categorization tool* replicates manual ways of grouping text segments and is very intuitive. This feature can be particularly attractive to experienced qualitative researchers who are familiar with manual methods of coding and categorization and therefore seek software which replicates that style of working.
- *Data and project management* options are not as wide ranging or as straightforward as other packages.

TRANSANA 2

Transana is a free, open source software package designed to facilitate the transcription, management and analysis of digital video or audio data. It was originally created by Chris Fassnacht, and is now developed and maintained by David K. Woods at the Wisconsin Center for Education Research, University of Wisconsin–Madison, USA. Here we review version 2 of Transana. Note: Transana is different from the other software packages reviewed here due to its primary focus on audio and video rather than text.

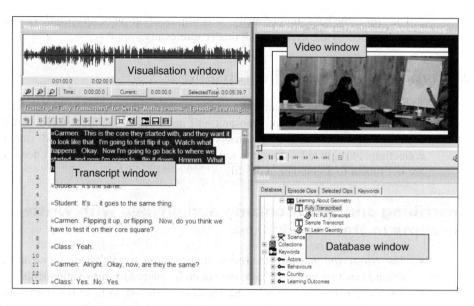

Figure C.7 **The Transana 2 user interface**

Minimum system specifications (recommended by developer)

MS Windows 2000 or XP, Mac OS/X 10.3 or higher; RAM 64 MB (minimum); minimum screen resolution 1024 × 768 pixels;
60–100 MB disk space for program, 10 MB space for database (the amount and quality of video used is the critical factor relating to required disk space).

Structure of work in Transana 2

Transana operates using 'external' database structure comprising three components: the application, the audio/video files and the database. The database contains the workings of the project: the transcripts, clips, key words, collections etc. Audio/video files are not altered in any way by Transana.

The Transana user interface (Figure C.7) comprises five elements: the *menu bar* houses the main program controls; the *video window* displays the video; the *visualization window* displays the audio waveform; the *transcript window* provides transcription tools and displays textual transcripts; and the *data window* provides an overview of the 'database tree', which houses various ways of organizing data and ideas (episodes, clips, collections, key words and searches).

The *clip* is the basic unit of analysis. A clip is a portion of an *episode* (a video or audio file) identified by the user as analytically interesting.

Data types and formats in Transana 2

Transana handles .mpeg1, .mpeg2 (which are the recommended video formats), most .avi video, .mp3 and .wav audio. Transana will not work with video stored on CD or DVD. Database and file manipulation tools facilitate the organization and storage of large collections of digitized video. It is not possible to create or import text documents which are not linked to a video or audio file.

Transcribing and synchronizing audio/video with written transcripts in Transana 2

- *The transcription mode* facilitates transcription for video or sound data. The auto rewind function and play back speed can be altered to suit requirements.
- *The waveform* is the visual representation of the intensity of the source data's sound, which Transana can generate automatically from the audio/video file.
- *Time codes* enable a point in the transcript to be linked to a frame in the corresponding video or audio file. This allows synchronized playback of video, sound and transcript. The positions of time codes are user defined and inserted manually at any point.

Closeness to data and interactivity in Transana 2

- *Synchronization* of audio/video, waveform and written transcript keeps the user very close to all three data representations simultaneously.
- *Interactivity is very good*: control video playback from any window; clicking on a particular point in one window takes you to the corresponding point in other windows.
- *Resizeable windows* enable focus on the required aspect. View clips individually or collectively, or view in context. Clips are independent segments of episodes, thus making it possible to work exclusively at the level of collections and clips, i.e. without applying key words.

Coding scheme in Transana 2

Coding processes happen in Transana by creating and applying key words to clips or collections. The process and functionality of key words in Transana is essentially the same as coding in the other software packages reviewed here.

The key word database tree is hierarchical in that key words can only be created within a key word group. Key words can, however, belong to multiple key word groups.

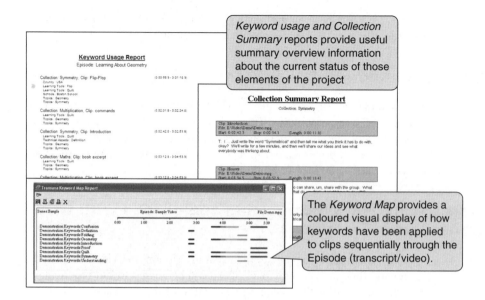

Figure C.8   **Examples of output from Transana 2**

The ability to create clips and collections can obviate the need to use key words for general sorting purposes, and any clip can belong to any number of collections. However, subsequent searches are based on the presence or absence of key words and key word groups rather than clips or collections. Reports are available (Figure C.8).

Coding processes in Transana 2

A data segment can only be assigned a key word if it is already a clip. This means that coding using key words must occur via the written transcript. Keywords can be applied to episodes, collections or clips. A clip can be assigned multiple Key words, and appear in multiple collections. Drag and drop to assign key word(s) to clips.

Basic retrieval of coded data in Transana 2

- *There are three ways to retrieve clips*: individually, by collection, or by using the search tool to find clips (regardless of collection) to which key word(s) have been applied. The first two ways are independent of the way the data have been 'coded' (application of key words).
- *Retrieval by collection* is a very quick and easy way to view all clips which have been grouped together sequentially.
- *Summary information* is very easy to access, providing an overview of which key words have been applied to the clips. The results of Boolean (AND, OR, NOT) searches can be converted into collections.

Data organization in Transana 2

Audio/video files and their associated transcripts are organized into series and episodes when assigned to the database. A series may have multiple episodes (which are likely to be separate audio/video files).

Socio-demographic characteristics are handled at the key word level, and can be assigned to series, episodes and clips in the same way as described above.

Writing tools in Transana 2

Transana provides relatively limited writing tools. *Notes* can be applied to series, episodes, transcripts, collections and clips (but not to key word groups or key words – to which definitions can be specified).

Teamworking in Transana 2

- *The multi-user version* of Transana is specifically designed for collaborative projects. It is a separate application and can run alongside the single user version. It allows multiple users (in different locations) to communicate and work on the same database (e.g. transcripts, clips, key words etc.) *at the same time.* This facilitates real-time analytic collaboration between distributed teams working on the same network and between networks. Multi-user projects can be worked on independently by researches or simultaneously with team members. There is therefore no need to merge databases.
- *The chat window* enables real-time communication with team members whilst working in a multi-user database. It is a synchronous text-based tool, facilitating collaboration as well as acting as a record of communication and decision making.
- *Presentation mode*: Transana includes a presentation mode to facilitate the demonstration of work with others. Video can be presented during playback in different ways: 'video only' displays the video window in full screen, and 'video and transcript only' displays the video and scrolling highlighting of synchronized transcript (if auto word tracking is enabled).

Comments on Transana 2

- *Transana is free, open source software,* developed for video analysis. Comments should be read in that context. Source code is openly available, so it can be customized to suit the needs of a project. Researchers primarily using video data are recommended to consider this software carefully.
- *Interactivity*: Transana is very easy to use. The ability to synchronize playback of video, sound and transcript and to control playback from any view is seamless and analytically helpful. Interactivity between windows and analytic functions is good.
- *Integration of additional data formats*: Transana currently does not easily enable the management and analysis of projects where textual data other than video transcripts are being utilized as a primary source of data.

- *The limited range of integrated writing tools* is its weakness in comparison to other software packages reviewed here.
- *The structure of the database tree system* is a little confusing at the outset as the organization on clips into collections can have a very similar function as the organization of key words into key word groups. In addition, each clip, collection, key word group etc. can have its own ID – so you need to be clear about the difference in the way you will use IDs and groups of other objects (collections, key words etc.).
- *The search tool* is not as sophisticated as in other packages reviewed here, only providing standard Boolean operators (AND, OR and NOT) for searching for the occurrence of key words in the dataset.
- *Teamworking*: the ability of the multi-user version to allow geographically dispersed researchers to work on one database simultaneously is unique amongst the software reviewed here and can significantly facilitate collaborative teamworking. Setting up the multi-user version is quite intensive, although information on the Transana website is useful in this regard. Whilst any team member can make changes to a database when using multi-user version, changes are not automatically tagged or logged according to who made the change. Therefore teams need to find ways of overcoming this if it is important to the progress of the analysis to hold on to 'who did what'.

Appendix D
Resources and Links

CAQDAS NETWORKING PROJECT

University of Surrey, ESRC Researcher Development Initiative Project

http://caqdas.soc.surrey.ac.uk

- Training and support in the use of a range of CAQDAS packages.
- Comprehensive bibliography relating to the use of CAQDAS packages.
- Links to online journals and articles.
- Links to software developer and distributor sites, including free and low cost packages.

ONLINE CAQDAS AND QUALITATIVE DATA ANALYSIS

University of Huddersfield and University of Surrey
ESRC Research Methods Project

http://onlineqda.hud.ac.uk

- 'Just in time' support for CAQDAS users.
- Information on qualitative methodologies.
- Comprehensive bibliography relating to qualitative data analysis and the use of CAQDAS packages.
- Links to broad range of relevant resources.

QUALITI: QUALITATIVE RESEARCH METHODS IN THE SOCIAL SCIENCES: INNOVATION, INTEGRATION AND IMPACT

School of Social Sciences, Cardiff University
ESRC National Centre for Research Methods Project

http://www.cardiff.ac.uk/socsi/qualiti/

- Promoting a step change in the quality and range of methodological skills and techniques used by the UK social science community.
- Providing support for, and dissemination of, methodological innovation and excellence within the UK.

ASSESSMENT AND DEVELOPMENT OF NEW METHODS FOR THE ANALYSIS OF MEDIA CONTENT

Loughborough University
ESRC Research Methods Project

http://www.lboro.ac.uk/research/mmethods/index.html

- The exploration and testing of computer software packages for the analysis of media content.

SOFTWARE FEATURED IN THIS BOOK

ATLAS.ti5 (throughout)
Scientific Software Development GmbH
http://www.atlasti.de

HyperRESEARCH 2.6 (Appendix C)
Researchware Inc.
http://www.researchware.com

MAXqda2 (throughout)
Verbi Gmbtt
http://www.maxqda.com

QDA Miner 2.0 and WordStat (Appendix C)
Provalis
http://www.provalisresearch.com/QDAMiner/QDAMinerDesc.html
http://www.provalisresearch.com/wordstat/wordstat.html

QSR NVivo7 (throughout)
Qualitative Solutions Research
http://www.qsrinternational.com

Qualrus (Appendix C)
Idea Works
http://www.ideaworks.com/Qualrus.shtml

Transana 2 (Appendix C)
University of Wisconsin–Madison
http://www.transana.org/

References

Abrahamson, M. (1983) *Social Research Methods*. Englewood Cliffs, NJ: Prentice-Hall.

Ackerman, F., Eden, C. and Cropper, S. (1992) 'Getting started with cognitive mapping'. Published in the proceedings of the 7th Young Operational Research Conference. University of Warwick. April. pp. 65–82.

Atkinson, J.M. and Heritage, J. (eds) (1984) *Structures of Social Action: Studies in Conversation Analysis*. Cambridge: Cambridge University Press.

Berg, B.L. (2001) *Qualitative Research Methods for the Social Sciences*. London: Allyn & Bacon.

Breakwell, G.M. (1986) *Coping with Threatened Identities*. London: Methuen.

Breakwell, G.M. (1992) 'AIDS generation, Thatcher's children: identity, social representations and action'. Inaugural lecture, University of Surrey, Guildford.

Brown, B.B. and Perkins, D.D. (1992) 'Disruption in place attachment', in I. Alman and S.M. Low (eds), *Place Attachment*. New York: Blenheim.

Buzan, T. (1995) *The MindMap Book,* 2nd edn. London: BBC Books.

Charmaz, K. (2000) 'Grounded theory: objectionist and constructionist methods', in N. Denzin and S. Lincoln (eds), *Handbook of Qualitative Research*, 2nd edn. Thousand Oaks, CA: Sage.

Coffey, A. and Atkinson, P. (1996) *Making Sense of Qualitative Data Analysis: Complementary Strategies*. Thousand Oaks, CA: Sage.

Coffey, A., Holbrook, B. and Atkinson, P. (1996) 'Qualitative data analysis: technologies and representations', *Sociological Research Online,* 1 (1), http://www.soc.surrey.ac.uk/socresonline/1/1/4.html (see also comment in Lee and Fielding 1996).

Denzin, N. and Lincoln, S. (eds) (2000) *Handbook of Qualitative Research,* 2nd edn. Thousand Oaks, CA: Sage.

East Surrey Health Authority (ESHA) (2000) *Health and social care needs of people over 50.*

Eden, C. (1988) 'Cognitive mapping', *European Journal of Operational Research*, 36: 1–13.

Eden, C. and Ackermann, F. (1998) *Making Strategy: the Journey of Strategic Management*. London: Sage.

Fielding, N. and Lee, R. (eds) (1993) *Using Computers in Qualitative Research* (1st edn 1991). London: Sage.

Fielding, N. and Lee, R. (1998) *Computer Analysis and Qualitative Research*. London: Sage.

Fisher, M. (1997) *Qualitative Computing: Using Software for Qualitative Data Analysis.* Cardiff Papers in Qualitative Research. Aldershot: Ashgate.

Gibbs, G. (2002) *Qualitative Data Analysis: Explorations with NVivo.* Buckingham: Open University Press.

Gibbs, G. (2005) 'Writing as analysis', Online QDA, http://onlineqda.hud.ac.uk/Intro_QDA/writing_analysis.php

Gibbs, G.R., Friese, S. and Mangabeira, W.C. (2002) 'The use of new technology in qualitative research', Introduction to issue 3 (2) of *Forum Qualitative Sozialforschung/Forum: Qualitative Social Research,* online journal http://www.qualitative-research.net/fqs-texte/2-02/2-02hrsg-e.htm

Giddens, A. (1984) *Constitution of Society: Outline of a Theory of Structuration.* Cambridge: Polity.

Glaser, B.G. (1978) *Theoretical Sensitivity.* Mill Valley, CA: Sociology Press.

Glaser, B.G. and Strauss, A. (1967) *The Discovery of Grounded Theory.* Chicago: Aldine.

Gulati, S. (2006) 'Learning in online and blended courses'. Unpublished thesis, City University, London.

Have P. ten (1990) 'Methodological issues in conversation analysis', *Bulletin de Méthodologie Sociologique,* 27 (June): 23–51. Available online at http://www2.fmg.uva.nl/emca/mica.htm

Holsti, O.R. (1969) *Content Analysis for the Social Sciences and Humanities.* Reading, MA: Addison-Wesley.

Kelly, G.A. (1970) 'A brief introduction to personal construct theory', in D. Bannister (ed.), *Perspectives in Personal Construct Theory.* London: Academic Chapter 1, pp. 1–29.

Layder, D. (1998) *Sociological Practice: Linking Theory and Sociological Research,* London: Sage.

Lee, R. and Fielding, N. (1996) 'Qualitative data analysis: representation of a technology. A comment on Coffey, Holbrook and Atkinson', *Sociological Research Online,* 1 (4), http://www.socresonline.org.uk/socresonline /1/4/ lf.html

Lewins, A.F. (2001) 'Computer Assisted Qualitative Data AnalysiS', in N. Gilbert (ed.), *Researching Social Life,* 2nd edn. London: Sage.

Mason, J. (2002) *Qualitative Researching,* 2nd edn. London: Sage.

Miles, M. and Huberman, A. (1994) *Qualitative Data Analysis: an Expanded Sourcebook.* London: Sage.

Novak, J.D. (1993) 'How do we learn to learn? Taking students through the process', *The Science Teacher,* 60 (3).

Novak, J.D. and Gowin, D.B. (1984) *Learning How To Learn.* New York: Cambridge University Press.

Opie, A. (1992) 'Qualitative research, appropriation of the "other" and empowerment', *Feminist Review,* 40 (1): 52–69.

Rich, M. and Patashnick, J. (2002) 'Narrative analysis of audiovisual data: video intervention/prevention assessment (VIA) and NVivo', *International Journal of Social Research Methodology: Theory and Practice,* 5 (3): 245–61.

Richards, L. (2005) *Handling Qualitative Data: A Practical Guide.* London: Sage.

Richards, L. and Richards, T. (1994) 'Using computers in qualitative research', in N. Denzin and Y. Lincoln (eds), *Handbook of Qualitative Research.* London: Sage. pp. 445–62.

Seale, C.F. (2000) 'Using computers to analyse qualitative data', in D. Silverman (ed.). *Doing Qualitative Research: a Practical Handbook.* London: Sage.

Seidel, J. (1991) 'Methods and madness in the application of computer technology to qualitative data analysis', in N.G. Fielding and R.M. Lee (eds), *Using Computers in Qualtitive Research.* London: Sage.

Seidel, J. (1998) *The Ethnograph v5.0: A User's Guide.* London: Sage.

Seidel, J. and Kelle, U. (1995) 'Different functions of coding in the analysis of textual data', in U. Kelle (ed.), *Computer Aided Qualitative Data Analysis: Theory, Methods and Practice.* London: Sage.

Silver, C. (2002) 'The development of school-based sex education in the Netherlands and England and Wales: culture, politics and practice'. Unpublished thesis, University of Surrey, UK.

Silverman, D. (2000) *Doing Qualitative Research: A Practical Handbook.* London: Sage.

Speller, G.M. (2000) 'A community in transition: a longitudinal study of place attachment and identity processes in the context of an enforced relocation'. Unpublished thesis, University of Surrey, UK.

Speller, G.M., Lyons, E. and Twigger-Ross, C. (2002) 'A community in transition: the relationship between spatial change and identity processes', *Social Psychological Review*, 4 (2): 39–58.

Strauss, A. and Corbin, J. (1998) *Basics of Qualitative Research: Grounded Theory Procedures and Techniques.* London: Sage.

Taggart, G., Whitby, K. and Sharp, C. (2004) *International Review of Curriculum and Assessment Frameworks – Thematic Probe. Curriculum and Progression in the Arts: an International Study.* Slough: NFER. Available online from http://www.inca.org.uk/pdf/final%20report%20amended %2012.8.pdf

Weaver, A. and Atkinson, P. (1995) *Microcomputing and Qualitative Data Analysis.* Aldershot: Avebury.

Weitzman, E. and Miles, M. (1995) *A Software Source Book: Computer Programs for Qualitative Data Analysis.* Thousand Oaks, CA: Sage.

Index

Note: In general index entries refer to aspects of generic software. References to features and functions specific to ATLAS.ti5, MAXqd2, and NVivo7 are under these headings. **Bold** page numbers indicate software overviews. *Italic* page numbers indicate 'getting started ' exercises.